.NET Enterprise Design with Visual Basic .NET and SQL Server 2000

Jimmy Nilsson

SAMS

201 West 103rd St., Indianapolis, Indiana 46290 USA

.NET Enterprise Design with Visual Basic .NET and SQL Server 2000

International Standard Book Number: 0-672-32233-1

Library of Congress Catalog Card Number: 10-93572

Printed in the United States of America

First Printing: December 2001

04   03   02   01   4   3   2   1

ASSOCIATE PUBLISHER
Linda Engelman

ACQUISITIONS EDITOR
Sondra Scott

DEVELOPMENT EDITOR
Shannon Leuma

MANAGING EDITOR
Charlotte Clapp

PROJECT EDITOR
Heather McNeill

COPY EDITOR
Pat Kinyon

INDEXER
Cheryl Landes

PROOFREADER
Jessica McCarty

TECHNICAL EDITORS
Deon Schaffer and Sundar Rajan

TEAM COORDINATOR
Lynne Williams

MEDIA DEVELOPER
Dan Scherf

INTERIOR DESIGNER
Gary Adair

COVER DESIGNER
Sandra Schroeder

Trademarks

Warning and Disclaimer

Contents at a Glance

Table of Contents

Foreword

I never asked Jimmy why exactly he asked me to write this foreword, but I am inclined to think that it was for "historical reasons:" Jimmy published his first article on MTS and COM+ development about two years ago on VB-2-The-Max, the site I run with other Italian authors and developers.

It was more or less Jimmy's first editorial experience, so I was prepared to do some editing before publishing the article. I am not talking about fixing grammar or style—after all, the combination of an Italian guy who edits an English document by a Swedish author isn't going to deliver exciting results—but I anticipated the need to reorganize the material, ask for further clarifications on key points, and so on. In short, the kind of things that make a technical article a good, readable article. To my surprise, I didn't find anything worth editing in the draft manuscript, and, in fact, the article went online in its original form. I was rather impressed, because it doesn't happen frequently—in general, and virtually never with first-time authors. (You can read it and the other articles Jimmy wrote for us at http://www.vb2themax.com/ ArticleBank.asp.)

I like to think that the good feedback Jimmy got from our readers encouraged him to propose his material to other sites, magazines, and conferences for developers, such as the European and U.S. editions of VBITS, where Jimmy now speaks regularly. This explains why I was so glad when Jimmy told me that he was writing a book. In my opinion, he *had* to write a book because it was the natural upshot of his ability as a writer and a teacher.

But Jimmy isn't just a teacher and an author; he is an experienced developer who has taken part in many programming projects of all sizes, including complex enterprise-level applications—and it shows in this book. For example, read Chapter 5 for a thorough analysis of the many approaches you can have while designing large-scale, multitier applications. The author obviously knows the theory and can combine it effectively with the constraints of everyday coding life. I believe he has a great talent for finding the appropriate midpoint between a rigorous and somewhat scientific approach and more practical, hands-on, tips-and-tricks-like techniques that all programmers must adopt to get the job done.

NET Enterprise Design with Visual Basic .NET and SQL Server 2000 is different from most of the .NET books you find on bookshelves today. While most of the offerings in this category describe the new language syntax or exciting technologies, such as Web Services, Jimmy preferred to focus on the options you have when you design a large-scale application, and the common mistakes you should avoid in this delicate phase. Of course, I believe that books that teach languages and the .NET internals are important—after all, I am the author of one such textbook—but it is evident that application design can have a far-reaching impact on performance, scalability, and extensibility. Your smartest solutions and the most efficient, hand-optimized code can easily be offset by a nonoptimal architecture. Even if you're code-addicted, this book won't disappoint you, because you'll find a lot of T-SQL and Visual Basic .NET code.

I especially like the way Jimmy explains the tradeoffs of each approach he introduces, teaching you to weigh all the relevant factors, and ultimately helping you select the most appropriate solution. If you're going to write complex, enterprise-level .NET applications, this book is for you.

—Francesco Balena

Author of *Programming Microsoft Visual Basic 6* and *Programming Microsoft Visual Basic .NET* (Microsoft Press).

Founder and editor-in-chief of `www.vb2themax.com`.

Contributing editor and Editorial Advisory Board member of *Visual Studio Magazine*, Fawcette Technical Publications.

Preface

To my knowledge, no book has yet been published that focuses on COM+ Component Services, stored procedures, and interactions. This book does just that, but within the new world of .NET Component Services, Visual Basic .NET, and SQL Server 2000.

The book discusses key problems that most developers will face as they develop enterprise applications for the targeted platform. I will offer some suggestions for solutions to these problems and discuss the pros and cons of each solution vis-a-vis performance, scalability, maintainability, data integrity, and so on.

Of course, it's risky to write a book and offer proposals for how to solve different problems at this early stage of life of the .NET platform. If I had waited a year, it would have been much easier, because many best practices would have had time to evolve and mature. Saying that, now is the time to read this book if you want to stay on the forefront of new technology. Just keep in mind that my recommendations are meant to provide you with inspiration rather than definitive solutions. The usefulness and applicability of a solution depends on the circumstances.

Unlike other books on the same subject, this book takes a software engineering approach and is focused on design. This design focus is relevant because it's more important when programming for Visual Basic .NET, for example, to be more design focused than for VB6.

Instead of describing different techniques found in the platform work, I mainly discuss how they can be used in solving key problems found in real-world applications. Thus, this book is problem-oriented instead of technique-oriented. You are asked to think about the proposals I present, consider how you will handle the problems on your own, and assess the pros and cons of any solution.

Target Audience of This Book

The target audience of this book is readers who want to learn more about building enterprise applications in the .NET platform. It's as simple as that. The book is written for architects, developers, team leaders, and technical managers.

I have tried to make the book component-oriented. That is, instead of repeating what every other book says about something, I have kept background information to a minimum and expect you to have some background knowledge before reading this book, including experience with the following:

- Visual Basic .NET or C#
- The .NET Framework

- Component Services from MTS, COM+, or .NET
- T-SQL in SQL Server 6, 7, or 2000
- ADO.NET

It will be helpful for you to have some experience of VB6, COM, and ADO as well. If you do not have background knowledge or experience with these topics, I point you in the direction of other books to read to get up to speed at appropriate times in the chapters.

Focus of This Book

Let's look at a picture that represents something that I assume you are used to, namely, a layered architecture. An example is found in Figure P.1.

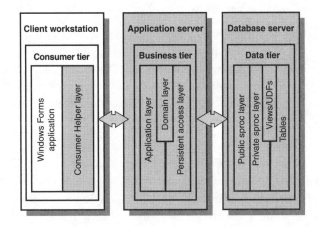

FIGURE P.1

A layered architecture: the focus of the book.

You can see in Figure P.1 that I demonstrate the architecture with Windows Forms for the client application. It could just as well have been an ASP.NET application, for instance. However, Windows Forms and ASP.NET are not the focus of the book. The shaded areas in the figure are the focus, including

- The components in the application server
- The stored procedures in the database server
- A helper layer at the consumer side

Why I Am Writing About the Chosen Platform

Instead of giving you a direct answer to this, I'd like to explain it in three parts. I'll discuss why I chose Visual Basic .NET and SQL Server 2000, but I will start with my reasoning behind using .NET Component Services.

Why .NET Component Services

For a couple of years now, MTS and COM+ Component Services have been very strong platforms for building enterprise applications. With .NET, it's becoming easier to write components for COM+ Component Services (or .NET Component Services, as it is now called) and you can express many design decisions in your code with the help of attributes. Just as before, you will benefit greatly from the infrastructure help you get from the services. And for VB developers, it's now possible to benefit from services such as Object Pooling for the first time.

Some of the Component Services—or Enterprise Services, as Microsoft often calls it— have equivalents in the .NET Framework. This isn't so strange because much of the .NET Framework was built by the same developers who built COM+. You don't have to make a choice between one or the other, as most often they complement each other. When using automatic transactions in the .NET Framework, COM+ transactions will be used. The same goes for activity-based synchronization, loosely coupled events, and so on.

As I write, there isn't much buzz being generated about Component Services. I think this is because there are so many new and exciting technologies coming with .NET, such as ASP.NET and XML Web Services, that are receiving most of the attention. My belief is that this will change very soon. Behind the entry point of XML Web Services and ASP.NET, COM+ components and Component Services will still be doing the lion's share of the work. It is as if the operating system has grown and is providing more services. For the most part, it's beneficial to use those services instead of writing similar ones of your own. I expect to see the programming model of Component Services being used for a long time in the future.

Why Visual Basic .NET

Before I started working on this book, I thought long and hard about moving from VB6 to C# instead of to Visual Basic .NET. I finally decided that I couldn't write a book for old C++ programmers. When you're mostly working in an environment such as VB, you get "assimilated" to it and talk and think in a specific way. (The opposite is also true. It would be hard for a C++ person to write a good book about Visual Basic .NET.) Therefore, I will focus on Visual Basic .NET. Still, programmers who focus on C# can still benefit from reading the book as long as they are prepared for its VB style. (This is especially true for C# programmers coming from VB, of course.) They just have to translate the code samples to their own language, which ought to be simple enough.

No matter what .NET language you choose, we are all .NET developers and we are all writing for the common language runtime.

Why SQL Server 2000

Around 1994, I thought relational databases would soon be just legacy products. I was wrong. Even today, relational databases are kind of state of the art for business applications, and SQL Server 2000 is a good example of such a product.

Although I could have chosen to write about a generic database platform, I would have lost one of my main points, namely that it's important to use the specific capabilities of the database if you want the highest scalability. I have chosen to write about SQL Server 2000 because SQL Server has been my favorite database platform for many years. It's competent, comparatively cheap, and widespread. However, most of the ideas I discuss can be converted, for example, to Oracle and DB2.

Organization of This Book

This book is divided into nine chapters and includes a separate appendix with suggestions for further reading.

In Chapter 1, "Introduction," I set the scene for the rest of the book by briefly discussing COM, COM+, VB6, and previous versions of SQL Server. I also describe the .NET Framework in general, .NET Component Services, Visual Basic .NET, C#, and SQL Server 2000. In Chapter 2, "Factors to Consider in Choosing a Solution to a Problem," I discuss the different criteria I will use throughout the book to evaluate my proposals to key problems.

In Chapter 3, "Testing," I start to describe key problems and solutions—a discussion that will continue throughout the rest of the book. This chapter looks at the extremely important—yet often forgotten—aspect of test applications thoroughly. In this chapter, I discuss and show a solution of how you can automate a good deal of testing, thus saving yourself time in the future. I also discuss strategies for using assertions. Chapter 4, "Adding Debugging Support," discusses important preparations you should consider when building enterprise applications, such as preparing for debugging. We look closely at adding tracing support, error logging, and how to handle configuration data.

Windows DNA has been a successful architecture for several years now. In Chapter 5, "Architecture," I describe a new architecture proposal (both similar and dissimilar to Windows DNA) that you can use to better take advantage of the new platform. I also discuss suitable code structures for the different layers in the architecture. Then in Chapter 6, "Transactions," we look at good transactional design and why it is crucial for building a successful enterprise application. In this chapter, I focus on how to write the most efficient transactions, while keeping correctness in mind. I also discuss methods for making the code easily to change from pure T-SQL transactions to COM+ transactions, if the need arises.

Moving on to Chapter 7, "Business Rules," I discuss different business rules, where they should be located, and how they should be implemented. In Chapter 8, "Data Access," I focus on a newly developed data access pattern and its helper. This pattern reduces round trips between the Business tier and the Data tier, and shortens transaction lengths and increases debuggability.

Finally, Chapter 9, "Error Handling and Concurrency Control," discusses strategies for error handling both in stored procedures and in .NET components. It also discusses strategies of concurrency control for situations when data is disconnected from the database, both optimistic and pessimistic protocols.

Topics That Aren't Covered

I decided early on that I wanted to write a concise and focused book. Therefore, I had to skip many interesting and important topics. Because the focus of the book is design and programming for the application server and the database server, I won't discuss Web Forms, Windows Forms, and Web Services in great depth. In addition, in-depth discussion of the following topics is beyond the scope of this book:

- .NET Remoting
- MSMQ, Queued Components (QC), Loosely Coupled Events (LCE), Compensating Resource Manager (CRM)
- Multithreading
- Delegates and Events
- ADO.NET

Each of these topics is interesting and important, but they can fill entire books on their own. I refer you to Appendix A, "Suggestions for Further Reading," for a list of suggested books should you want to read about these topics.

The Book's Web Site

You'll find the Web site of the book at www.samspublishing.com. This site includes the following:

- Results of several performance tests, executed after version 1 of .NET has been released
- A continuously updated list of suggestions for further reading
- The code from the samples and the tools discussed in the book
- The errata for the book

A Few Final Comments

When you read the book, you will find that the source code has almost no comments at all. This is not how I think you should program, of course. I have done it this way for reasons of brevity alone. If you download the complete source code from the book's Web site at www. samspublishing.com, you will find that the code is heavily commented.

I have tried to ensure that the content in this book is as correct as possible. However, there is always a risk for errors, especially because I wrote the book early on. If you find an error, please e-mail me and I'll post a correction on the book's Web site.

In sum, I've tried to write a book that I would love to read myself. Hopefully, you will enjoy it too.

Jimmy Nilsson

www.jnsk.se

Jimmy.Nilsson@jnsk.se

Ronneby, Sweden

September 2001

About the Author

Jimmy Nilsson is the owner of the Swedish consulting company JNSK AB. He has been working with system development for 13 years (with VB since version 1.0) and, in recent years, he has specialized in component-based development, mostly in the Microsoft environment. He has also been developing and presenting courses in database design, object-oriented design, and so on at a Swedish university for six years. Jimmy is a frequent speaker at Fawcette and Wrox Conferences and has written numerous technical articles. Even so, he considers himself to be mainly a developer.

Dedication

I dedicate this book to my wonderful wife Lotta, our great son Tim, and our second child whom we are expecting early next year. I love you guys and without you, nothing would mean anything!

Acknowledgments

There are so many to whom I owe thanks. I am indebted to them for providing feedback, for being sounding boards, and for being sources of inspiration. It is impossible to thank them all, but I would like to mention four people in particular who have meant more to me than anybody else during this project.

To Francesco Balena: For being my mentor throughout my writing career and for writing such a nice foreword.

To Dan Byström: For being a great sounding board and source of inspiration throughout the whole of my professional life as a developer.

To Ingemar Lundberg: For providing more feedback and participating in more discussions than anybody else while I was working on this book.

To Shannon Pahl, Program Manager for COM+, Microsoft: For answering my many questions, but mostly for reading through the book and providing feedback.

There are a great many more people whom I would like to thank. The following list isn't at all complete, but those who have meant the most to me when writing the content are (in alphabetical order):

Mike Amundsen, Rickard Bengtsson, Joe Celko, Martin Forsberg, Tommy Grändefors, Kenneth Henningsson, Peter L. Henry, Tibor Karaszi, Martti Laiho, Joe Long, Michael D. Long, Tom Moreau, Per-Ola Nilsson, John Robbins, Enrico Sabbadin, Egidio Sburlino, Charlie Svahnberg, and Johan Svanström.

I also owe a big thanks to the team that helped me transform my ideas into something understandable, the Sams team with whom I've been working very closely.

Sondra Scott, Acquisitions Editor, talked me into writing the book in the first place and has been a tremendous support throughout the entire project. Lydia West, Language Editor, transformed my "Swenglish" into English. Shannon Leuma, Development Editor, made wonders of each and every chapter, both in terms of structure and the clarity. Heather McNeill, Project Editor, was in charge of the production side of the book. Deon Schaffer and Sundar Rajan, Technical Editors, checked the content for technical errors and proposed numerous improvements. And finally, Pat Kinyon, Copy Editor, helped me clean up the mistakes the rest of us missed.

Tell Us What You Think!

As the reader of this book, *you* are our most important critic and commentator. We value your opinion and want to know what we're doing right, what we could do better, what areas you'd like to see us publish in, and any other words of wisdom you're willing to pass our way.

As an Associate Publisher for Sams Publishing, I welcome your comments. You can fax, email, or write me directly to let me know what you did or didn't like about this book—as well as what we can do to make our books stronger.

Please note that I cannot help you with technical problems related to the topic of this book, and that due to the high volume of mail I receive, I might not be able to reply to every message.

When you write, please be sure to include this book's title and author as well as your name and phone or fax number. I will carefully review your comments and share them with the author and editors who worked on the book.

Fax: 317-581-4770

Email: feedback@samspublishing.com

Mail: Linda Engelman
          Sams Publishing
          201 West 103rd Street
          Indianapolis, IN 46290 USA

Introduction

IN THIS CHAPTER

In this chapter, I will briefly discuss the history of the Component Object Model (COM) up to the state of .NET today. In this discussion, I will tell some horror stories from the dark ages of COM, Visual Basic 6 (VB6), and COM+, and will look at the advances made in the industry in recent years. I will also touch on key technologies, such as .NET Component Services, Visual Basic .NET, C#, and SQL Server 2000, that I intend to use for my examples and discussions throughout the book. To understand this chapter and the rest of the book, I assume that you are somewhat familiar with Visual Basic .NET, common language runtime, and so on, and so I won't discuss these topics in detail in this chapter. With that caveat out of the way, let's get started.

The History of COM, MTS/COM+, VB, and SQL Server

Although we all know that programming didn't start with COM, a major shift in the industry occurred when COM became popular in the mid-1990s, so it seems a good place to start our look at the technology's history. From there, we'll move on to MTS/COM+ Component Services, before touching on VB and SQL Server.

COM

Perhaps one of the most important ideas behind COM was to make it a technique for moving away from monolithic applications toward component-based applications. As such, COM is a binary model, not a source-code model. This might make frequent reuse a little easier to accomplish, because you reuse binary components instead of source-code classes with COM. Another important benefit is the user's ability to take advantage of black-box reuse, which means that the reuser only pulls some ropes to make the component behave as wanted without knowing how the code is written for the component. Black-box reuse was not possible to achieve when source code was reused. If you, as a reuser, are able to view the code you are reusing, it might be more acceptable for the vendor to require knowledge of the implementation of the reused code instead of totally hiding all implementation details, which most often makes life easier for the reuser. That means that the reuser must have a firm grasp of the inner workings of the component it wants to reuse before he or she can make it work correctly.

Another idea behind COM was that it needed to be language-independent; in essence, with COM, programmers are able to choose among several different languages. To make this work, certain rules need to be complied with, and the interfaces of the components must be described with Interface Definition Language (IDL), which is then compiled and transformed into type libraries.

The designers of COM were of the opinion that object-orientation was the way to go, and that object-orientation provided a sound base from which to work. One problem COM addressed was versioning, so that a component could be extended while still being compatible with existing consumers. Meanwhile, COM (or rather DCOM for Distributed COM) also focused on creating a method to split applications so that different parts of the workload can be executed on different machines.

MTS/COM+ Component Services

COM was a big leap in the right direction, but Microsoft Transaction Server (MTS) took COM to the next level. MTS added some runtime services for COM components, such as declarative distributed transactions, declarative role-based security, administrative support, and resource pooling, to name a few. In a way, MTS added services to the operating system that developers who wrote distributed applications previously had to build on their own. Soon after MTS was released, pure DCOM applications became a rarity in the industry.

A friend of mine who works as a project manager often asks me how long it will take me to write a certain program. I always tell him that it will take two days. (That *is* the universal answer, right?) His response is always one of shock: "How can it possibly take two days to check a check box?" he asks. In fact, with MTS's attribute-based programming, my friend's shock is a bit more justified, because more programming can be accomplished through simple declaration or by setting an attribute value. Transactions in COM+ is one example, referential integrity in SQL Server another.

With Windows 2000, MTS was upgraded to COM+. While MTS was actually an add-on to Windows NT, COM+ was natively supported by Windows 2000. This simplified the programming model quite a bit. It was often said that MTS + COM = COM+. In essence, COM+ joined these two previously separated parts. In addition, COM+ added component services, such as Object Pooling (OP), Compensating Resource Manager (CRM), and Queued Components (QC).

VB

I started my adventures in Windows programming with VB1. I still remember my first major mistake in that environment. It's actually rather embarrassing to share, but it makes me sentimental in a nice way. I was supposed to build a menu application from which several other applications should be started. It was an early "portal" of sorts. My boss wanted me to use pictures instead of text on the buttons, so I used picture boxes instead of command buttons. Unfortunately, I managed to insert pictures, each having a size of approximately 200KB, but only 1KB was actually of interest and shown from each of them. The exe was over 2MB large, which made for very slow startup on the hardware at that time, especially in relationship to what a rocket-science application it was.

Several years and many mistakes later, VB4 was released. It was the first really COM-competent version of Visual Basic. Still, it wasn't until VB5 and VB6 that the COM programming in VB became popular. One of the great (but sometimes also negative) aspects of VB is that it hides several details of COM, such as class factories, reference counting, user-defined interfaces (if desired), IDL, and QueryInterface. You can't achieve as good a performance out of VB as you can from C++, but the productivity is very good. Still, in some camps, VB is considered more of a toy than a tool for a professional programmer. In fact, I've been asked more than once if I get paid to program in VB. The good news is that Visual Basic .NET will change the opinions of some of those who see VB as just a toy. So you no longer have to be embarrassed to admit it if it is your favorite programming language.

SQL Server

I learned SQL at the university in the late 1980s, and it is still useful today. Actually, it's more important to master than ever, especially if you find scalability vital for your applications. Since I started working with SQL Server (version 4), its programming model, with its triggers and stored procedures, has remained quite consistent. For example, the shift from version 6.5 to version 7 was a major one at the engine level, but T-SQL didn't change that much at all.

A friend of mine once said, "Database design is important. Databases are used in 102% of all applications today." I think many developers agree that databases are used a lot. I also think that there is a large difference in opinion regarding whether the database tier—such as SQL Server 2000, for example—should be used for data-focused logic.

I fall on the extreme yes side. You will see me present my position throughout the book; stored procedures, for example, will have a central role in several of the proposed solutions. However, even though I am fond of using database capabilities, I definitely want to encapsulate the access calls to them so they are not visible to more layers than necessary.

Now, let's turn our attention to .NET, which can be seen as the fourth version of COM (after pure COM, MTS, and COM+). Saying that, COM is dead, but long live COM (now called .NET)!

A Few Important Definitions

Before we get too far along in the book, I'd like to define a few terms I will be using in these chapters that have many different meanings in the industry:

- *Component*—If you agree with Szyperski[5], the word "component" refers to a COM server, such as a DLL or a .NET assembly, that is a binary collection of classes. The COM+ definition of the word refers to one single binary class. I prefer this COM+ definition.

> • *Tier and layer*—I used to think the terms tier and layer were synonyms. Over the last few years, I have come to understand that layer is logical, while tier is physical. Unfortunately, this explanation isn't very distinct. For example, I like to think of the server-side components as one tier and SQL Server as another, but sometimes they execute physically at the same machine. Therefore, in this book, I will use the word tier to refer to an execution environment and layer to refer to a logical slice of a tier. Typical execution environments include ASP.NET, SQL Server, COM+, Web browser, XML Web services, and Ordinary Win32 exes.

The New World of .NET

Now that we have taken a look at the history of the technology, we're ready to look at the many changes that have come about with the introduction of .NET.

.NET: A Whole New Platform

I remember when I first read Mary Kirtland's articles, "Object-Oriented Software Development Made Simple with COM+ Runtime Services"[1] and "The COM+ Programming Model Makes it Easy to Write Components in Any Language,"[2] in *Microsoft Systems Journal* in 1997. In her articles, Mary discussed many of the things we know of today as .NET, but she called it COM+. At that time, it felt like a huge step and, as it turned out, it was probably too big a leap for Microsoft to take; with COM+ 1.0, they didn't leverage more than a handful of the things Mary discussed. I also remember thinking that several of the concepts were familiar to me as a COM programmer in VB, and that the C++ guys now would have some of these productivity-enhancing features too. This was also the first time I heard the expression "You can think of metadata as a type library on steroids." How many articles and books can you list that have used that expression since?

.NET Features

The following are some of the concepts that Mary discussed in her articles but that weren't fulfilled in COM+ 1.0:

- A common runtime that could be used from any programming language.
- Full interoperability between languages.
- Attributes with a central role.
- Rich metadata.
- No need for manual code regarding garbage collection, class factories, and so on.
- Methods used directly on classes and not only via interfaces.

- Implementation inheritance.

- No deterministic finalization, which means that you don't know when an object is finalized because the garbage collection may happen immediately or, most often, much later. (Yes, deterministic finalization was already mentioned at this time. I wonder why it didn't upset developers as much then.)

- A strong security model for the components.

- Functionality similar to `SqlDataAdapter` in ADO.NET. (An `SqlDataAdapter` can be used to register which stored procedure should be called for inserting new rows that have been added to a `DataSet`, for updating, and so on.)

- No need for a separate interface language (such as IDL).

- All languages decide on a common set of types.

- Parameterized constructors and overloading.

The good news is that .NET does deliver on all of these ideas and, even years later, it's an impressive list. Although Mary's discussion was based on the idea to build the runtime and everything else on COM, .NET isn't written on COM; it's a completely new platform.

In addition, .NET also includes the following features:

- Remoting (for example with SOAP)

- ADO.NET

- ASP.NET

- Windows Forms

- Web Forms

- XML Web services support

- Base Class Library (BCL)

- A new and a much more competent versioning schema

- A new language called C#

- Many changes to VB6 (or rather a rewrite) to make it Visual Basic .NET

It's important to note that even though the common language runtime is extremely important in .NET, it does not replace COM+. This means if your components written in managed code (that is, code managed and executed completely by the common language runtime) need component services, such as declarative transactions, you will still use our old friend COM+. We will discuss serviced components (components that use component services) further in a minute.

In the end, you may be asking yourself whether it is an advantage or a disadvantage to have prior experience with COM and COM+ when you enter the new world of .NET. In my opinion, it's definitely an advantage.

.NET Component Services

.NET isn't really an evolution, it's a revolution. Even so, writing serviced components (that is, using component services in .NET) is, in essence, evolutionary. If you have worked with writing components that use COM+ component services, you will be well prepared.

Listing 1.1 shows what a very simple serviced component would look like as a class in Visual Basic .NET. (For it to work, you must set a reference to `System.EnterpriseServices.dll`.)

LISTING 1.1   A Simple Serviced Component in Visual Basic .NET

```
Imports System.EnterpriseServices

Public Class MyFirstSample
    Inherits ServicedComponent

    Public Function GetTime() As String
        Return Now.ToString()
    End Function
End Class
```

When this class is used for the first time, it will automatically be registered as a configured COM+ component, which comes in handy at development time. Still, at deployment time, this feature is most often not useful, because the user running the application must have administrator privileges to have it registered. You can use RegSvcs to manually register the component as a configured COM+ component.

COM+ object pooling will now be available to the majority of COM+ programmers, namely those who use VB6, when they shift to a .NET language, such as Visual Basic .NET or C#. An added plus is that the components you write with Visual Basic .NET and C# will not have the thread affinity problems—which means, for example, that an object of a VB6-written class can only be used from the same thread as the one that instantiated the object because of the heavy use of Thread Local Storage (TLS)—and Single Threaded Apartment only threading model of VB6.

A very handy feature of .NET is that the attributes can be written in code. Listing 1.2 shows an example in which a class is decorated with attributes for object pooling.

LISTING 1.2   Attributes Decorating a Class

```
<ObjectPoolingAttribute(Enabled:=True, _
MinPoolSize:=2, MaxPoolSize:=3, _
CreationTimeout:=20000)> Public Class MyPooledClass
```

Special Considerations

You may be wondering whether the .NET programmer has to consider anything special when writing serviced components. Indeed, several things differ between writing ordinary .NET components and writing serviced ones, including the following:

- You should call Dispose() when you are done with an instance of a serviced component. (Most often it's not a must, but recommended.)
- You should not use nondefault constructors.
- Static methods are not serviceable.
- Services flow between machines, but only when DCOM is used. (That means, for example, that you must use DCOM instead of .NET Remoting if you want to use a COM+ transaction that spans two machines.)
- During runtime, the user executing the COM+ application must have permission to run unmanaged code.

As usual, consumers won't have to know whether the used component is serviced or not. Of course, the consumers can be unmanaged code, such as VB6-written code. In fact, using .NET to write better COM+ components for unmanaged consumers will likely be a common scenario in the near future.

COM+ 1.5 Component Services

Windows XP and Windows .NET Server will contain COM+ 1.5 and with it a lot of new functionality, including:

- Process recycling
- Configurable isolation level
- Applications as Windows services
- Memory gates
- Pause/disable applications
- Process dumping
- Moving and copying components
- Public/private components
- Application partitions
- COM+ applications exposed as XML Web services

We will discuss each of these features in the rest of this section.

Process Recycling

A simple way of escaping the problems with memory leakage is to restart the server process now and then. With process recycling, you can declaratively tell how and when this should happen—for example, after a certain amount of requests or every night.

> **NOTE**
>
> I once wrote a Web application that had a memory leak. The customer thought it was a cheap solution for them to just reboot the machine every weekend because they had people working then anyway. I preferred to try to solve the problem instead of using a Band-Aid, but they didn't see this as a problem at all. Of course, process recycling would have been more convenient for them.

Configurable Isolation Level

In COM+ 1.0, the transaction isolation level was always SERIALIZABLE for COM+ transactions against SQL Server. (Oracle gets the same request to set the isolation level to SERIALIZABLE, but neglects this and uses READ COMMITTED instead. This is because Oracle uses versioning instead of locking for concurrency control, and then READ COMMITTED is most often enough.)[3] In the past, this has been a major constraint to keep in mind when designing for COM+, but in COM+ 1.5, it will be possible to configure the needed isolation level.

Applications as Windows Services

Some of the component services, such as queued components, need a started COM+ application to work. In COM+ 1.5 it is possible to run COM+ applications as Windows services. This also comes in handy if you like to run the application as the local system account, to make it possible to act with the privileges from that user. This is also a solution to the short delay that might otherwise be apparent when the first request is made to a COM+ server application after system boot (or after the application has been shut down).

Memory Gates

The Memory Gates feature prevents the creation of objects when the amount of free memory falls below a certain level. The reason for this functionality is to avoid adding objects when there's not enough memory to support their operations. Strange errors occur when a system runs out of memory, and it is hard to trap for errors in components in this environment. In fact, most components aren't tested for low memory conditions, so it is better that they don't get called at all if the system has run out of memory.

Pause/Disable Applications

In COM+ 1.0, you can't pause a COM+ application. Instead, you have to delete the component if, for any reason, you don't want anybody to use it for a certain amount of time. In COM+ 1.5, you can both pause and disable applications.

Process Dumping

To make debugging easier in COM+ 1.5, it will be possible to take a snapshot of the process without having to stop the process. This snapshot can then be used with a debugger to examine the exact state when the problem occurred.

Moving and Copying Components

Often, it is useful to be able to let the same component appear several times, in several applications. That is especially the case for helper components. Assume that one helper component is used by five different COM+ applications. In COM+ 1.0, all five applications have to be upgraded at the same time to use the new version of the helper. I generally prefer to upgrade step-by-step instead. Therefore, it's common that helpers are reused in source-code form instead of as binary components. In COM+ 1.5, it will be possible to configure the same physical component several times and in different ways.

Public/Private Components

In COM+ 1.0, all components are public. In COM+ 1.5, it will be possible to set a component to be private to the current application. The less you expose externally, the easier it is for you to make changes in the future to the application.

Application Partitions

The purpose of application partitions is to partition a machine so that applications don't disturb each other. A typical situation when application partitions are of great use is in data centers. Consider the possibility of running several instances of SQL Server 2000 in one single machine.

COM+ Applications Can Be Exposed as XML Web Services

If you want to expose some functionality of a COM+ application as XML Web services, COM+ 1.5 makes that easy. You can achieve that automatically with the help of the Component Services Explorer.

> **NOTE**
>
> Now that I have sounded like a salesperson for a while, I'd like to say that I was told by Microsoft that there are no plans to add the functionality of COM+ 1.5 to Windows 2000. Only time will tell.

Visual Basic .NET

I, for one, have been longing for Visual Basic .NET for a long time. Why, you ask?

Problems Solved with Visual Basic .NET

VB has always had great ideas for how applications should be built, but the implementations have had quirks. The following are a few examples of problems that were found in VB6 but that are now solved in Visual Basic .NET:

- WithEvents *can't be used with user-defined interfaces*—The first time I tried to use WithEvents with user-defined interfaces, it took me half a day to decide that it just wasn't possible. A call-back solution solves the problem, but it's still irritating that the system-plugged solution doesn't work.

- *Single-threaded apartments (STA) are not always a sufficient model for multithreading*—VB6 protects us from ourselves. Most of the time, this is a good thing. On the other hand, when we have advanced needs and know what we are doing, it would be nice to have the capability to move into dangerous grounds. Using free threading is a typical example. This is definitely interesting for COM+ components. The built-in synchronization support in COM+ helps a lot with writing thread-safe code without STAs.

- *When* GlobalMultiUse *is used, the class must live in another DLL*—I have also had problems with GlobalMultiUse in COM+ applications. Therefore, I instead use old-style code modules for my helper routines in VB6. That means I often employ code reuse instead of binary reuse, but I also skip some instantiation overhead (both when I write the code and when the code is executed).

- *The class editor isn't made for writing user-defined interfaces, and VB creates an ugly type library*—Because of this, although it is possible to take some control of the interfaces with VB6, serious VB6 developers often write the interfaces in IDL and compile them with Microsoft Interface Definition Language (MIDL, the compiler that transforms IDL into, for example, a typelib). There is not a lot of "VB feeling" in that approach, but it is the preferred way.

- *There is a lack of strong typing*—If I forget to declare the data type for a variable or parameter, I consider this a bug, and I definitely want the compiler to tell me about it. VB6 forgives and offers a `Variant` instead. Another example is that VB6 forgives when I forget to do an explicit cast. It makes an implicit one automatically. Is it good to be forgiving? No, not in this case. Hiding risks and bugs is not a good thing.

- *There is a weak error-handling scheme*—The error handling in VB6 is quite weak and definitely not well understood. Unfortunately, it's not uncommon to find insufficient or incorrect error-handling code in articles published by Microsoft, either.

- *The implicit cleanup is shaky*—Especially in a highly stressed server-side scenario, there have been several reports that the implicit cleanup of VB6 isn't cleaning up correctly. There is also the more well-known circular reference problem of COM that you have to break up manually. (To understand the circular reference problem, assume that you have two objects, each of which keeps a reference to the other object. It's not enough to set one of those objects to `Nothing` explicitly. The reference counting–based cleanup algorithm in COM will keep both objects alive.)

- *There is a lack of shared (or class or static) members*—I tried to implement an ordinary Singleton[4] (which means one single object, reused over and over again, similar to a global object) without any luck when VB4 was released, because VB4 didn't have members that belong to the class rather than the objects. The same goes for VB5 and VB6.

In addition to these problems, there has also been a lack of other object-oriented concepts too. The most common complaint in that area is probably the lack of implementation inheritance. (Implementation inheritance means that a class can inherit the implementation from another class. When a programmer refers to "inheritance," he or she is probably referring to this type of inheritance.) At first, I thought Microsoft was "creating" a truth when they said that large projects would suffer if you used implementation inheritance. (Over the years, I have developed an ability to see conspiracies everywhere.) A few years later, I read Clemens Szyperski's *Component Software: Beyond Object-Oriented Programming*[5] and I understood that it was a well-known fact in academic research. Since then, I've been happy using user-defined interfaces and separating the interface from the implementation. I will use user-defined interfaces a lot in .NET too, but there are situations for implementation inheritance. Inheritance is good if you want to inherit the *implementation* from the base class, but that is actually the only case. We also only have single inheritance in .NET and, therefore, you have to be careful to not "waste" the single inheritance possibility.

As I mentioned earlier, these problems have all been solved with Visual Basic .NET. Visual Basic .NET = the VB way, with fewer quirks.

New "Problems" with Visual Basic .NET

Unfortunately, even though Visual Basic .NET solves a lot of problems, it introduces some as well. For one, Visual Basic .NET is a much harder language to learn for newcomers than VB6. It is more competent, but also full of advanced concepts. Formal training and/or much experience are a must. In fact, for this reason and others, some developers don't like Visual Basic .NET at all. In my opinion, it's a huge and great leap forward. One thing that does irritate me is that between beta 1 and 2, Microsoft suddenly announced that they were changing Visual Basic .NET so that is was more consistent with VB6. They based this decision on the feedback (or, rather, criticism) they got from the VB MVPs. When I discussed this with Microsoft, I was told that these changes would only increase backward compatibility, and that this wouldn't affect the future at all. I don't agree. We will have to live with those mistakes a long time.

The following are the changes Microsoft made between beta 1 and beta 2 of Visual Basic .NET:

- `True` *should be represented as* `-1` *in numerical form, not as* `1`—In my opinion, if you have coded so that you are dependent on the numerical representation, you should be prepared to make changes in the future.

- `And` *and* `Or` *will not be short-circuiting*—The main risk was said to be if a user had written an `If` clause as follows:

  ```
  If a = 1 And InitializeSome() Then
  ```

  Assume that `InitializeSome()` sets some global variables. If `And` would be short-circuiting and `a = 1` is False, `InitializeSome()` would not execute in Visual Basic .NET. In my opinion, this type of coding is a hack, and the programmer should be prepared for ugly code like this to break in the future. It won't happen in Visual Basic .NET.

  If you want a short-circuiting `And/Or`, you should use `AndAlso/OrElse` instead. I always want it to short circuit, so I have to get used to using those new syntactic elements.

- `And/Or` *will be bitwise operations again, as in VB6*—(Before this change, they were purely logical operators and `BitAnd/BitOr` had to be used for bitwise operations.)

- *Array-declarations should set the upper bound, not the number of elements*—If you declare an array as follows:

  ```
  Dim x(5) As Integer
  ```

  you get an array of six elements, not five. Over the years, this has irritated me repeatedly. It's not intuitive, and I can't see the point in doing it like this.

Despite these changes, the MVPs are still unhappy with Visual Basic .NET. The only thing Microsoft achieved was to make the language weaker and to irritate a large and quiet part of the VB community.

I decided on Visual Basic .NET as my .NET language of choice quite early. After that, when Microsoft did their movement back, I almost decided to use C# instead. It's actually not a dramatic decision. You can be switching between Visual Basic .NET and C#, and still be quite productive. I will probably work mostly in Visual Basic .NET, despite some irritating details, because of my background. I'm sure that I'll use C# quite a lot as well.

C#

Although some would argue that C# is Java-based, it is primarily rooted in C++. There have been some restrictions and a lot of cleanup in the language in the transition. C# has also been VB-ified to a large degree, which made it simpler and more productive to use than its ancestor C++.

Although they do differ, C# and Visual Basic .NET are very much alike. If you master one, it's quite easy to use the other. A lot of your time investment will be put in the Base Class Library (BCL) and, because it is shared by both C# and Visual Basic .NET, you don't have to spend time relearning its concepts.

C# Versus Visual Basic .NET

The differences between C# and Visual Basic .NET are mostly to suit different programmer's backgrounds. Unfortunately, there are some other differences. The following is a list (other than those that were mentioned when I discussed Microsoft's "going back") of some examples of the differences between C# and Visual Basic .NET:[6]

- *C# warns you if a function is missing a return statement*—This catches a few bugs automatically.
- *C# requires XML-tagged documentation to be written in the code*—Seems to be a good idea to drag out the comments from the code and use it for different scenarios.
- *C# can switch to Unmanaged mode*—This can easily be achieved in Visual Basic .NET by just calling a C# class that takes care of it. Still, I find it nice to have the same possibilities in both environments.
- *You can use* Using() *in C# to tell that an object should be automatically* Dispose()*ed when going out of scope*—That is very handy, for example, for connections and file objects that you don't want to wait for being garbage collected.

To be fair, Visual Basic .NET has some advantages over C# too:

- *Visual Basic .NET differs* Inherits *from* Implements—In C#, it's written in both cases with a colon.
- *The event syntax is simple in Visual Basic .NET*—It's as clean and intuitive as in VB6. In C#, you have to take care of more by hand.

- *Visual Basic .NET is not case sensitive*—This is a matter of taste, but I prefer non–case sensitive. Otherwise, there is always somebody that will have two methods in a single class named something like getData() and GetData().

> **NOTE**
>
> Despite the differences between C# and Visual Basic .NET, you can use this book with either C# or Visual Basic .NET. The book is probably more "direct" if you have your background in VB6, because that is what I have too. I think and reason more as a VB programmer than as a C++ programmer.

SQL Server 2000

Compared to Visual Basic .NET, SQL Server 2000 is almost an old-timer. Still I think it's important to discuss some of its new features. Although you may think that the leap from SQL Server 7 to 2000 would be a big one, the real changes aren't all that dramatic. However, there are some interesting features for developers to consider, including XML support, user-defined functions, and distributed partitioned views, among others.

XML Support

I'm a geek, and so I love to use new technology. When XML came on the market a couple of years ago, I used it as the file format in a project for a customer of mine. (Hey, I know what you think, but my customer actually thought—and still thinks—it was a good solution!) However, I soon learned that XML—especially its tool support—was not the wonder technology I had first envisioned. The project worked out fine in the end, but I became reluctant to use XML for some time. Since then, the standards and tool support for XML have gone through tremendous development, and are sure to continue into the future.

I became re-interested in XML with SQL Server 2000. There is a lot of XML support in SQL Server 2000. The following are the most interesting features:

- *You can now pass XML documents to stored procedures and open them for further processing*—That gives, for example, a good solution for the problem of handing over several rows to a stored procedure in one call.

- *You can fetch results from* SELECT *statements as XML documents*—In some situations, it will be a good solution to create the result in XML directly at the database server instead of converting it at the middle tier or at the client.

Perhaps the XML support is the reason that SQL Server 2000 now is called a .NET server. It's not written in managed code and nothing has changed since it only was called SQL Server 2000, but hey, it can talk XML! What can I say? Marketers…

User-Defined Functions

In SQL Server 2000, we finally had User-Defined Functions (UDFs). Since we have waited so long, Microsoft was kind enough to give us three different versions of UDFs:

- *Scalar Functions*—These can be used for creating functions to be used the same way as columns in SELECT statements, similar to, for example, CONVERT().
- *Inline Table Valued Functions (ITVFs)*—ITVFs are similar to views, but can take parameters. The result is created with one single SELECT statement.
- *Multistatement Table Valued Functions (MTVF)*—In this case, the result can be created with multiple statements. MTVFs are, for example, a good solution in situations where you normally use temporary tables.

The UDF implementation in SQL Server 2000 is a typical first version, with several quirks. For example, it is not possible to use RAND() and GETDATE() in MTVFs. The same goes for touching temporary tables and calling stored procedures. Microsoft will probably fix some of the rough edges in an upcoming version.

Distributed Partitioned Views

With distributed partitioned views (DPVs), a table can be partitioned over several machines and it will be completely transparent to the clients. This is currently the technique Microsoft is using to achieve shared-nothing clustering with SQL Server.

> **NOTE**
>
> I will discuss DPVs more in Chapter 5, "Architecture."

Other Interesting New Features

The following are some other new features of SQL Server 2000, of high interest to developers:

- *Improved replication support*—It is now possible to use queued updates with MSMQ. In addition, merge replication doesn't have to be reconfigured from scratch, for example, every time you need to change the structure of a table.
- BIGINT *and* TABLE *data types*—The ordinary INT (32 bits) is sometimes too small a data type. The typical example is for primary keys. Four billion rows (assume both positive and negative values) aren't enough in many cases. BIGINT (64 bits) will probably come in handy in these situations. The TABLE data type can be used instead of an ordinary temporary table to create a temporary table in memory instead of in the tempdb. By doing this, you can save overhead. This data type is also important for the UDFs. Unfortunately, the TABLE data type can't be used as a parameter between stored

procedures. Another limitation is that a stored procedure can't be the source when adding rows to a variable of TABLE type.

- *Declarative cascading referential integrity*—People have been waiting for this SQL92 feature a long time.

> **NOTE**
>
> In my applications, declarative cascading referential integrity isn't very important. I prefer taking care of this explicitly in the stored procedures that are responsible for the deletions. I will discuss this more in Chapter 7, "Business Rules."

- INSTEAD OF *triggers*—INSTEAD OF triggers execute instead of a specific UPDATE operation, for example (in other words, the original UPDATE will not execute). This is the only kind of trigger you can use on a view.

- *Multiple instances*—It's possible to have several SQL Server instances on a single machine. This is great for testing an application on several versions of SQL Server, on a single box. It is also very useful in consolidation scenarios.

- *Extended properties*—Extended properties make it possible for you to add your own metadata to the schema, such as adding documentation for each column in each table, storing edit masks, and so on.

- *Indexed views*—An indexed view will have an index of its own and not only a stored query definition as with an ordinary view. This can greatly enhance performance for some queries.

- *New built-in functions*—These include GETUTCDATE() and SCOPE_IDENTITY(), which will return the last IDENTITY value that is created in the current scope, such as the stored procedure. This way, the problem with @@IDENTITY, in which a trigger could have added a row to another table with an IDENTITY that changed the value of @@IDENTITY, is avoided. (Once again, if you don't use triggers, this is not a problem anyway.)

- *Save* TEXT, IMAGE, *and so on in row value*—Quite often, the data for a TEXT or IMAGE column is quite small. In these cases, it would be beneficial from a performance point of view to store that data with the rest of the row, instead of in its own structure, as was always the case in previous versions of SQL Server.

- *Several productivity enhancements in Query Analyzer*—These include support for templates, object browser, and built-in debugging.

And, as is tried with every version, there have been a lot of improvements when it comes to performance and scalability. One example is that each connection is now consuming less memory than before.

Outstanding Problems with SQL Server 2000

Unfortunately, the T-SQL programming language still feels weak and old-fashioned. The following are some of the basic problems it still has:

- You cannot directly define ordinary constants.
- You can't use statements (such as @x + @y) as parameters.
- You can't directly send arrays as parameters. (The XML support in SQL Server 2000 is one possible solution that partly solves the problem. I will discuss this further in Chapter 8, "Data Access.")
- The error handling is very old-fashioned and has many quirks.
- There are some hindrances for centralizing code.

Beyond SQL Server 2000

There hasn't been much talk about the next SQL server version yet, code named Yukon, but the following are the features that I've heard of so far:

- The possibility to store XML documents in columns and being able to index the content
- Better administrative support for DPV
- The possibility to use the .NET languages to write the "stored procedures"
- The possibility to let SQL Server store the file system

Time will tell which or all of these features come to fruition.

What's Next

In the next chapter, I will discuss the factors I will use to evaluate my proposals to key problems that we will discuss throughout the rest of the book.

References

1. *Microsoft Systems Journal*, November 1997, http://www.microsoft.com/msj/1197/complus.htm.
2. *Microsoft Systems Journal*, December 1997, http://www.microsoft.com/msj/1297/complus2/complus2.htm.

3. T. Ewald. *Transactional COM+: Building Scalable Applications*. New York: Addison-Wesley; 2001.

4. E. Gamma, R. Helm, R. Johnson, J. Vlissides. *Design Patterns: Elements of Reusable Object-Oriented Software*. New York: Addison-Wesley; 1995.

5. C. Szyperski. *Component Software: Beyond Object-Oriented Programming*. New York: Addison-Wesley; 1997.

6. D. Appleman. *Visual Basic.NET or C#? Which to Choose?*, `http://www.desaware.com/Ebook2L2.htm`.

Factors to Consider in Choosing a Solution to a Problem

IN THIS CHAPTER

If you're like me, you sometimes get the feeling that most customers think that the only factor to consider when designing an application is raw performance. When you think about this more and discuss it further with your customers, however, you soon realize that it's not as simple as that. After all, why else would such a large percentage of the world's developers use VB in their work when it's possible to write faster programs in assembly language? And why are Oracle and SQL Server such popular database platforms? Memory allocations are much faster, as is writing to raw files. The answer is simple: There are always several factors to consider when designing an application, and it's a matter of give and take between them, because you can't optimize for them all.

Starting with the next chapter, I will be discussing several problems you can encounter when building enterprise components. In each example, I will discuss several different proposals for solutions and give arguments for and against each of them. In this chapter, I will present and describe the factors I will use throughout the book to evaluate the advantages and disadvantages of these different solutions. This should help you see how I have decided on my preferred solution. In explaining my reasoning, I hope to make it easier for you to make a choice, depending on your unique environment, situation, and personal taste.

As you read this chapter, you will find that the factors that must be considered in making your decisions are a bit like apples and oranges (or apples and pears, as we say in Sweden). I often find it hard to categorize these factors, because there are always too many dimensions that seem important, and any simple method of categorization fails. In addition, most developers will have their own definition of each of these factors, as well as their own means of categorization. However, think of my categories merely as a means to organize the evaluations in this book.

Portability

Although it might seem strange, I'm not going to discuss portability much in this book. This is because this book focuses on how to solve key problems when developing enterprise systems using .NET Component Services, Visual Basic .NET, and SQL Server 2000. As you read, you will also find that there is a lot of emphasis on stored procedures.

At the time of writing, .NET is designed for the Windows OS. Although there have been some rumors and announcements about support for .NET on other operating systems, nothing concrete has been developed. And when it comes to SQL Server stored procedures, there aren't even any rumors. Okay, T-SQL in Microsoft SQL Server looks a lot like it does in Sybase SQL Server, but there are numerous differences. If you choose those programs that the book is focused on, portability isn't your main concern, at least not if you like to take full advantage of the platform, which is what I intend to do. Thus, portability isn't a factor I consider when evaluating my proposals in this book.

Type of Consumer

I used to refer to the first tier in n-tier architectures as the presentation tier. However, this term is a bit too narrow. After all, what about batch processes and XML Web services, for example? I think a better term is "consumer tier" rather than presentation tier. Depending on which consumer type you plan to use, your design will have to adapt to it. Although I believe the general rule should be to let your design be as consumer-independent as possible, in reality, you'll have to make at least some decisions based on the consumer type. When I speak of specific types of consumer, I'm referring to whether the consumer of your components will be, for example, Web Forms, Windows Forms, XML Web Services, or just other components. However, while it's important to keep the type of consumer in mind, don't look solely at the current situation. It can, and does, change rapidly. Be prepared for these changes as you design.

Need for Coarse-Grained Methods

To further emphasize the notion that the consumer types of your client can change quickly, it's important to keep in mind that the design should be usable by all types of consumers. However, it's often possible to make design changes that are optimized for a specific consumer type. One good example of this is the need for coarse-grained methods exposed to the consumer. Assume that you have a component that accepts an order to be created, products to be requested, and shipment information to be handed over, and that this order will be saved. (Let's assume that it is only the Save() method that will need a database transaction in this example.) Even in this simplified version, there are four different methods used and, because the user typically requests, say, 10 different products, you will have 13 method calls for each order. Figure 2.1 demonstrates how the call stack might look when a fine-grained call design has been used.

If Web Forms is the consumer, a typical deployment schema would be on the same machine as the components. If the components are to live in a COM+ Library Application (which means that the components will execute in the same process as the ASP.NET application), having so many method calls will carry quite low overhead. You can see an example of this deployment schema in Figure 2.2.

In the case of Windows Forms as the consumer, each method call to the application server is costly, because the component I'm discussing here typically lives at the server, while the Windows Forms lives at the client computer. There is high overhead in this case. (The solution could mean that some fault tolerance is built in so that, if the client goes away prematurely, the server could remember the state until the client gets back.) You can see an example of this deployment schema in Figure 2.3.

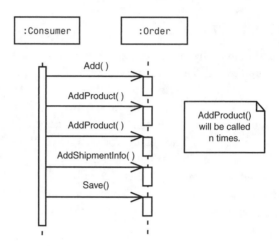

FIGURE 2.1

Interaction diagram showing a fine-grained call design.

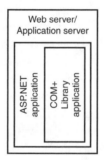

FIGURE 2.2

Deployment schema for when Web Forms are the consumer.

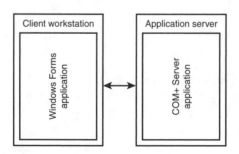

FIGURE 2.3

Deployment schema for when Windows Forms are the consumer.

There will also be much overhead if we create an XML Web service more or less directly out of the Order component. Then, the consumer of the XML Web service will have to make several calls to the XML Web service to have the service fulfilled, in this case over the Internet, which can be slow and unreliable.

A simple and typical solution would be to add a Facade[1] to help the Windows Forms and XML Web services by providing a single method (to be called once for a complete order) that will take care of making the 10 fine-grained method calls. By doing this, you create a solution that is optimized for Windows Forms and XML Web services, but Web Forms doesn't gain much. While there are some drawbacks to the consumer, such as a little less intuitive interface to use, there are also some advantages, such as deployment flexibility. The application could be deployed as a COM+ server application (in a process of its own) instead of as a COM+ library application without terribly degrading performance. In Figure 2.4, you can see the call stack for the same order example again, this time using a Facade to get a coarse-grained call design in perspective of the consumer.

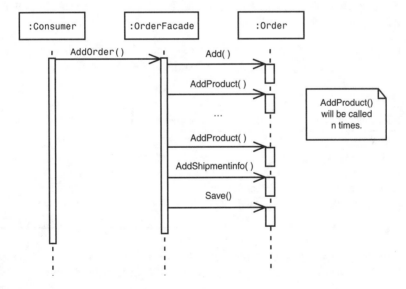

FIGURE 2.4
Interaction diagram showing how a Facade can solve the problems associated with fine-grained call design.

Concurrency Control

Let's take a second example in which the chosen consumer type will affect the design of concurrency control. (With concurrency control, I mean a mechanism that does not allow different transactions to affect the result of the other transactions, even though they run in parallel. The result should be the same as if the transactions had been executed after one another instead of at the same time.) Assume that you want to use optimistic concurrency control, which is that you expect to be able to update a row even though you don't keep a lock on the row and disconnect from the database between the fetch from the database and when it's time for updating. One typical solution would be to remember a ROWVERSION value (called TIMESTAMP in versions before SQL Server 2000) found at the fetch of the row until it's time to save the row. The UPDATE statement might then look like the code found in Listing 2.1.

LISTING 2.1   UPDATE Where ROWVERSION Is Used

```
UPDATE ordermaster
SET deliverycountry = @deliveryCountry
, deliveryaddress = @deliveryAddress
WHERE rv = @rv
AND id = @id
```

Note in Listing 2.1 that if @@ROWCOUNT is 0 and @@ERROR is 0, someone else has probably changed the row, since we fetched it.

Another typical solution would be to reuse the values that were found at read time in the WHERE clause, as is demonstrated in Listing 2.2. Note that the variables with Old as a suffix are the values found in the read.

LISTING 2.2   UPDATE Where "Complete" Comparison Is Used

```
UPDATE ordermaster
SET deliverycountry = @deliveryCountryNew
, deliveryaddress = @deliveryAddressNew
WHERE deliverycountry = @deliveryCountryOld
AND deliveryaddress = @deliveryAddressOld
AND id = @id
```

There are some advantages to the solution found in Listing 2.2. For example, if someone else changes a totally different column, it won't interfere with our UPDATE. Assume that you use a DataSet from a Windows Form. You can then keep an instance of the DataSet in the Windows Form and make all the changes to the DataSet. When it's time for updating, the DataSet could be sent to the component that will take care of the UPDATE. In the DataSet, both the old values and the new values are found and can be used for calling the stored procedure that will take care of the UPDATE for each row.

> **NOTE**
>
> In Chapter 8, "Data Access," I will discuss how I access the database. There you will see that instead of directly using `SqlDataAdapter`, I use a custom helper.
>
> I will discuss concurrency control in depth in Chapter 9, "Error Handling and Concurrency Control," where I will also show other possible techniques.

On the other hand, when it comes to Web Forms and XML Web services as consumers, it is less probable that the consumer will keep the `DataSet` between the fetch and the request for `UPDATE`. Instead, the `DataSet` is typically released after the values have been used for rendering the Web Form page or returning the result from the XML Web service. When the user asks to save some changes, perhaps a new `DataSet` is fetched from the database. The changes are then made to that `DataSet`. However, in this `DataSet`, there is a big chance you will fetch values different from the first fetch; the protocol doesn't work here. Instead, the original values must be kept somewhere else until it's time for the `UPDATE`.

Finally, assume that you have 25 columns to `UPDATE`—not an unheard-of situation at all. This will create a lot of work and require more memory than using a single `ROWVERSION`.

Physical Restrictions and Possibilities

Of course, as I'm sure you are aware, it is extremely important to keep the physical restrictions in mind regarding your design decisions when you allocate responsibilities to different layers and tiers. On the other hand, as was the case in considering consumer type, it's important to not look too narrowly at the current situation in this case either. If you use a new, more powerful server for the data tier instead of an old tired one, the situation has changed. The best strategy is to try to put the responsibilities where they belong: to make the most sense in the most common case, not only where they will give the best resource utilization in the current configuration. This is especially true if you're building something that you plan to sell to several customers and you don't know for sure what configuration the other customers have.

Still, what is considered a good design in the most common case could give painfully slow response times in a specific configuration. Assume that you build a system for a company that has its offices spread over 10 different cities all over the country. A pretty slow Wide Area Network (WAN), let's say 256KB, connects the offices. A new application is to be built and a rich client environment is needed. It has also been decided that there will be only one database server, which will be located at one specific office where there is a huge amount of traffic. In addition, each office has a Local Area Network (LAN) and an application server running the server components.

Perhaps you are wondering what the reason for having only one database server is instead of having one database server at each location and using merge replication. Assume that the application has one queue of requests from which each office worker will choose a request with which to work. They will, so to say, compete for the requests, and there is no geographical or organizational categorization of requests. (This way, load balancing of work is easily achieved.) This alone will make it difficult to replicate the database over several database servers.

This configuration is schematically depicted in Figure 2.5. As you can see, Application Servers 2–*n* are connected to the database server via a WAN, while Application Server 1 is connected via a LAN.

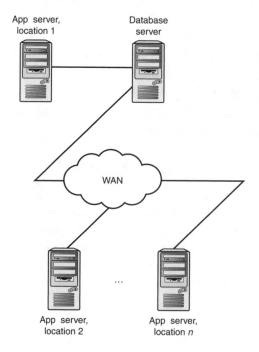

FIGURE 2.5
Sample configuration of n *application servers connected to one database server.*

When connecting an application server to the database server via a WAN, there's a performance penalty when hitting the database with many small calls.

NOTE

A round trip is, for example, a request sent from the application server to the database server and the answer going back again. I will discuss the importance of and how to reduce the number of round trips in depth in Chapters 5, "Architecture," and 8, "Data Access."

From a performance perspective, it's normally positive to check the data-focused business rules in the database tier. In this case, assume that as much as 20% of the UPDATE requests fail because a business rule is not met. It would probably then be disadvantageous to have the business rules checked in stored procedures in the database. A lot of the scarce bandwidth will be consumed without any use.

As I have said, I believe a good strategy is to put responsibilities where they make most sense in the most common situation. If you need to optimize for certain other configurations, then, of course, it's nice if you make it configurable so that different customers can configure the application for their specific situations.

Let's take another example of a physical restriction. Client-side caching of static data is normally very beneficial—both from the performance and the scalability perspective—because you can save network round trips. However, if the client computers have a shortage of memory, it's not a good idea to use a lot of memory-consuming, client-side caching.

Performance

Although Moore's Law states that computing power will be doubled every 18 months, more often than not, performance is still a very real problem. Why? There isn't one single answer to that question. Possible reasons could be

- Users' expectations for functionality and interactivity are growing all the time.
- Designs, tools, and languages are exchanging efficiency for productivity. Hardware is becoming cheaper all the time; consultants' hourly fees are not.
- Networks (both fast and slow) are more often a component of the runtime environment than they were before, which affects performance. Network round trips can be a real bottleneck.
- There is increasingly more data to process. Because the price for fast secondary storage is dropping all the time, there is less reason to delete old data. Instead, it is kept for future analysis, among other usages.

There is definitely a difference between real and perceived performance. Often, perceived performance is the more important of the two. However, improvements in perceived performance often degrade the real performance. A typical example is using a message queue. As soon as users have had their request written to the queue, they think the work is done and that they can continue on to something else. Actually, the real performance has been degraded slightly because the complete operation will take more time because queuing and dequeuing add some overhead.

A good metaphor to keep in mind when speaking about performance is that a chain is only as strong as its weakest link. When you try to optimize performance, you are trying to track down the bottlenecks—or weakest links in the chain—and remove them. In this respect, it's important to start designing with performance in mind. A well-designed system can typically get good enough performance automatically or with minor fine-tuning. A badly designed system will probably need a rewrite. To determine if you have reached the goal for performance, you must do stress testing. You must ask yourself, "When and where will the chain break?"

The Importance of Test Results

As you know, it's extremely important to use the target system (or one that is identical) when you do performance (and scalability) testing. Because of this, some people think that it is useless to read test results for other systems or configurations. I don't agree. Published test results provide important information about a variety of topics, and the relative differences between solutions are often quite similar for different configurations. Consequently, I have done a lot of tests when writing this book. However, be careful about drawing any conclusions from the test results I give; to get more accurate results, execute the tests in your own environment. The test results and all code can be found at the book's Web site at www.samspublishing.com. (Microsoft doesn't allow publication of test results from beta versions and I think that makes sense. Therefore, all published results will be from version 1 of .NET.)

You will find that in my solutions proposals throughout this book, I focus a lot on performance and scalability. One example of this is my fondness for stored procedures and for relying heavily on SQL Server. Letting SQL Server complete tasks for which it is suitable is an excellent way of getting good performance and high scalability, which brings us to the next topic on our agenda, namely, scalability.

Scalability

Engineers love definitions. My favorite definition of scalability is "How well a solution to a problem will work when the size of the problem increases."[2] No, as we've all heard before, performance and scalability aren't synonymous. As an example, take a fairly common question in the COM+ newsgroups, "Why isn't an application giving shorter response times when part of it is ported to COM+ Component Services?" The simple answer is that COM+/.NET Component Services don't really try to increase performance, only scalability.

What do I mean by this? Assume that there is a user running the application. .NET Component Services will not help him or her by splitting his or her requests into several parts that can execute in parallel to achieve a shorter response time for the total request—not even if there are multiple CPUs of which several have free capacity. On the other hand, if there are hundreds of users, .NET Component Services will do some tricks to try to serve all the user requests with response times for each request as close to the single user scenario as possible. Thus, .NET Component Services focuses totally on helping applications get good scalability; performance is not its design goal.

An example of how it is easy to intermix performance and scalability is illustrated in the following story. A couple of months ago, I was invited to a brainstorming activity at a company where I tried to come up with ideas on how to improve the throughput for a single client scenario. The client was a batch program that executed a use case over and over again, as quickly as possible. This was actually more of a performance problem, but I also gave several ideas that would only help in the scalability sense, such as when more simultaneous users were present. A typical example of this was me trying to shorten the length of the transactions relative to the complete use case. It didn't have any effect at all. I guess I got stuck in scalability ideas, because this is usually the problem at hand. (Still, the client will be able to use those ideas when it's time for the next phase, namely having several real users together with the batch program.)

Sometimes, performance and scalability do go hand in hand. If an action has good performance, it will release the used resources fast and, in that way, someone else can use the resources quickly. Good performance also often leads to good scalability.

However, sometimes performance and scalability are in opposition to each other. An example of this is using client-based caching in ASP.NET. If you save a lot of data in the Session object for each user, it could lead to very good response times for each user (depending on where the Session object lives). On the other hand, that data will consume a lot of memory for each user and thereby limit the number of simultaneous users that can be serviced with a certain amount of hardware.

As I mentioned previously, bottlenecks are the main enemy. A typical example of this is blocking, where several requests wait for a shared resource that requires serialized access. For example, it's extremely important to design for short and small transactions against the database; otherwise, this will kill the scalability. As you can see in Figure 2.6, it doesn't matter how wide the road is for miles and miles if a couple of meters are narrow.

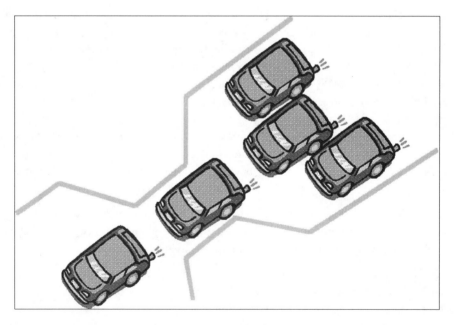

FIGURE 2.6
Bottlenecks effectively decrease throughput.

Scaling Up and Scaling Out

Developers often tend to solve problems by enhancing the code. That goes for problems in scalability too. When you check the pricelist for hardware, you see that your customer will get a lot of memory or CPU for the same money as if he or she buys one week of programming from any consultancy shop. Of course, not all problems should be solved by adding hardware, but quite often it's a cheap and safe solution.

> **NOTE**
>
> Don't try to add hardware if your customer has decent hardware and your application only scales to five users or so when the requirement is hundreds of users. There is probably a design problem or two that you should solve instead.

Microsoft often uses the terms "scale up" and "scale out" when discussing scalability. (As I understand it, Sun uses the terms "scaling vertically" and "scaling horizontally" instead.) What Microsoft means when they refer to scaling up is to add hardware to your current box—perhaps another CPU, more memory, another network card, a faster controller, and so on. This is a simple and efficient technique to use, because, for example, the administration will be no more difficult. Still, there is a limit to how far a single machine can be extended, and sooner or later there will be no single machine that can cope with the load you want to execute. Then it's time for scaling out.

Scaling out is about adding more machines and having them work together. The general concept is that several small machines could scale better than a single large one. Processes running on different machines will not compete, for example, for the same bus and the same memory because each machine has a bus and memory of its own. As long as the request can be handled totally by the machine that receives the request, the scalability will reach higher levels with scaling out.

However, there are several problems with scaling out, one being administrative in nature. It's simply much harder to take care of several machines instead of a single one. Are they all running the same version of the DLL, for example? In addition, all the tools needed for providing a single system image aren't currently available. Still, this looks very promising for the future, but your application won't be suitable for scaling out automatically. You have to prepare for it. I'll continue this discussion later in this chapter.

The Database and Performance

Earlier, when I discussed various performance issues, I mentioned SQL Server's role in getting good performance and scalability. I'd like to discuss this a bit more. As VB-programmers, we will finally get a strong environment and platform with Visual Basic .NET, and we can at last use all the good-to-have object orientation features. Still, database-close tasks most often can't be done faster and more efficiently than by the database.

> **NOTE**
>
> Database-close tasks are tasks that work a great deal with the data stored in the database. For example, such a task could be to join two tables or to search for a specific customer.

When I worked at a university, I was responsible for the courses in database design. I was quite alone in that field in my department. Most of my colleagues were more orthodox, object-oriented guys. Day after day, I heard that the database was just a place where the state should be spooled out to, just as to a file system. The database design wasn't important. Perhaps they were just teasing me, but I don't think so. It was more of a strong, underlying opinion. My opinion also is strong, and I still believe that I'm right—at least for the type of applications that I build, namely information systems taking care of large amounts of data. The opposite of information systems would probably be embedded technical control systems, such as programming robots or digital phone switches.

So, don't be fooled. If you have business rules that need to be evaluated, and if the rules require something to be read from the database, it will be more efficient to have the rules in the stored procedure that will take care of the UPDATE itself instead of in a .NET-component living on another tier.

To balance my favoritism of stored procedures a little, I'd like to point out that the database tier is often the one that is hardest to scale out. That could be one reason for not putting a lot of logic in stored procedures. The reason for the scaling out problems is that the database will have to hold state. This is the nature of the database. Therefore, pure cloning of the database isn't as simple as of Web and application servers.

> **NOTE**
>
> I will discuss scaling out the database in more depth in Chapter 5, "Architecture."

Using the Database

Watch out. What I just said isn't that it's more scalable to move the requests for reading data from the stored procedures to another tier. If the data still has to be read, all you have achieved as a result is worse performance and lower scalability. You are not saving resources in the database tier. As an example, assume that you have a simple business rule saying that you can't let the customer add another order if he or she has the status of "not trusted." In the stored procedure for adding a customer, you have a simple check to see whether he or she is trusted, which might look like the code in Listing 2.3.

LISTING 2.3 Simple Business Rule Evaluated in Stored Procedure

```
SELECT @aTrustedCustomer = c.trusted
FROM customer c
WHERE c.id = @customerId

IF @aTrustedCustomer = 1 BEGIN
  INSERT INTO ordermaster
  (customer_id, orderdate, ...)
  VALUES
  (@customerId, GETDATE(), ...)
END
ELSE BEGIN
  --Report the error...
  ...
END
```

You could rewrite the code in Listing 2.3 in Visual Basic .NET so that you first call a stored procedure that will tell you whether the customer is trusted. If so, you call another stored procedure that inserts the order. You may even decide to skip stored procedures and complete this task with direct SQL from your Visual Basic .NET code instead. All that you buy yourself in scalability terms is a worse result. And keep in mind that this is an extremely simple example. Finally, sometimes I get the feeling when I read books and articles that everybody is building applications for large corporations such as VISA and the like. Of course, most of the processing being done isn't of that scale. Even so, it's important to think about scalability from day one if you are reaching for a higher load than initially estimated.

2

FACTORS TO
CONSIDER

Other "-abilities" (Such as Maintainability, Reliability, Reusability, Testability, Debuggability, and Interoperability)

In the software engineering field, there is a lot of discussion about "-abilities." Other collective names for them are "quality attributes" and "nonfunctional requirements." Unfortunately, they are often hard to measure, but, even so, they are extremely important to consider.

In addition, it's often difficult to get customers to discuss the nonfunctional requirements. If you ask them if you should add support for "debuggability," for example, they often turn away from the idea as soon as they understand that it will cost them in the short run. They will tell you to not create bugs instead. To a large extent, the "-abilities" are something you have to think long and hard about for yourself, to be as professional as possible.

> **NOTE**
>
> If you are interested in these topics, there are plenty of books for further reading. Two examples are Frank Buschmann, Regine Meunier, Hans Rohnert, Peter Sommerlad, and Michael Stal's *A System of Patterns: Pattern-Oriented Software Architecture*[5] and G. Gordon Schulmeyer and James I. McManus's *Handbook of Software Quality Assurance*.[6]

Maintainability

Is it possible to change the system and extend it to meet new requirements without eroding the original architecture? For this to happen, the initial architecture must be flexible enough to adapt to unknown changes in the future. Compare it to a building. If you don't like the basic architecture and you decide to move a wall, there is a lot to consider if the alteration wasn't prepared for up-front. The result might be that the whole building collapses. More often than not, problems don't arise that quickly. As new functionality is added, some of the originally planned details will not be used anymore, and others will be used differently than what was planned. After a while, you can't recognize the original architecture.

> **NOTE**
>
> Some of you might feel that *Extreme Programming*[7] says the opposite to what I just said. I don't agree. *Extreme Programming* states the importance of having the chance to make changes. Don't plan for all possible changes, but be prepared for them.

It's also important that the architecture isn't so flexible that it is impossible to understand. Sooner rather than later, the changes will then conflict with the architectural vision. Of course, documentation is also very important to communicate the architecture so developers won't unintentionally destroy it. Test drivers and assertions that I discuss in depth in Chapter 3, "Testing," will also add quality parts to the documentation.

Another very important aspect of maintainability is to consider whether it is dangerous to make a change somewhere due to a large risk of side effects somewhere else. A high degree of encapsulation will take you a long way, because there will be fewer side effects if you make changes to an encapsulated implementation compared to one that, for example, uses a lot of global variables. Strong typing will also help to lessen any danger in making a change because the compiler will tell you if you, for example, try to make an implicit cast. This can be a reason for thinking more about typed DataSets, for example. In Figure 2.7, you can see an illustration of a "system" that isn't maintainable at all. Take out a card and the card house will crash.

FIGURE 2.7
A house of cards is an obvious example of something with low maintainability.

Yet another aspect of maintainability can be from the administrator's point of view. Is it easy to switch connection strings? Are there semaphores (flags) that will on occasion stay "up" and require an administrator to take them down every now and then? Is it possible to examine custom performance counters and such?

> **NOTE**
>
> In Chapter 9, "Error Handling and Concurrency Control," I will present a solution that demonstrates an administrator-friendly technique for providing pessimistic locking in a disconnected scenario.

Reliability

Reliability is often discussed in terms of fault tolerance and robustness, but it is also looked at in terms of recoverability. Hardware can provide you with some fault tolerance, but in this book, I will only discuss software aspects of reliability. In an effort to avoid confusion due to the myriad terms that are used in the industry, I'll discuss reliability in terms of

- Using preventative measures
- Actively taking care of a problem
- Using recovery/fail over when a problem occurs

Using Preventative Measures

As I'm sure you know, instead of letting a problem occur before taking care of it, you can take precautions to make it less probable that a problem will occur at all. For example, most of us would rather change the oil in our car's engine every now and then instead of replacing the engine when it crashes because of bad oil or lack of oil. A typical example of a preventative measure in a technical sense is to use the new feature in COM+ 1.5 to request recycling of your server processes, say, once a day.

Actively Taking Care of a Problem

You can also think of good error handling with automatic retry mechanisms as a way of achieving fault tolerance. It's no use that the user has to click a Retry button to make a new try because there was a locking conflict; the program should instead retry several times on its own. Another proposal is to use message queuing often. If the message has been written to the queue, many retries can occur.

Another way to see it is that the system will be able to cope, for example, with incorrect input, and will just tell the client that the input wasn't acceptable, without going to an unexpected state.

> **NOTE**
>
> I will address such reliability aspects in Chapter 3, where I discuss assertions and design by contract.

Using Recovery/Fail Over When a Problem Occurs

.NET Component Services will help a great deal when problems occur. For example, if there is a serious exception, the process will be nailed down and a fresh process will automatically be started. Meanwhile, one way to get safe recoverability is to use a transaction log, as SQL Server 2000 does. Another way is to expect fail over to do the job; that is, when one machine faults, another machine takes over. A typical product that helps with fail over support is Microsoft Cluster Services in Windows 2000.

> **NOTE**
>
> Products need to be cluster-aware to benefit from Microsoft Cluster Services. One example of such a product is SQL Server 2000.

Let's end this section with yet another example. Using lazy initialization is less efficient than making the initialization once at startup. (An example of initialization could be to read the connection string to use from a configuration file.) On the other hand, because there is a check before each usage that the initialization has been done and that the instance is okay, you can easily make a refresh action if a problem is found.

Reusability

From the beginning of the object-orientation hype, reusability has been its nirvana. So far, the promises haven't lived up to expectations. There are probably several reasons for this. For example, some might argue that components are a better reuse unit than classes in code. In any case, reuse requires a lot of work and won't happen automatically.

Another way to think about reusability is to not create reusable components in advance, but to try reuse when you face the problem again.[7] Nevertheless, you shouldn't create barriers, and I will be evaluating the proposals in light of this in the coming chapters.

It's important to understand that there are several granularities for where reuse is possible. You can reuse components or complete assemblies, stored procedures, user-defined interfaces, or whole layers. The location of your business rules is a major factor to consider when you think about reuse. Take, for example, the portion of an architecture as shown in Figure 2.8. There you can see that the business rules are living in a layer "before" the stored procedures.

> **NOTE**
>
> An assembly in .NET is a package of classes, and there is typically a one-to-one mapping to a DLL. An assembly contains one or more namespaces, and assemblies are also the smallest versionable units.

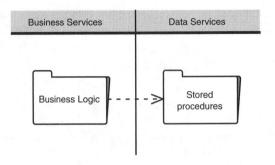

FIGURE 2.8
Example of an architecture where the stored procedures can't be reused without also reusing the components in the business logic layer.

For a design as shown in Figure 2.8, reuse of stored procedures that takes care of updating is impossible (or at least unsuitable) because the business rules are located in the business logic layer. The only layers that are reusable are the business logic layer and consumers to that layer—at least as far as operations that run transactions against the database go. (If you reuse a method that fetches some rows, that doesn't matter.) If, on the other hand, you move the business rules to the stored procedures, you can reuse every layer, including the stored procedures.

> **NOTE**
>
> I will discuss business rules in more detail in Chapter 7, "Business Rules."

In a way, reusability overlaps with interoperability, which I will discuss later in this chapter. You can, for example, reuse a VB6-written component from a .NET component. This is a typical example of interoperability between unmanaged and managed code. (Managed code is executed and managed by the common language runtime. Unmanaged code is the opposite; a typical example of unmanaged code is COM components written in VB6.) In addition, you can definitely design to get more reusable components. A classic problem is how and where to control transactions, which can affect the possibility of easily achievable reuse.

> **NOTE**
>
> I will discuss transactions in the face of reusability in Chapter 6, "Transactions."

Don't forget that it's not only the implementations that can be reused. Reusing design elements can be a real time-saver too, and can also help increase quality. One example of this is well-designed, user-defined interfaces. Another example is design patterns.[1,5]

Testability

Some people say that debugging and testing are the same thing. I don't agree. Testing is what you do to see if you can find errors in the application. Debugging is what you do when you try to locate a known error and correct it. Still, some techniques work for both testing and debugging. One example of this is using assertions, which tell you that you have an error. The program is testing itself, in a way. At debugging time, assertions will also be a signal to you about where you should start looking for the problem.

If you create a loosely coupled system, that is, when the different parts aren't tightly dependent on each other, but can interoperate with other parts instead and can be used in isolation without all the parts it is normally interoperating with, you will also increase testability, because each component can be more easily tested in isolation. The same goes if you see to it that you write stubs that return reasonable values early on, even though the real implementation hasn't started yet. (A stub in this context is an empty method, but with the correct signature. The stub can also deliver dummy values, to simulate the real method.) Components depending on those stubs can be tested early on.

Caching may decrease testability, because race conditions might give intermittent problems that may only show themselves once until the server is shut down and restarted. This means that caching will decrease the exposure of the risks, which makes it harder to find problems. You can rest assured that the bug will show itself in an important demo or at production time!

> **NOTE**
>
> An example of a race condition can be two threads that both want to initialize a value. The first thread checks to see if the value has been initialized and finds out that it hasn't, so it starts to gather information so it can set the value. Meanwhile, the second thread has also seen that the value hasn't been initialized; so, it starts to gather information too.

> **NOTE**
>
> I will discuss testing in more detail in Chapter 3.

Debuggability

I asked a friend who is a researcher in software architecture if they talk about "debuggability" too, and, although he understood what I meant immediately, he had never heard of the term. Perhaps I have invented the word.

There are several things you should do to prepare your application for easy and efficient debugging, but the single most important technique, in my opinion, is to add tracing support so that your application can tell you what is going on. For example, say a distant customer calls you and says he has a problem with the application you built. Because it seems to be a strange problem, the only answer you can give him is that you will have to add tracing to the application and send him a new version in a couple of days. It would be much better for you (and your customer) if you could just tell him to "turn a switch" (for example, by adding a row to a .config file) to turn trace calls on, run the scenario, and send you the trace log. You haven't solved the problem yet, but you have gotten off to a very quick start.

The interactive debuggers that we are now accustomed to should, of course, be used as much as possible, but they have shortcomings that tracing helps to solve. Examples of shortcomings that tracing solves include easier debugging of multiuser scenarios and debugging online and/or offsite without interfering (too much) with the system. With a tracing tool, you will also get a better overview when you start debugging than with a debugger, where you're in detail mode directly.

Another way to increase the productivity of debugging is to have the application log as much information as possible when there is an unexpected situation. That way, you can hopefully reproduce the situation when you investigate the problem.

> **NOTE**
>
> Chapter 4, "Adding Debugging Support," is dedicated to increasing debuggability.

Interoperability

Although interoperability can mean several things, I will use it in the sense of .NET components coexisting with COM (and COM+) components created in VB6 and with purchased components. In doing so, I assume that most of us will use VB6 for at least another few years. It just doesn't make sense to rewrite all the old components in a .NET language directly when there are so many other projects that must be developed for the first time. Microsoft is aware of this and has invested a lot of time and money in creating strong interoperability in .NET with existing COM components. The way I see it, this is crucial for the wide acceptance and success of .NET.

The coexistence and interoperability between .NET and COM components is really twofold. It's important that .NET components are able to use COM components and vice versa. Although it is possible, just how good will the interoperability in certain situations be? And how will the need for coexistence with COM components affect your design decisions? These are questions I will try to answer in the evaluations of the various solution proposals throughout this book. I will also focus on how to let .NET components interoperate with your stored procedures. In my opinion, there has been too little said about this over the years.

The common language runtime also has a lot to do with interoperability. For example, the garbage collector will help make interoperability easier to achieve. Using the common type system and the Base Classes Library (BCL) are two other ways to affect interoperability. In addition, there are interoperability aspects (few, but some) to think about even between languages, such as Visual Basic .NET and C#. For example, if you code in C#, remember that Visual Basic .NET is not case sensitive.

Yet another aspect of interoperability, namely coexistence with third-party components, is of course hard to target in specific terms, but I will give some general comments here and there throughout the book. One example that can help tremendously is the possibility of declarative transactions, which is one of the .NET component services.

One rule I try to adhere to is not to use distributed transactions (which is what you get if you use declarative transactions) if there is only one Resource Manager (RM), such as SQL Server. In this case, I use local transactions instead, so as not to waste resources and to get better scalability. One exception to this rule of thumb is when you have to deal with a component where the implementation is unknown to you and where there is no way of adding the component's behavior into your local transactions. Then, distributed transactions come to the rescue.

> **NOTE**
>
> I will devote a lot of time to discussing transactions and tips on how to optimize for each case in Chapter 6, "Transactions."

Don't forget that interoperability aspects have a great influence on writing serviced components, because the services will still be in unmanaged code and your components will be in managed code. Because of this, you can't expect static methods as root methods to be serviced, for example.

Productivity

Computers are getting faster all the time, but our productivity isn't growing at the same pace. Meanwhile, the productivity factor might be in conflict with, say, the performance factor. An example of this is that you need to know the names of your methods during execution time. This is used for tracing, for example, which I'll discuss in greater detail in Chapter 4. It would be very fast to hard-code the name of the method as a constant and hand that over in every trace call in the method, but when it comes to productivity, it would be less effective than using reflection to get to the metadata. You will find an example of how that can be done in the code snippet in Listing 2.4.

LISTING 2.4   Finding the Name of the Calling Method

```
Dim st As New StackTrace(1)
Dim sf As StackFrame = st.GetFrame(0)
Dim aBuffer As String = sf.GetMethod.Name.ToString()
```

It's very common that developers copy and paste code (commonly referred to as editor or clipboard inheritance) and, with the meta data approach, you won't get any extra copy-and-paste problems. (As you know, there are other more serious problems with copy and paste, but that's another story.)

Another example of productivity being in conflict with performance is that you don't have the chance of creating global constants when programming in T-SQL. The closest solution is probably to have a table with all the constants and then encapsulate the table with the help of a User-Defined Function (UDF) for each constant. This gives very readable and maintainable code, but this example, too, sacrifices performance.

You don't want to make a choice? Well, one way to have the best of both worlds could be to keep the source code intact with the productive solution. When it is time for final optimization, you copy the source code and execute a simple search-and-replace tool on it that exchanges some code snippets for hard-coded snippets. For the previous examples, it would probably take you less than an hour to write such a tool.

Another great way of increasing productivity without sacrificing performance is to use generators and templates. Then, writing the code is faster. Of course, running it will be as fast as if it has been written by hand.

How can productivity suffer because of the design? A typical scenario is that an overlayered architecture has been chosen. Layering could be good for productivity because several groups can more easily be working in parallel, but "lagom är bäst," as we say in Sweden: "All things in moderation."

Finally, two of the most productivity-killing features of a project can be when testing and debugging haven't been planned for up front. The bad news is that this often won't become evident until late in the project.

Security

Let's face it. Developers find security difficult and "in the way." Firewalls are often wrongly configured and cause problems at deployment time. An authentication problem adds another task to the already-delayed project plan, the need for certificates was not a requirement up front, and so on, and so forth. Still, security is a reality, and the way to cope with it is to think long and hard about it. Because of this, I will evaluate all the solution proposals in the book with regard to security, discussing whether any extra security risks will be created by a given solution.

Let's take a few examples. Could the localization of the business rules open up a security problem? Assume that some of the business rules are put in the stored procedures. The way to send the user identification is as an ordinary parameter to the stored procedure (because you shouldn't let the end users log in to the database with their own identity due to connection pooling reasons, for example). This is less secure than if no user identification has to be sent to the data tier. Usually, the problem is probably not big at all, but it's there because if somebody could intercept the call, he or she could change it so that his or her own credentials are used instead. Suppose that you use data caching a lot, and for sensitive data, too. Is the data cache as secure as your data tier? Probably not. We'll discuss more about this and other security-related issues throughout the book.

Farm- and Cluster-Enabling

Of course, I could have discussed how to farm- and cluster-enable components in the "Physical Restrictions and Possibilities" section, but I feel it is of such importance and such a long discussion that it's important to look at it separately. I started discussing scaling out earlier in the chapter. Let's continue with this discussion a bit more.

As I said, letting several small machines work together in an intelligent way can give extremely good scalability, especially if the shared-nothing model is used. In Figure 2.9, you can see that each database server has its own disk system, memory, bus, and so on. That way, there is no bottleneck because of several machines competing for the same bus, for example.

There are three basic ways of achieving "shared nothing:"

- Cloning
- Partitioning
- Replication

I will discuss each of these, as well as shared disk clustering next.

2

FACTORS TO
CONSIDER

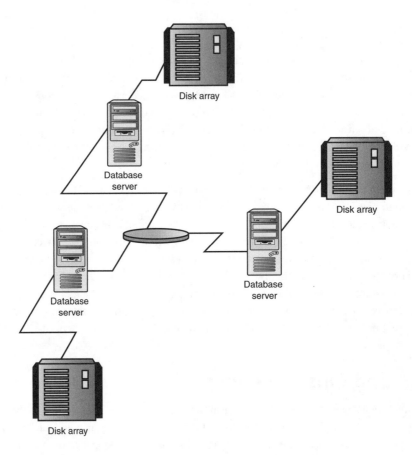

FIGURE 2.9
A schematic picture of "shared nothing."

Cloning

In cloning, a Web server and application server is duplicated so that the load is split between two or more machines instead of one. Some load-balancing mechanism is needed, but when that is in place, cloning is often easily used. The load-balancing mechanism is simple to set up and gives some fault tolerance (as fail over) automatically. Note, in Figure 2.10, that the Web and application servers are all equal and it doesn't matter which one the user hits.

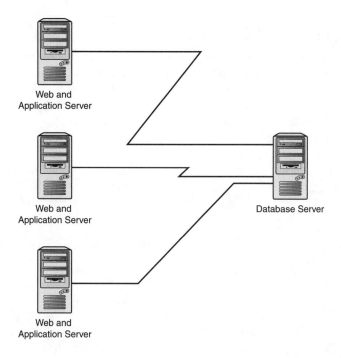

FIGURE 2.10
Cloning.

Partitioning

Another common approach is to partition the application server over several machines so that some components live on one server and some on another. Unfortunately, this will suffer from performance and scalability problems. It will also be more vulnerable because if one server is down, it won't be possible to use the application at all. It's most often preferable to use cloning instead of partitioning for the application server, at least when it comes to performance. On the other hand, there could be other reasons for partitioning the application server, such as when you want to process some of the logic inside of the DeMilitarized Zone (DMZ) and some of the logic outside of it. As always, it's a tradeoff. In Figure 2.11, you can see an example of partitioning where the application server has been partitioned between business logic and data access.

The DeMilitarized Zone (DMZ) in Software Architecture

The idea of the DMZ is to create a semisecure zone between the firewall and the Internet and the firewall and the corporate intranet. For example, if you want to put a sensitive Internet Web application in the DMZ, you can dictate that the only time that traffic goes through the second firewall to the corporate intranet is when the Web server has to contact the database server for accessing data.

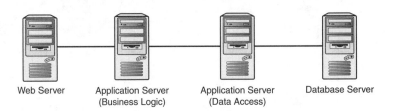

Web Server   Application Server   Application Server   Database Server
                  (Business Logic)   (Data Access)

FIGURE 2.11

Partitioning example 1. In this example, the application server is partitioned in two.

Even though I think cloning is a very good strategy for scaling out Web and application servers, it doesn't work well automatically for the database server. The reason for this is a matter of state. Because the components running on the Web server/application server could be designed to be stateless, it doesn't matter which server the user will hit the next time. There aren't any differences as far as the user is concerned. When it comes to the database, it's an entirely different story. The database is inherently stateful, so the user must hit the correct database server each time to find the state he or she needs. If all database servers look alike, so that each of them has the same state, there will be another problem, namely with the UPDATEs that must be propagated.

Instead, the database can be partitioned over several servers so that the part of the database that takes care of orders can occupy one server, the shipments can occupy another server, and so on. Then you have a major design influence. A more recent possibility found in SQL Server 2000 is Distributed Partitioned Views (DPVs) that let you split a table, such as ordermaster, over several machines. The partitioning is transparent to the layer closest to the database. It can also be built by hand, but then the layer closest to the database must know how the partitioning has been completed. Either way, it's extremely important to find a distribution key that splits the data, or rather the load, evenly. You can see that the customer table has been split over three database servers—East, Central, and West—in Figure 2.12.

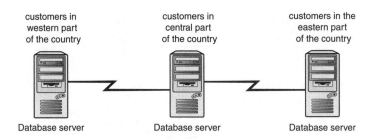

FIGURE 2.12
Partitioning example 2. In this example, the database server has been partitioned.

Replication

In several partitioning scenarios, there will be a need for duplication of lookup tables (and duplication of the rows in those tables) because there will be referential integrity relationships that need to be checked. When those lookup tables are to be updated, a two-phase commit transaction is needed if "real-time consistency" is a requirement. Replication can give a "real-enough time consistency" solution to the problem.

One problem with DPVs is that all queries can't always be answered by one machine. Instead, several machines have to cooperate to produce the result, which decreases performance. A more high-performance solution would be to clone the databases instead so that all data will be found at every server. The reading will be very fast and the solution will be very scalable—that is, until you take UPDATEs in consideration. If you need real-time consistency between the databases, you need to use two-phase commit transactions (distributed transactions), which are not only very costly but also vulnerable. If one server is down at the time of the transaction, the transaction can't be fulfilled. Figure 2.13 shows a schematic description of replication. You can see that the workstation is only talking to one of the database servers, but the changes will be replicated to the second database server.

Shared Disk Clustering

So far, I've discussed "shared nothing" clustering. Another clustering model is the shared disk technique. One way to use the shared disk technique is to have a disk system with the database that is shared by several servers acting as database servers. Figure 2.14 provides an example of how shared disk clustering might look.

As Microsoft sees it, the main reason for shared disk clustering nowadays is to get fault tolerance by using fail-over techniques. With shared disk clustering, you don't have to think so much about fault tolerance when you design your components as you do with shared-nothing scenarios.

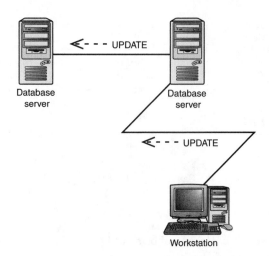

FIGURE 2.13
Replication.

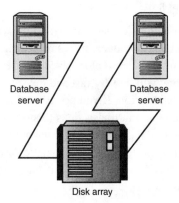

FIGURE 2.14
Shared disk clustering.

It will probably be quite common to combine shared disk with shared-nothing so that each database node will use a shared disk cluster. Figure 2.15 shows such an example. In general, shared-nothing is used for scalability and shared disk is used for reliability.

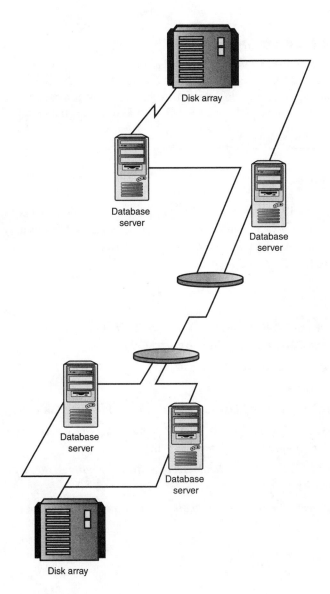

FIGURE 2.15

Combination of shared disk and shared-nothing.

> ### Caching and Clustering
>
> At the same time you start with farms and clustering, you must be careful with your caching solutions. Assume that you cache data at a cloned Web server and that piece of data is changed. How can you make the change to hit the cache at all the Web servers at the same time? Do you have to? If you do, it's probably better not to use caching.

What's Next

In the next chapter, I will start discussing key problems when building enterprise-scale applications. First up is testing. I will focus on how you can automate tests to cheaply increase the quality, with only a small effect on productivity. I will also discuss assertions as a technique for the code to test itself.

References

1. E. Gamma, R. Helm, R. Johnson, J. Vlissides. *Design Patterns: Elements of Reusable Object-Oriented Software*. Addison-Wesley; 1995.

2. http://wombat.doc.ic.ac.uk/foldoc

3. http://www.tpc.org

4. G. F. Pfister. *In Search of Clusters, Second Edition*. Prentice Hall PTR; 1998.

5. F. Buschmann, R. Meunier, H. Rohnert, P. Sommerlad, M. Stal. *A System of Patterns: Pattern-Oriented Software Architecture*. Wiley; 1996.

6. G. Schulmeyer, J. McManus. *Handbook of Software Quality Assurance, Third Edition*. Prentice Hall; 1999.

7. K. Beck. *Extreme Programming Explained: Embrace Change*. Addison-Wesley; 1999.

Testing

IN THIS CHAPTER

Although most system architecture books include a chapter on testing toward the end of the book, I believe that testing should be considered in the beginning of every project and at every step along the way. Therefore, I am including a chapter dedicated to testing early on in this book, in the hope that you will plan and design your projects with testing in mind.

Often, in real-world projects, testing isn't used as much as it should be and, when it is used, it is considered extremely time-consuming. Meanwhile, developers often claim they need a third-party testing tool to get started on their testing work. However, testing is more about organizational attitude than about fancy tools. If you value testing in the beginning of a project, it will help you in the long run, regardless of the tool you use. I firmly believe that the amount of testing you do is inversely related to the stress level in your project. In addition, you probably create more bugs under pressure than when you are working in a calm environment.

Most of this chapter will be devoted to making testing automatic to inexpensively increase the long-term quality of your application. We will start by looking at the various types of testing available. I will then present a proposal to automate testing that you can adapt to your own projects. Next we will look at how assertions can be used to make the code test itself. Finally, we will discuss a diagnose/monitor tool as well as important testing tips. I will conclude the chapter by evaluating the automatic testing and assertions proposals I have made based on the factors I presented in Chapter 2, "Factors to Consider in Choosing a Solution to a Problem."

A Short Introduction to Testing

This section is not meant to be used as a guideline for the Quality Assurance folks; rather, it is a recap of testing issues for developers—both considering the testing level and the type of testing needed—before we start getting our hands dirty.

Considering the Testing Level

Before you begin testing any project, you must first consider the level at which you want your testing efforts to be applied. You could test the entire application (and you definitely should) but it's important to consider individually the parts of the whole and to test them early on. If you postpone testing until the application is done, you're in for trouble. It will be too late to fix serious problems, and you most likely won't be able to conduct enough testing due to lack of time. I highly recommend you test the subsystems as they are being built, but even that is too granular and too "late" a level if it is the first one at which you test. Start testing directly at the unit level for components and stored procedures, and test all of them.

A couple of years ago, I had a heated discussion with my wife, who was working as a project manager for a test group at the time. She said that her group was in a wait state because they couldn't start testing their subsystem because it was dependent on another group's subsystem that hadn't been built yet. I told her that they should create stubs to simulate the delayed subsystem, giving the throughput that was to be expected and so on. (Stubs are empty methods but with the signature of the real methods. They are used to simulate the finished methods, to make dependent parts testable early in the process.) However, my wife thought it would be too expensive for her group to create the stubs and so wanted to wait until the other group's subsystem was complete. As you might guess, I didn't agree with this. I think that creating the stubs would have been cheaper than delaying the tests. (On the other hand, as I tried to remind myself, the less you know about a problem, the easier it is to solve. I guess I ought to say this should my wife ever read this book.) The bottom line is: Test at the unit level, and then at the subsystem level (by testing all the components in that subsystem), and finally at the complete system level, with all the subsystems working together.

Determining the Type of Testing

Depending on the level at which you will test your system, you can and should use different types of testing. It's important to note that no single technique will be the only one needed. Let's take a look at the different types of testing you should consider.

Development Testing

As developers work with a component, they obviously must test the component from different perspectives. Does it work in this case? Do I get the result I expect for a bunch of different combinations of input? And so on.

Historically, VB has been a great tool for writing code, testing it, and correcting problems as you test, continuing to write more code as you go. This is a very productive approach. What is *not* a productive approach is to have only the final User Interface (UI) as the test driver when you build the components. There are several problems with this, including the following:

- The UI might not be finished yet.
- Clicking through several dialogs before you get to where you can test your method is not just time consuming and frustrating, it can also lead to carpal-tunnel-syndrome-like symptoms.
- It will seldom be easy to test all the functionality of your component, as a lot of it will be "hidden" by the UI. (This is especially true for error-handling code.)

Most developers conduct development testing as they go along. However, the process of development testing may need to be formalized. We'll discuss this in more detail later in the chapter.

Code Reviewing

One powerful testing technique is simply to review your code. This is especially efficient if you ask someone else to review your code. In my first real-world project, a mentor came in to check on us now and then. One time he said to me, "Jimmy, show me your best function." I quickly guessed that he wanted to see some code with a lot of comments, and I remembered one function I had recently written that was heavily commented. (Yes, all my code was commented, but this function was more so than average.) I proudly showed him that sample. After half an hour or so, I wasn't so proud of the code anymore. He had given me feedback on how I could improve every single aspect of the function. Perhaps he was too tough on me, given that it was so early in my career, but on the other hand, it helped me improve the quality of my code greatly. Not only did his ideas inspire me, I was also afraid that he would ask me to show him my best function again!

A few organizations have formalized code reviewing so that every component must be signed by a reviewer, for example. On the other hand, the majority of organizations have only just begun to discuss implementing a code-reviewing policy. I recommend you start conducting code reviewing if you haven't already done so. Let somebody read your code for an hour; you will be surprised by the amount of potential problems that someone other than yourself can see easily.

I've encountered many examples of the importance of code reviewing. One in particular stands out. A colleague of mine once built an application that was to be used on a national television show that was collecting money for charity. My colleague had a hard time convincing the customer that it was important to test the application, and so he was very anxious about his application failing during prime time. Therefore, he asked me to review the code. Although he is the most skilled programmer I know, and had reviewed the code several times himself and carried out stress tests and such, nevertheless, in two hours I was able to point out three major risks that he was able to remove before using the application. The application ran with no problems on the show. (Perhaps it still would have without my review, but it was a much smaller "perhaps" with the review.)

Code review does involve some problems you have to watch out for. For example, you must take care that programmers don't feel personally insulted by the review process. Also, be careful that the code review doesn't focus solely on checking formalism, such as that the naming convention is followed and so on. Such reviewing is important, of course, but it is less important than finding parts of code that may be risky, especially if all the review time is spent debating on how a vague naming rule should be applied.

Finally, most of what I've said about code review can be valuable and should be used for reviewing the project's design as well. As you know, the earlier a problem is found, the easier and cheaper it is to fix.

Integration Testing

Although each unit should be tested separately, they must obviously work together when you integrate them. Therefore, it's important to test the components after they have been integrated.

I suggest that you schedule integration tests at specific points in time—perhaps once a week, perhaps as a nightly build with automatic integration—by automatically extracting the code from the version control system you use. If you don't schedule such testing, you risk getting into the situation I've been in several times. Say I'm about to integrate my code with a fellow programmer's. I go over to his or her office and ask if he or she is ready for integration. The response is that he or she needs another hour, and so I go back to my office and start fixing something. Two hours later, my fellow programmer comes to my office and asks me if I'm finished. I say that I need another hour, and so we continue like this for a week or more. Avoid this trap by scheduling integration tests, and stick to your schedule.

It's important to note that, as is the case in other levels of testing, if integration testing is not done until the end of the project, you are asking for trouble. Start doing integration tests as soon as the components take shape—they don't have to be finished. In fact, they don't even have to be programmed at all except for the interfaces and a minimal amount of fake code. This will allow for integration as early as possible.

Stress Testing

Yet another type of test that you definitely shouldn't put off until the end of the development cycle is stress testing. (In reality, it's very common that this isn't done until after the system has been shipped and the customer complains about performance and/or scalability problems.) A good approach is to make a proof of concept stress test for one or two key use cases as soon as the design is set. If you can't reach your throughput goals at that point, you probably won't for the other use cases either, so you'll have to rethink the design.

Stress testing is also a good opportunity to conduct recovery testing. What happens if I pull the plug? When does the system hit the wall, and is there a convenient interval between the expected load and the wall? Will the system continue working at peak when it hits the wall? Asking these questions and testing for answers now will save time later.

A few years ago, Microsoft hired Vertigo to create the sample application Fitch and Mather Stocks,[2] which simulates a stock trading Web site. The purpose of creating the sample application was not only to see how well an application built with Microsoft tools such as ASP, VB6, COM+, and SQL Server could scale, but also to show developers around the globe the best practices for how to write scalable applications with these tools. When Vertigo thought they were finished, they shipped the application to National Software Testing Labs (NSTL) for the initial stress tests. The stress testing was done with four IIS/COM+ servers and one database server. NSTL found that the application crashed at 16 simultaneous users. After some fine-tuning by Vertigo, the application could handle approximately 15,000 simultaneous users with less than one-second response time, still using the same hardware. In this specific case, most of the tuning effect was reached because Vertigo used a workaround for an NT bug, but that's not my point here. My point is that if you don't do early stress testing, you don't know what the limits of your application's scalability are. One bottleneck, and you're in trouble.

Regression Testing

Sound object-oriented and component-based design will, thanks to a high degree of information hiding, make it more possible to change components without breaking other parts of the system. Still, as soon as you change anything in an application, there is a risk that something else will stop working. You have probably said something like, "The only thing I changed was X, but that doesn't have anything to do with this new problem" only to find that the change actually was the reason. The more encapsulated your system is, the less often you encounter a problem like this, but for every n^{th} change, you will create a problem. Therefore, when you change something, you should perform regression testing to see that nothing else has been tampered with. Most often, you have to decide to test only the closest parts of the code change; otherwise, it would take too long, at least if you have to test by hand. In my experience, regression testing is one of the most important forms of testing, but many programmers do not take much time to do it.

This brings us to the next section: support for automatic testing.

Support for Automatic Testing with a Standardized Test Bed

Do you know the most common reason developers give for why they haven't tested their components? Well, it depends on when they are asked. Early on in the project, they may say, "It's no use testing my own code. Someone else has to do it." If they are asked after the project is completed, they may say, "There wasn't enough time." I've used both of these responses myself at one point in time or another. And although I know it *is* more likely that someone else will find problems with my components than I will, on the other hand, if I leave easily detectable errors to the tester, he or she won't have time to find the more important, nasty problems. So of course, as a programmer, I must remove as many simple bugs as possible as early as possible. Perhaps the singlemost efficient way to achieve this is to add support for automatic testing to your components.

> **NOTE**
>
> Although in this chapter I discuss a custom solution for making testing more automatic, there are several third-party solutions that are very interesting too. Two common examples are the tools from Rational and Compuware.

When you build components, the final UI often isn't available, and it would take too long to use it for all your testing because it often takes several actions in the final UI before your component is used. A common approach is to build a dummy UI instead with 48 buttons that have to be pressed in a certain order to test your component. Unfortunately, only the original developer will know how to use this dummy UI, and not even he or she will know how to use it after a couple months. Why not skip that specially built UI as a test driver and use a standardized test bed instead? It doesn't have to be very fancy. The important thing is that you have something that you (and your colleagues) use. While you're building the components, you also write a test driver for each component, so the test suite for the test bed is being created too. Bugs will be found early on and the test suite can be used repeatedly. You will be most happy about it when you make a small change in a component and re-execute all the tests, just in case, and the tests tell you about a newly introduced bug.

Test Driver, Test Bed, and Test Suite

Before we get any further in our discussion, it's important you understand the meaning of the following terms:

- *Test driver*—A test driver is a program that executes some tests of one or more components or one or more stored procedures.
- *Test bed*—A test bed is a container or a controller that can execute the test drivers.
- *Test suite*—A test suite is a couple of test drivers that are related in some fashion.

Developers of the source code are usually the best persons to write a test driver for the component. This test driver should be able to handle as many cases as possible and should expose the most sensitive parts of the code in the component, something with which the original developers are familiar. The developers of the components can also complete this faster than anybody else because they know the code inside out, and it will rarely be as quick or efficient to write the test driver as when the code itself is being written.

NOTE

When the tester knows about the implementation and doesn't just see the unit as a black box, it is commonly referred to as white-box testing. (The opposite is black-box testing.) If the developer of a component also writes the test driver, white-box testing is being used.

It's important to note that there is no silver bullet when it comes to testing. Creating test drivers according to some rules for all the components will not solve every problem. However, doing this will increase the quality of your application if your organization isn't using something similar to it already. By using a test bed like the one I will discuss in this chapter, you will take care of development testing, integration testing, stress testing, and regression testing. The test drivers will also provide great documentation, showing you how the components should be used, for example. After all, an example is often the most helpful documentation.

> **NOTE**
>
> Remember this simple rule: The component or stored procedure isn't finished until there is a well-written and successfully executed test driver that follows the rules established by the standardized test bed.

Working with the Test Bed

Let's look at a simple test bed that I've used to test the code in this book. The test bed is called JnskTest. The general requirements that I had for the test bed were that it should

- Log the test results in a database
- Log who executed the tests, when they were started, and when they ended
- Be usable for testing stored procedures, .NET components, and components written in VB6
- Have test drivers that are possible to use (without logging) from another test tool that logs data on its own, such as Microsoft's Application Center Test 2000 (ACT)
- Make it possible to schedule execution, for example, after the nightly build

In this section, I will demonstrate how you can work with the test bed. Please note that the tool itself isn't really important; it is the principle I hope will inspire you or give you some code to start with that you could then expand. I also want to make it clear that the following few pages aren't typical of the book. I'm *not* going to fill the book with a lot of screenshots. I'm including these screenshots only as a means to communicate the ideas behind this tool.

> **NOTE**
>
> You'll find all the source code for this chapter on the book's Web site at www.samspublishing.com.

In the following sections, I'm going to show you each of the forms in the test bed application JnskTest. The first is the overview form, which is the main form. Keep this in mind when you read through the explanation of the tool. The idea is that you create test drivers for your components and stored procedures. Those test drivers are orchestrated to test executions. The test executions are listed in the overview form.

The Overview Form for the Test Bed

The JnskTest tool is "operated" through the overview form, where test executions are listed. Here, you can set a filter to see only certain executions, such as those that were executed during a certain time interval or those that haven't been executed yet. Before the form shows, you are asked for ordinary login information and what database to use. Figure 3.1 shows how the overview might appear. Here you can see the test executions based on the current filter.

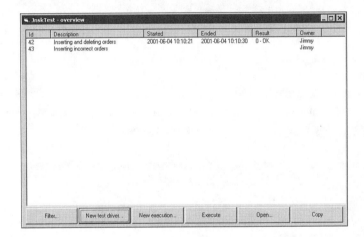

FIGURE 3.1
An overview of test executions based on the current filter.

> **NOTE**
>
> As you can see in Figure 3.1 (and coming figures), the user interface for the test bed application is currently built in VB6. When the book has been published, you can find a version of the test bed where the user interface is written in Windows Forms at the book's web site at www.samspublishing.com.

The Form for Registering a Test Driver

Before you can get started, you must register your test drivers. (You also must have your test drivers written, but we will discuss that shortly.) It would be possible for the application to autoregister test drivers by examining the database for specific suffixes among the stored procedures and checking the classes at the machine if they implement Jnsk.Test.ITestDriver.

However, I have skipped that for now and instead will show you how to register the test drivers by hand. Figure 3.2 shows how the appropriate dialog appears. In the example, a stored procedure test driver is being registered.

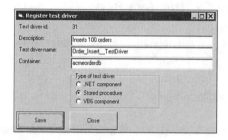

FIGURE 3.2

Registering a stored procedure test driver.

Registration and Execution

After you have registered your test drivers, you can register an execution by pointing out which test drivers to use. The registration of an execution is shown in Figure 3.3.

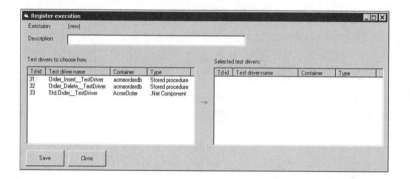

FIGURE 3.3

Registering the test drivers that should be used for an execution.

When you have registered one or more executions, you can execute them from the overview form (refer to Figure 3.1) by selecting the desired rows and clicking the Execute button. After a while, you will get the result of the execution. At this point, you can see how long the execution took and whether it worked out as you expected. You can then open each execution to get more details about the test driver used in the execution. Figure 3.4 shows the subsequent dialog in which you can add a comment to the result as documentation for the future.

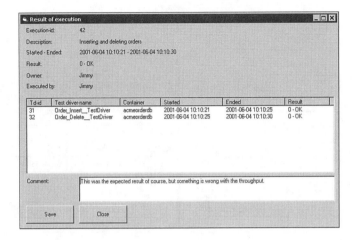

FIGURE 3.4
Viewing the result for each used test driver in a specific execution.

NOTE

The GUI calls stored procedures as the technique to access the database. The stored procedure interface can be used directly by the user of the test bed, as can the underlying tables (which will be described in the following section). For more information about this topic, you can download the tool from the book's Web site at www. samspublishing.com.

Understanding the Database Schema for the Test Bed

Whenever I design a component, I try to keep in mind the idea that simplicity is beautiful. You will find that the database schema I use for the test bed is quite simple. The tables are as follows:

- `jnsktest_td`   In this table, each test driver (regardless of whether it is a test driver for a stored procedure or for a component) will be registered before it can be used.

- `jnsktest_execution`   In this table, a certain execution request will be registered. A row in this table is the master to the detail rows in `jnsktest_executionrow`. After the test has been executed, you will find the overall result about the execution here.

- `jnsktest_executionrow`   A row in this table carries information about one step of a certain execution request and what test driver to use. Afterward, you will find the result of each test driver used in the execution in this table.

The database schema just described is shown in Figure 3.5.

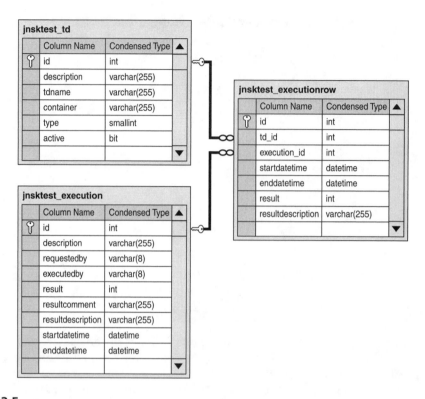

FIGURE 3.5
Database schema for test bed.

There are several points that need to be made about using the database for logging data. For one, I've asked myself more than once how long a certain scenario took in an earlier version. If I have the data about that easily accessible, I have an answer to this question. Another advantage is that it is easy to run statistic reports to determine, for example, whether the problem frequency is decreasing over time.

Using the Test Driver to Test Stored Procedures

It's simple to write a test driver to a stored procedure. Just write a stored procedure that returns 0 for success and another INTEGER value, typically the error code, for failure. (You should also use RAISERROR() to give some contextual information as text, such as exactly where the problem occurred.) Take care that you stop execution if you find a problem and return the error code. If you execute another test instead, there is a risk that the second test will be successful and you will never find out that there was a problem.

Listing 3.1 displays the first part of the code for a sample test driver. Some standard declarations of local variables are done first, followed by a few initializations. (This will be discussed in depth in Chapter 5, "Architecture.") After that, a specific local variable is declared, called `@anOrderId`, that will be used to receive the order ID of a newly added order.

LISTING 3.1   Example of a Test Driver for Stored Procedures: Part 1

```
CREATE PROCEDURE Order_InsertMaster__TestDriver AS
  DECLARE @theSource uddtSource
  , @anError INT
  , @anErrorMessage uddtErrorMessage
  , @aReturnValue INT

  SET NOCOUNT ON
  SET @anError = 0
  SET @anErrorMessage = ''
  SET @theSource = OBJECT_NAME(@@PROCID)


  ----------------------------------------------------


  DECLARE @anOrderId INT
```

In the second part of the test driver, shown in Listing 3.2, the stored procedure to be tested is called. In this case, `@aReturnValue` of 0 is expected, meaning that an order registration for customer 42 at a certain date executed just fine. As you can see by the error-handling model, the execution of the test driver will be ended by a GOTO to the `ExitHandler` if there is an error.

LISTING 3.2   Example of a Test Driver for Stored Procedures: Part 2

```
  EXEC @aReturnValue = Order_InsertMaster 42
  , '2001-04-30', @anOrderId OUTPUT

  SET @anError = @@ERROR
  IF @anError <> 0 OR @aReturnValue <> 0 BEGIN
    SET @anErrorMessage =
    'Problem with inserting order (1).'
    IF @anError = 0 BEGIN
      SET @anError = @aReturnValue
    END
    GOTO ExitHandler
  END
```

In the third part of the test driver, shown in Listing 3.3, the stored procedure to be tested (`Order_InsertMaster()`) is called again, but this time it is called with parameters that force an error. If @anError equals to 8114, everything is fine and it won't be treated as an error by the test driver. Otherwise, there was an unexpected error, which will be reported by the test driver.

LISTING 3.3 Example of a Test Driver for Stored Procedures: Part 3

```
EXEC @aReturnValue = Order_InsertMaster 42
, 'xx', @anOrderId OUTPUT
SET @anError = @@ERROR

IF @anError = 8114 BEGIN
  SET @anError = 0
END

IF @anError <> 0 OR @aReturnValue <> 0 BEGIN
  IF @anError = 0 BEGIN
    SET @anErrorMessage =
    'Problem with inserting order (2).'
    SET @anError = @aReturnValue
  END
  ELSE BEGIN
    SET @anErrorMessage =
    'Unexpected value for @@ERROR'
  END
  GOTO ExitHandler
END
```

In the fourth part of the test driver, shown in Listing 3.4, you can see the ExitHandler. If an error has been found, it is reported through a centralized stored procedure called JnskError_Raise(). Finally, the stored procedure is ended with RETURN() of the error code.

NOTE

The error-handling model will be discussed in detail in Chapter 9, "Error Handling and Concurrency Control."

LISTING 3.4 Example of a Test Driver for Stored Procedures: Part 4

```
ExitHandler:
  IF @anError <> 0 BEGIN
    EXEC JnskError_Raise @theSource
```

LISTING 3.4   Continued

```
  , @anError, @anErrorMessage
END

  RETURN @anError
```

I suggest that you give your test driver the name of the stored procedure that is tested with a
_TestDriver suffix. That way, you can easily see the stored procedures that lack a test driver.

> **NOTE**
>
> I originally had two versions of the controller for the execution: one for stored proce-
> dures and one for components. I have dropped that design and let the overview form
> in Figure 3.1 (together with a .NET class) be the controller for all types of test drivers
> instead. This is easier and cleaner. To make it as easy as possible to write the test dri-
> vers, the controller will take care of all the logging.

Using the Test Driver to Test .NET Components

When you are testing .NET components with the test driver, you will use the same tables as
were discussed earlier and shown in Figure 3.5. The test drivers will be Visual Basic .NET
components, a sample of which is shown in Listing 3.5. In the sample, a method called
SalesOfToday() is tested in an Order class.

LISTING 3.5   Example of a Component Test Driver

```
Public Class Order__TestDriver
    Implements Jnsk.Test.ITestDriver

    Public Sub Execute() _
    Implements Jnsk.Test.ITestDriver.Execute
        Dim anOrder As New Order()

        Try
            If anOrder.SalesOfToday() < 100000 Then
                Throw New ApplicationException _
                ("Strange SalesOfToday result.")
            End If

        Finally
            anOrder.Dispose()
```

LISTING 3.5   Continued

```
        End Try
    End Sub

End Class
```

As you can see, the test driver component must implement `Jnsk.Test.ITestDriver`, but except for this, there is nothing else special required. You can even skip `Try`, `Catch`, and `Finally` if you want, because the controller will take care of unhandled problems. If the test driver catches exceptions, it's important to `Throw()` an exception also, so it is popped to the controller.

> ## Change of Style
>
> For several years, I've been a fan of prefixing variables with data types and adding prefixes for the scope of variables and for `ByVal`/`ByRef` of parameters. For the .NET languages, Microsoft recommends camelCase (first letter lowercase, initial letter in the next word uppercase) as the naming convention for parameters—no data-type prefixes. (Microsoft actually only comments on public elements. Variables and so on aren't important in Microsoft's view of standardizing.)
>
> Because VB6 did not have strong typing, data-type prefixes were very important. We now have strong typing at our disposal, so I typically add an a, an, or the prefix for variables. (For parameters, I follow Microsoft's recommendation.) For member variables, I use m_ as the prefix instead. (I also use btn for buttons, and so on.) This is my choice, and you should follow the standards you think are appropriate. However, I strongly recommend standardizing public elements if you are creating a coding standard at your company, and it's probably a good idea to follow Microsoft's recommendation then.
>
> I use the same convention for my parameters in my stored procedures. In the past, I used the same data-type prefixes in my stored procedures as for my VB6 components. That was probably not good for database administrators, because it is not at all a defacto standard in the T-SQL field.

> **NOTE**
>
> You could (and it's not uncommon) add your test driver code as a method to the class itself. Then you wrap that method with a conditional compilation directive so it's not in the release version of the code. I prefer *not* to use this solution because if I have

the test driver as a method in a separate class, I get the interface tested too because this question will be answered: Can the test driver call the other component and its methods? In the COM world, it has helped me on numerous occasions to have the test drivers code in separate classes.

Understanding the Controller of the Test Bed

The UI will act as the controller of the test bed (refer to Figure 3.1). The controller will call JnskTest* stored procedures to fetch information about test drivers, log what is going on, and save the final result. The same goes for calling the stored procedure test drivers. The technique that is used for calling component test drivers by name is found in the snippet from the controller code starting in Listing 3.6. In VB6, you could accomplish the same thing easier using CreateObject(), but if you use CreateObject() in Visual Basic .NET, you pass the interoperability layer and use the test driver as a COM object.

In Listing 3.6, the assembly with the test driver is loaded by using the name of the assembly for where the test driver is located (container), for example, AcmeOrder. Then, the classname (for example, Std.Order__TestDriver, where Std is the namespace) is used for getting the class.

LISTING 3.6 Sample Controller Code: Part 1

```
Dim anAssembly As System.Reflection.Assembly = _
System.Reflection.Assembly.Load _
(container)

Dim aType As Type = _
anAssembly.GetType(testDriverName, True, True)
```

NOTE

The container parameter may contain a fully specified reference to an assembly, for example,

```
AcmeOrder, Culture=neutral, PublicKeyToken=abc123..., Version=1.0.0.0
```

Then, as you see in Listing 3.7, the test driver class is instantiated and then cast to the Jnsk.Test.ITestDriver interface. Finally, the Execute() method is used to run the test scenario in the test driver.

3

LISTING 3.7   Sample Controller Code: Part 2

```
Dim aTestDriver As Jnsk.Test.ITestDriver = _
CType(Activator.CreateInstance(aType), _
Jnsk.Test.ITestDriver)

aTestDriver.Execute()
```

NOTE

This tool is fully usable for components written in VB6 as well as for components written in another .NET language, such as C#. You'll find test driver templates on the book's Web site at www.samspublishing.com.

Writing the Test Drivers: Issues to Consider

So far we have discussed how to use a test bed and write the test drivers. Now it's time to discuss some issues you should think about when you write test drivers to make them as useful as possible. But before we do that, I'd like to share a tip for choosing test cases in addition to the testing you do for each and every component and stored procedures. The use cases are a great source to use. If each and every part of your use cases—both the normal and those with expected exceptions—works fine, you have come a long way.

I've often heard that the part of the system that is most often full of errors is the error-handling code. Although it is rarely used, it is still important that it works correctly. Make sure that you handle different error situations, including unexpected ones, when creating the error-handling code.

In addition, you should set a goal for how much code should be executed, or covered, in the tests. Because you will write the test driver together with the component, it is the best opportunity to ensure such code coverage. You should also check it with a tool. (There will soon be several third-party tools to use with .NET components.) When it comes to stored procedures, I don't know of any streamlined tools to use. One proposal I came across was to add uniquely numbered trace calls after each line of code that can be executed.[3] That way, you can collect all the trace calls and calculate the percentage of the code that was visited.

NOTE

I will discuss tracing in depth in Chapter 4, "Adding Debugging Support."

It's also important that you test at the limits if there is an interval of possible values. Try the smallest value, the largest value, and the values just outside the interval. Another example of where it is important to test at the limits is Arrays. This is due to Microsoft's decision to let developers define the size of Arrays in Visual Basic .NET the same way that they defined them in VB6. I'm sure that will lead to bugs, especially among the many programmers who don't program exclusively in Visual Basic .NET, but also in C#.

You should be ruthless when you write test drivers. Remember that a good test driver is one that finds a problem, not one that says that everything seems to be running smoothly.

"Combinatorial bugs" are hardest to find in my opinion. By combinatorial bugs, I mean bugs that only happen when there is more than one circumstance occurring. Assume you have two variables, A and B. The bug is only occurring when A equals 10 and B equals 20, and never in any other situation. Finding that bug is, of course, much harder than if it occurs both when A equals 10 *or* B equals 20. Think about how to find such bugs when you write the test drivers so that you don't only test each case in isolation. When a bug is found, you should try to extend your test drivers so that you catch similar bugs the next time.

Test your test drivers with test drivers that you test with… Sorry, I got carried away there. What I mean is that you may want to introduce saboteurs that check that your tests work well. Insert some bugs in your stored procedures and components. In your components, I recommend you wrap the saboteurs within a specific compiler directive so that you don't forget to change the problem back. Unfortunately, a similar feature to compiler directives doesn't exist for stored procedures.

Test the transactional semantics as much as possible. Simulate problems in the middle of transactions and check that the system handles this gracefully. Also be sure to test concurrency situations. For example, you can add wait states in your components/stored procedures and execute two or more test drivers simultaneously to force the testing of concurrency situations.

Create fake components that your component is dependent on to make early testing possible. You can, of course, do the same with ADO.NET and DataSets. To make this productive, spend an hour or so writing a tool to generate the fake code because writing it by hand can be tedious. In sum, this is a good idea of how to achieve parallelism in your development project. For example, the UI group can immediately get components that return data (even if it is only fake data). When the components have real implementations, they are switched and the UI works just fine.

Write your test drivers (at least some of them) so that they can also be used for stress testing and not just for functional testing. That way, you can use the same test drivers in several different scenarios.

3

TESTING

Finally, write a couple of generators that can create stubs for test drivers very quickly. That way, you can increase the productivity even further for the testing.

Discovering Problems with the Test Bed Proposal

Of course, test drivers do introduce some problems. One problem is that you will find yourself making code changes in two places—first in the code itself, and then in the test drivers. If you don't change the test drivers as the system evolves, they will quickly become obsolete.

Another problem is that in the kind of systems I build, I interact a lot with the database. Therefore, the tests, too, will be database-centric, so they must know something about what data to expect. If you delete all the rows in a table, for example, the test drivers will probably not work as expected. You could take proactive steps in the test drivers and add and delete rows to the database so it appears as you want it to before the real tests start, but then it will be more time consuming to write the test driver. I believe a better approach is to keep several instances of the database running, with one version specifically for the test bed. That way, most of the experiments will be run in other developer-specific databases instead, and the test database can be quite stable. You need to test your upgrade script anyway, so the test database will work fine for that. Just don't forget to make backups of the test database—it's as valuable as your development databases.

In the proposal for a test bed that I've given here, I haven't said anything about parameters to the test drivers. It might be a good idea to add support for this. That way you can, for example, let a test driver call another test driver with specific parameters to get a specific task done. When it comes to stress testing, it's important not to read the same piece of data over and over again (if this isn't a realistic situation). Otherwise, you will only hit the data that SQL Server is caching and you get an erroneous test result. This is yet another situation for which parameters could be handy, using a client that creates random values for the parameters. Of course, you could use a similar technique within the test drivers themselves to create random customer ID criterions, for example. In any case, it's important to add support for logging the exact values that are used so that a detected problem can be duplicated easily.

Finally, because the components and stored procedures will evolve, it could be wise to add some version information to the test results so that you don't compare apples and oranges. Otherwise, you will get strange comparisons when you see that a certain test driver took 1 second in one instance and 10 seconds in the next. How come? Even the test drivers will evolve, and, most probably, they will execute more tests over time. Thus, there are actually two version series to track.

> **NOTE**
>
> As you saw before, it's possible to give version information for the assembly of a test driver in the version of the test bed that I have discussed here.

Assertions

If you expect a variable at a certain place to have a value between 1 and 4, for example, you can express this in the code. In VB6, the Debug object has a method called Assert() that you can use to test your assumptions. Unfortunately, that method will not be compiled into the executable, and, in my opinion, this makes the method useless. Because of this, I wrote my own version of Assert() for my VB6 components.

The .NET Framework (and therefore Visual Basic .NET) has a new version of Assert() in the System.Diagnostics.Debug and Trace classes. (Use the Trace class if you want the calls to stay in the release version.) This new version is much better than the VB6 equivalent. You can use the .NET version, as shown in Listing 3.8. In this example, the someParameter parameter is expected to be different from zero. Otherwise, there is a bug.

LISTING 3.8   Example of How the Built-In Assert() Can Be Used

```
Trace.Assert(someParameter <> 0, "someParameter <> 0")
```

> **NOTE**
>
> There is another, security-related Assert() method in the Base Classes Library (BCL), but that's another story.

Although the built-in Assert() is quite good, I have written my own one as well. This is because

- *I want the tool to integrate with my tracing solution*—When you sit listening to your application (by using tracing), it's important to get broken assertions as trace calls too. (I will discuss my tracing solution in depth in the next chapter.)
- *I prefer a similar tool for both Visual Basic .NET components and stored procedures (and for VB6 components as well)*—Although this feature is not paramount in importance, it is useful.

- *I want a centralized solution that I can easily change*—For example, I like a broken assertion to terminate the application for the user and I want to have the problem logged. I also prefer to have it integrated with my own logging solution.

> **NOTE**
>
> For server-side development, using the built-in assertion solution can be a real show-stopper. You will get a `MsgBox()`, and the execution waits for somebody to accept the message. Because the message will pop up at the server, and typically at a virtual screen, nobody will press Enter.
>
> John Robbins presents an ASP.NET-specific solution to this problem in his article called "Bugslayer: Handling Assertions in ASP.NET Web Apps."[4]
>
> According to the documentation, you can also disable broken assertion signals to pop up, by adding a row to the `<switches>` section of the `.config` file as follows:
>
> `<assert assertuienabled="false" />`
>
> I will discuss `.config` files more in Chapter 4. In that chapter, I will also show a solution for how to handle configuration settings on-the-fly that comes in handy for my own assert solution.

Before I describe my solution for assertions in more detail, let's discuss the assertions in general. Although I spend a lot of time describing my own solution for assertions, the most important thing is that you use the concept somehow.

Getting the Basic Idea

Regardless of whether you use my assertion tool or the built-in one, you must consider where you should use assertions in your source code. I suggest you create a plan for when assertions will be used.

Before doing so, let's take a step back for a minute. In another programming language called Eiffel, created by Bertrand Meyer[5], a concept called design by contract (DBC) is used a great deal. The idea of DBC is to set up contracts between consumers and servers (a consumer uses a class and its methods; a server is the class). The server says what it expects (require) and what it promises (ensure). The consumer promises to fulfill the server's expectations; otherwise, the server doesn't have to fulfill its promises.

Assume that you are the consumer and the U.S. Post Office is the server. The contract between you and the Post Office is that you want them to deliver a certain item of mail to the correct person. For you to get that service, they expect to receive the mail before 5 p.m. that day, a valid stamp of the correct value on the letter, and the correct address on the envelope. If all this is fulfilled, the mail will be delivered to the correct person, and, hopefully, on time. Although in reality you actually don't know when the mail will be delivered and don't really have any form of contract between you and the Post Office, this example expresses the general idea well.

What we want is to transfer this contract-based thinking to software construction. The software can check itself to see if any nasty bugs have been introduced, and the contracts, which are often implicit, will be made explicit to show which part is responsible for what. This way, you can avoid defensive programming. In defensive programming, everything is checked every-where. Both the consumer and the server must check the value of the parameter. With DBC, the server can set a requirement and then expect that to be OK. Only the client has to perform a test; the server doesn't. That way the code will be robust but with far fewer lines of code, and the number of code lines is often directly correlated to the number of bugs.

> **NOTE**
>
> As a side note, Eiffel is going through a renaissance right now, at least when you con-sider how often it's mentioned in the Microsoft community compared to before. I guess that's because it's an example of a language that is compliant to the common language runtime, but probably also because it's a very solid language.

To make the design-by-contract concept a little bit more concrete, a method called `Deliver()` in a `Mail` class is shown in Listing 3.9. There you can see that all the expectations of the method are checked before anything else is done. Then, before the method is exited, the promise is checked too.

LISTING 3.9   Example of How Assertions Can Be Used

```
Public Sub Deliver()
  'Require------------------
  Trace.Assert(OnTime(), "OnTime()")
  Trace.Assert(CorrectAddress(), _
  "CorrectAddress()")
  Trace.Assert(CorrectStamp(),"CorrectStamp()")
  '--------------------------

  'Do the real delivery stuff
  '...

  'Ensure--------------------
  Trace.Assert(CorrectlyDelivered(), _
```

LISTING 3.9   Continued

```
"CorrectlyDelivered()")
'- - - - - - - - - - - - - - - - - - - - - - - - - - -
End Sub
```

You could naturally use ordinary If statements instead and Throw() exceptions when you find a problem, but the code in Listing 3.9 is cleaner. You also have the ability to disable the checks without deleting all the code lines. This is very important because one of the major positives with assertions is their value when you maintain the code. They will tell you if you make a change that breaks some other code.

Understanding Class Invariants

Bertrand Meyer's DBC includes a concept called "class invariants." If we take the U.S. Post Office example discussed earlier, we will find that there are "social" contracts and laws that say we're not allowed to send, for example, narcotics and explosives by mail. However, this does not mean that every time you send a letter you need to sign such a contract. Indeed, the process would be extremely long if we had to repeat those contracts and laws over and over again. The same goes for classes in software. If a class for a person has a member variable called m_Age, for example, the variable may never have a value of less than 0 and more than 125. This condition shouldn't have to be expressed repeatedly in all the methods of the class. Still, it should be checked in every Require and Ensure section to help discover any nasty bugs. How do we arrange for this? A possible solution would be to have a sub, as is shown in the class in Listing 3.10.

LISTING 3.10   Example of Class Invariants Helper

```
Private Sub AssertInvariants _
(ByVal source As String) _
Implements Jnsk.Instrumentation.IAssertInvariants.AssertInvariants
    'Call Assert() for each contract-part to check.
End Sub
```

The sub in Listing 3.10 should be called from the Require and Ensure sections in all the Public methods. You can add the calls through a utility to a copy of the code, or you could add it manually. The implementation of AssertInvariants() is a no-brainer—just call Jnsk.Instrumentation.Assert.Assert() once for every part of every social contract.

Most assertions in your code will be quite basic—for example, checking that a value is always in an interval or that there is a certain relationship between some variables. Sometimes, however, you need to create complete functions that return True and False to provide more advanced logical expressions. I will discuss conditional compilation and similar techniques in the next chapter.

Examining My Solution for Assertions in Visual Basic .NET

As you have probably suspected by now, I centralize my assertions to `Jnsk.Instrumentation.Assert.Assert()` to get several positive benefits (such as those you usually get out of generalized code). The call then looks like that shown in Listing 3.11.

LISTING 3.11   Call to Customized `Assert()`

```
Jnsk.Instrumentation.Assert.Assert _
(a < b, "a < b", exeOrDllName, theSource)
```

My customized `Assert()` could just wrap the ordinary `System.Diagnostics.Trace.Assert()` or it could do customized work. (If I use the ordinary `Trace.Assert()` version, I will get one extra level in the call stack, but that is not such a big problem.) My current version appears in Listing 3.12.

LISTING 3.12   Customized `Assert()` Method

```
Public Class Assert
    Public Shared Sub Assert _
    (ByVal resultOfLogicalExpression As Boolean, _
    ByVal logicalExpression As String, _
    ByVal exeOrDllName As String, _
    ByVal source As String, _
    ByVal userId As String, _
    ByVal raiseException As Boolean)
        If Not resultOfLogicalExpression Then
            Dim aMessage As String = _
            String.Format _
            ("Broken Assertion: {0} ({1}.{2}) For {3}.", _
            logicalExpression, _
            exeOrDllName, source, userId)

            'Send a trace call.
            Jnsk.Instrumentation.Trace.TraceAssert _
            exeOrDllName, source, logicalExpression)

            'Instantiate a custom exception.
            Dim anException As _
            New ApplicationException(aMessage)
```

LISTING 3.12   Continued

```
        'Log to applications own error log.
        Jnsk.Instrumentation.Err.Log _
        (exeOrDllName, source, anException, userId)
        'Log to the usual event log.
        EventLog.WriteEntry(source, aMessage, _
        EventLogEntryType.Error)

        'Show message box, depending upon
        'the current configuration.
        ShowMessageBox(aMessage)

        If raiseException Then
            Throw (anException)
        End If
    End If
End Sub


End Class
```

As you see in Listing 3.12, the output from a broken assertion will be written to the event log, the log for the application, as a trace call, and as a `MsgBox()`. John Robbins created a solution that you could use to determine if the application is executed from the IDE or not.[6] The solution I have used instead uses the same solution for handling configuration data as is discussed in the next chapter.

> **NOTE**
>
> In Listing 3.12, several methods were used, such as `TraceAssert()` and `WriteToLog()`, which will be discussed in depth in Chapter 4.
>
> Also note that I `Throw()` an `ApplicationException` instead of a custom `Exception`. The reason for this is that I don't want the consumer to have to reference my `Instrumentation` assembly (or another assembly with my custom `Exceptions`).
>
> Finally, there is an overloaded version of the `Assert()` method that is used most often. It doesn't have the `raiseException` parameter, and it calls the method shown in Listing 3.12 with `raiseException` as `True`.

Examining My Solution for Assertions in Stored Procedures

Unfortunately, T-SQL doesn't have built-in support for assertions, but you can easily come up with a solution on your own. Listing 3.13 shows an example of an assertion being checked.

LISTING 3.13 Call to Stored Procedure Version of `Assert()`

```
IF NOT (@someParameter <> 0) BEGIN
  EXEC JnskAssert_Assert
  '@someParameter <> 0', @theSource
END
```

I expect that `@someParameter` will always be different from 0 at that particular point in the code. Therefore, I call my homegrown `JnskAssert_Assert()` stored procedure. As you know, I can't have the logical expression directly in the procedure call in T-SQL. Therefore, I have to evaluate the logical expression before I make the stored procedure call. Because of this, the assertion looks a bit unintuitive. Please observe that I use `NOT` in the `IF` clause. Doing it like this gives an assertion solution that doesn't require that many lines of code per assertion. The `JnskAssert_Assert()` procedure is shown in Listing 3.14.

LISTING 3.14 Stored Procedure Version of `Assert()`

```
CREATE PROCEDURE JnskAssert_Assert
(@logicalExpression VARCHAR(255)
, @source uddtSource
, @userId uddtUserId = '') AS

  DECLARE @anError INT
  , @aMessage VARCHAR(600)
  , @theNow DATETIME

  SET NOCOUNT ON

  --Trace the problem.
  EXEC JnskTrace_Assert @source
  , @logicalExpression, @userId

  --Log the problem.
  SET @anError = 99999
```

3

LISTING 3.14   Continued

```
SET @aMessage = 'Assert broken: '
+ @logicalExpression

SET @theNow = GETDATE()

EXEC JnskError_Log @source, @anError
, @aMessage, @theNow, 'unknown', 'unknown'
, @userId

--Finally, raise an error that closes the connection.
SET @aMessage = @aMessage + ' (' + @source + ')'
RAISERROR(@aMessage, 20, 1) WITH LOG

RETURN @anError
```

As you see in Listing 3.14, the same output will be used as for the Visual Basic .NET solution (except for a message box). The call to RAISERROR() will make broken assertions visible in the SQL Server Query Analyzer, and because severity level 20 is used, the connection is closed. The reason for that degree of violence is to directly terminate the operation, but also to make it easy to use calls to JnskAssert_Assert() because no error checking is necessary after the calls, as you saw in Listing 3.13.

Use Other Ways for Checking Arguments

Microsoft recommends that you check arguments for validity and raise ArgumentException (or a subclass exception). Listing 3.15 gives an example where a parameter called size isn't allowed to be less than zero.

LISTING 3.15   How to Check for an ArgumentOutOfRangeException

```
If size < 0 Then
    Throw New ArgumentOutOfRangeException _
    ("size must be >=0.")
End If
```

As I see it, this is defensive programming. Still, to comply with the standard, I do this in the methods that are entry points for the consumer. With methods in layers that are only internal to my own code, I use assertions instead of checking arguments. That seems to be a happy medium.

Creating Documentation

A bonus to the methods we have just discussed is that the contracts written in the code will provide great documentation. I've seen the use of contracts even without the automatic and built-in testing that I've discussed here, just because the contracts express much of the semantics of the classes and their methods. You can, for example, easily build a utility that drags out the method signatures together with the assertions to create one important part of the documentation of your application. This documentation is very valuable for public components.

The same goes for cooperation between different developers. Those contracts express responsibilities in a natural way. The assertions may also be a handy instrument at design time. They help you to be detailed about the responsibilities of the methods without writing all the code.

Checking for Traps

The most common trap is that your assert checks change the execution in any way. Be careful of this. A typical example is that the assert code moves the "cursor" in a DataSet, for example. Make sure you use a clone in that case. No matter what, there will be some minor differences when you use assertions and when you don't, because the code isn't the same. Just be careful that you're not affected.

Summing Up: Final Thoughts About Assertions

I mentioned earlier that I prefer the consumer application to terminate if an assertion has been broken. In this case, I don't want the application to continue with unpredictable and probably damaging results. To make termination happen, I Throw() an exception in the Jnsk.Instrumentation.Assert.Assert() method and I use RAISERROR() in JnskAssert_Assert() stored procedure with a severity level that closes the connection. In both cases, the consumer can continue to run, but hopefully, he won't want to continue when unexpected error codes are coming in.

Should the assertions be left in the compiled code so that they execute at runtime? There is a cost in overhead, of course. On the other hand, most often the cost is quite small, and it's great to have the system tell you when it's not feeling good and even what is wrong sometimes. Let's face it, most development projects are run in Internet time, and there aren't six months of testing before the components are rolled out. Why not distribute both a version with assertions active and one without them to the customer? You can also use a configuration solution, similar to the one I discuss in the next chapter, to activate and deactivate assertions on-the-fly. In the case of stored procedures, it's easy to toggle whether assertions should be active by just commenting/uncommenting the body of the JnskAssert_Assert() central routine. (You can also customize the behavior, of course. For example, you may want to do this if you don't want the

3

connection to be closed and no error to be raised, but want only the broken assertions to be logged.) Anyway, it's important to leave the assertions in the code. You will need them again!

> **NOTE**
>
> I will show you some real-world examples of assertions in the coming chapters. In addition, you can download the code samples from the book's Web site at www. samspublishing.com.

The Diagnose/Monitor Tool

Another tool that comes in handy when you have a problem that is hard to understand is a diagnosing tool. This can help you capture basic and essential information to get you on the right track.

Most developers I know have at least once spent hours thinking about a problem only to find, for example, that the customer has changed something vital in the environment. Or, perhaps you have had to ask a customer to check this and that before you start thinking about the problem. In my opinion, a much better approach is just to execute a diagnosing tool to collect all the interesting information to a file, which you can then analyze before you do anything else. Typical information to gather is

- Performance monitor metrics
- Items in the event log, SQL Server's error log, and your application's error log
- Version information for certain DLLs, OS, and so on
- Hardware information (for example, the number of CPUs)

Most of this information is quite easily caught with the help of System.Diagnostics namespace. You can also reuse some of the test drivers from the in-house testing that checks diagnostic matters. Why not ship a complete test database and all the test drivers to check the complete test suite at the customer location? It may also be wise to expand these thoughts a little, not only to execute the diagnosing tool to find information about the site after a problem has occurred, but also to monitor the site all the time. Log some of this information every hour or so. That way, you will easily see trends and can take action before a problem occurs.

Of course, this is a lengthy discussion, but hopefully I have whetted your appetite.

Miscellaneous Tips

Finally, the following are two additional tips for testing:

- Security issues are often "forgotten" by developers. The same applies to testing too. Spend some extra time on testing security issues and the deployment will run more smoothly.

- Perhaps the most important tip of all regarding testing is to have a similar testing environment—hardware, communication, size of database, and so on—to the one you will have in the real situation. A common problem is that the customer has a Symmetric MultiProcessing (SMP) machine—a machine with several processors—but you don't have that in your testing environment. It's common to find problems that only show up with an SMP machine. At the same time, it's unusual that companies have these kinds of machines in their testing environment. I can't say this enough: It is important to have a realistic testing environment. Period.

Evaluation of Proposals

Now it's time to wrap up this chapter by evaluating the proposals I have presented against the factors we discussed in Chapter 2. I hope it is clear that all the proposals are good in terms of testability because they all have this as their primary focus. Apart from that, let's dig into the evaluation of each of the proposals in more detail.

Evaluation of the Test Bed Proposal

The test bed will not directly improve the performance and scalability of your project. However, it won't decrease it either, because the test drivers are not in the binary that will be used by the application—the test drivers are separate units. On the other hand, you do get a tool that can help you to get on the right track and to find out bottlenecks in different situations. You can test to increase performance and scalability, and you can carry out the testing with good productivity.

The test bed is also good for easily checking how physical restrictions are affecting the application and to see that the application is working correctly, say, in a farm environment. Meanwhile, reliability is definitely addressed with the test bed because you can check a lot of "totally" impossible situations, for example. You can, and should, unplug network cables, the power supply, and such to see that the components act as expected.

In terms of productivity, it probably won't increase in the short run. In fact, it can actually suffer. But it will most often increase in the long run. The possible maintenance side effects are addressed greatly.

The test bed can help improve debuggability because it can be hard to set up a certain problem situation with only the application's ordinary UI. You can also use the test bed to localize a problem when you know that something has stopped working. I think even reusability could be improved because you can easily test to see how a component behaves in another context. Security problems can also be found by using the test bed. And when it comes to coexistence and interoperability, I've emphasized making the test bed possible to use for both COM and .NET components as well as for stored procedures.

Even if I'm only partially correct, can you afford not to give these ideas a try?

Evaluation of Assertions Proposal

As with the test bed, assertions will increase testability and debuggability a great deal. In a way, assertions are to finding bugs as the compiler is to finding syntax errors. I also think reusability will benefit because the assertions will tell you if the reused component doesn't work correctly in the new context.

The price for my solution to assertions is some added overhead. Interoperability with VB6 and stored procedures is addressed because the solution works in all three cases. (Actually, there isn't anything stopping this from being used with old ASP either.) Productivity can be both positive and negative, but in the long run, I believe it will be positive. Contracts as documentation will increase maintainability, and reliability is addressed by ending the scenario in case of broken assertions.

What's Next

In the next chapter, I will discuss a topic closely related to testing, namely debugging. When you have proved that something is broken with the help of testing, debugging will help you to determine what is wrong. I will focus on how to prepare for debugging.

References

1. K. Beck. *Extreme Programming Explained: Embrace Change*. Addison-Wesley; 1999.

2. http://msdn.microsoft.com/library/techart/fm2kintro.htm.

3. DMS Reengineering Toolkit at
   http://www.semdesigns.com/Company/Publications/TestCoverage.pdf.

4. J. Robbins. "Bugslayer: Handling Assertions in ASP.NET Web Apps," *MSDN Magazine*; October 2001; Microsoft.

5. B. Meyer. *Object-Oriented Software Construction, Second Edition*. Prentice Hall; 1997.

6. J. Robbins. "Bugslayer: Assertions and Tracing in .NET;" *MSDN Magazine*; February 2001; Microsoft.

Adding Debugging Support

IN THIS CHAPTER

My house has a small garden. When my wife and I bought the house, I actually wanted a much bigger garden. However, after having lived here for almost a decade, I now realize that we don't have enough time even for the small garden we do have.

Besides producing an occasional edible vegetable, I have learned something from our garden. What we don't do in the autumn we have to do in the spring, and by then the problem has grown into something much larger and more time consuming to fix. And if we don't get rid of the weeds early in the summer, they are out of control by August.

The same goes for software. If you don't prepare for debugging early on in a project, it will take much more time to do a couple months later. You could just skip debugging preparations altogether, but sooner or later, you'll have a debugging nightmare.

This is especially true for distributed applications, which are often tricky to debug. Some of the material I discussed in Chapter 3, "Testing,"—the information relating to assertions, for example—is also useful when it comes to debugging. In this chapter, I will propose some ideas for what you can do up front to ensure a pleasant debugging experience when you need it. (Note that I said "when," not "if.") I'll start the chapter by discussing tracing. Next, I'll examine error logging, after which I'll turn the attention to using attributes to create a more pleasant debugging experience. After that, I discuss different solutions for how to deal with configuration data. I'll close the chapter with an evaluation of the tracing and error-logging proposals I've presented.

Tracing

If you're like me, you've had more problems at customer sites with your applications than you'd like to admit. Many times, I've had to guess what was going wrong in my application and, after a few guesses and code changes, I've managed to solve the problem. But for more pesky issues, I've had to add tracing to the troublesome part of the application and, bit by bit, eventually track down the problem. Having this happen to me a number of times, I decided to create a standardized tracing tool that I could use over and over again. Now, when a customer reports a problem, I can just ask him or her to activate tracing and send me the trace log. This is much faster and more professional than having to add trace code in selected places first, send the customer a new binary, and so on. Indeed, probably the most important debugging support you can take advantage of is tracing. By adding tracing to your components, you can listen to what is going on, what code paths are taken, and where any strange behavior is occurring.

Why not just stay with the debugger, you ask? Ordinary debuggers are great, but they have shortcomings when it comes to tracing execution after deployment. For one, customers often won't allow you to install a debugger on their database server, and there are a slew of potential licensing problems. The debugger also interferes with the production system, killing processes and bringing execution to a halt. Yet another problem with debuggers is that you are in detail mode directly. Tracing allows you to see the bigger picture before you look at the details. You don't eat soup with a fork, even though forks are great tools; you need different tools for different situations.

Tracing tools also provide you with primitive profiling capabilities for free. That way, you can see where most of the time is spent in your code and where you should spend your optimization resources. While simple tracing tools do not replace real profiling tools, I use them quite often for locating bottlenecks quickly.

You can also use trace logs for review purposes. As I mentioned in the last chapter, I'm a big fan of design and code review processes; reading trace logs is sort of like taking the review process to the next level. Once when I was teaching my COM+ Component Services and VB course, one of my students had an idea of how he could use tracing. He would use a trace log to automatically check whether the documentation he had created as interaction diagrams in Rational Rose was correct. (Rational Rose is a modeling tool for creating UML diagrams. It is the full version from which Visual Modeler was excerpted.) This would allow him to obtain better documentation and to check that the documentation had evolved with the system.

Tracing in the Dark Ages

In the old world with VB6, there were several solutions from which to choose for tracing. Because it didn't work outside the Integrated Development Environment (IDE), only a few developers used `Debug.Print()`. Other developers just logged to files. However, as these developers often discovered, this can create a huge bottleneck at the server-side when you have several simultaneous users hitting the application, opening and closing the file for every trace call.

Perhaps the most common solution was to call the `OutputDebugString()` Win32 API function instead, which could be listened to by a debugger, such as the one that comes with Visual Studio 6. The cost for `OutputDebugString()` calls is comparatively low when no one is listening, so it's often possible to leave these calls in the code all the time. (This was the basic technique that I based my own custom tracing solution on back in the dark ages.)

These three techniques—`Debug.Print`, log to file, and `OutputDebugString()`—represent only a small selection of the available techniques. There are also many third-party solutions.

> ## Avoiding Trace Calls When Nobody Is Listening
>
> It's extremely important that debug tools interfere as little as possible with the execution. Otherwise, there is a risk that they will hide bugs that are dependent on timing. My friend, John Robbins[1,2] (the "Bugslayer" himself), says that OutputDebugString does some work, regardless of whether you are under a debugger. "Disassembling W2K's OutputDebugStringA shows it calls RaiseException with an exception code of 0x40010006," John says. "That's a guaranteed trip into kernel mode and a context switch." He continues: "All this work in OutputDebugString happens whether you are under a debugger or not. Given that context switch, you can see why Microsoft combed the W2K source code and ensured that they only call OutputDebugString when absolutely, positively necessary."
>
> So, contrary to what most developers think, it's not without interference to the system to leave OutputDebugString() calls in the executable, even when you are not listening to them.

The Built-In Tracing Solution in .NET

As with so many other things, Microsoft took a totally new tack on tracing in the .NET Framework. The solution is effective and represents a big leap forward. In this section, I will briefly introduce how to use the built-in solution.

Classes

In the System.Diagnostics namespace, there are two classes, called Debug and Trace, that can be used to send trace calls. You should use the Debug class if you only want the trace calls in your debug version and not in the release version. Calls to methods in the Trace class will stay in both versions.

Trace Calls

Making a trace call is easily done. Listing 4.1 shows an example of how trace calls can be made with the built-in solution.

LISTING 4.1   Making Trace Calls with the Built-In Solution

```
Trace.Write("Hello World! This time as a trace call.")

Trace.WriteLine _
("Hello World! With a line feed this time.", "Begin")
```

As you can see in Listing 4.1, you can choose whether you want to have a linefeed after the trace call. You can also set a category (see the `"Begin"` parameter in Listing 4.1) for each call.

Listening

Now you know how to send messages. However, that won't help you much if you can't listen to them. This hole is what the `TraceListener` class fills. By default, there is a `DefaultTraceListener` in the trace `Listeners` collection. It listens to your trace calls and sends them on via `OutputDebugString()` to, say, a debugger. The `DefaultTraceListener` also makes a `Log()` call to a debugger if one is attached.

If you want, it's very easy to add another listener to the trace `Listeners` collection. You could create a `TraceListener` on your own by inheriting from `TraceListener`, or you could, for example, instantiate the `TextWriterTraceListener` and add the instance to the `Listeners` collection.

In Listing 4.2, I have added a `TextWriterTraceListener` that listens to trace calls and then writes output to the console.

LISTING 4.2   Adding a Listener That Writes Output to the Console

```
Dim aTextWriter As New _
TextWriterTraceListener(System.Console.Out)
Trace.Listeners.Add(aTextWriter)
```

The first time I heard about the listener concept, I totally misunderstood it. I thought it could be used for listening systemwide for trace calls, but that is not the case—it will only listen to the same process. The purpose is to decouple the sending of the trace calls from the format of the trace calls. For example, some trace listeners need another "listener," such as a debugger, while others write to a file or the event log.

Configurable at Runtime

I began this section by saying that you can choose between the `Debug` and `Trace` classes depending on whether you want the trace calls to stay in the release version or not. Most of us would prefer to have the trace calls left in the binary so that it's easy to enable them when we need to listen to what is happening. The built-in solution gives you that functionality if you use `WriteIf()` and `WriteLineIf()` instead of `Write()` and `WriteLine()` as the methods. Then you add a `TraceSwitch.Level` enumerator as a parameter, indicating at what level the message is. Table 4.1 lists the levels you can choose from and their numeric representations, while Listing 4.3 presents a code example. As you see in Listing 4.3, the trace calls can be configured so as not to be sent, depending on the settings in the `.config` file.

TABLE 4.1   `TraceSwitch.Levels` and Their Numeric Representation

TraceSwitch.Level	*Numeric Representation*
TraceLevel.Off	0
TraceLevel.Error	1
TraceLevel.Warning	2
TraceLevel.Info	3
TraceLevel.Verbose	4

LISTING 4.3   Using a `.config` File for Configuring Trace Calls

```
Dim aSwitch As New TraceSwitch("aSwitch", _
"Description to this traceswitch")

Trace.WriteLineIf(aSwitch.TraceError, _
"An error trace call.")

Trace.WriteLineIf(aSwitch.TraceVerbose, _
"A verbose trace call.")
```

You can set the `TraceLevel` by using an application `.config` file similar to the one shown in Listing 4.4. This is also where you can use the numeric representation mentioned in Table 4.1.

LISTING 4.4   Using a `.config` File Where `TraceLevel` Is Set to `Warning` (Including the Lower Level `Error`)

```
<configuration>
    <system.diagnostics>
        <switches>
            <add name="aSwitch" value="2" />
        </switches>
    </system.diagnostics>
</configuration>
```

With the code shown in Listing 4.3 and the `.config` file shown in Listing 4.4, only the first trace call actually takes place.

NOTE

I will discuss some difficulties with using `.config` files from serviced components later in the chapter.

My Proposal for a Custom Tracing Solution

Does the world really need another tracing solution? I can think of a number of shortcomings the built-in solution has:

- It is not directly possible to trace the complete execution path over all the tiers. (Windows Forms/ASP.NET, .NET serviced components, stored procedures).

- It does not directly "force" developers to give a standardized set of information.

- It is not directly configurable at runtime without having to restart server processes.

- There is no built-in sender-side filtering.

- There is no built-in viewer User Interface (UI).

- It is not directly possible to receive trace calls from a remote computer in real time.

- Writing trace calls to a file has drawbacks. If each call is written individually, it is a slow and laborious process, especially if each call is written to a share. If you skip to set `AutoFlush()` to `True` and call `Flush()` manually, there's a risk that some calls will be lost during problems because the typical writer solution will be in process.

- It doesn't work well with serviced components because of the surrogate process called `Dllhost` that will execute all the COM+ server applications. What is worse is that `Dllhost` is not written in managed code and it doesn't know it should load a `.config` file.

Because of these and other shortcomings in the built-in tracing solution, in this chapter, I'll present you with a custom solution that solves these problems. Along the way, I'll also show how to put several interesting .NET techniques to good use. Thus, even if you already have a tracing solution that you are comfortable with or prefer to use the built-in solution, this section will be useful to you.

Because my original VB6 solution fits the new requirements quite well, I have expanded it and transferred it to the new world of .NET. But before we get into the implementation for the different tiers, I'd like to briefly discuss some basic design principles that I have applied to the implementation.

Centralization

The most important design decision I made in my custom tracing solution is to centralize the calls through a number of custom methods. That way, I can change the call mechanism in a few minutes if I want to. I typically use `OutputDebugString()` via Platform Invocation (P-Invoke) as the transport mechanism, but if I want, I can change that to ordinary .NET trace calls in my .NET components, for example. The centralization also makes it easy to use a mechanism for activating and deactivating the trace calls during runtime. (Even if you don't listen to the trace calls, there is some overhead involved. By disabling them, this overhead can be decreased.)

Another big advantage of using centralization of code is that you can easily add the "poor man's interception" code. Before anything specific actually happens, you can intercept the call and do something else first or instead. A typical example is when you want to add a trace call just before an error is raised, which is easily done if all errors are raised in a general method.

In my opinion, it's almost always a good idea to centralize code. The drawback is efficiency, but most often the overhead is negligible compared to the time it takes to execute the ordinary code. Another minor drawback relates to reflection. The context will be different when reflection is used in a centralized method instead of inline.

Categorization

The built-in tracing solution in .NET makes it possible to categorize trace calls in Error, Warning, Information, and Verbose. I can understand the benefits of this use, but in general, I prefer to categorize in another way. Basically, I want to know the reason for a call. Is it because of a method being entered or exited? Is it because of an error or a broken assertion? Or is it perhaps just because it is showing that a certain piece of code has been used and that a particular variable's values are interesting to look at? In my custom tracing solution, I have let the developer choose the categorization. If the built-in solution is used under the hood, one of the built-in categorizations is used as well. Table 4.2 lists the methods I use as well as the .NET categorization used for each of them.

TABLE 4.2   My Trace Methods and Corresponding .NET Trace Levels

My Trace Methods	*.NET Trace Levels Used*
TraceBegin()	TraceVerbose
TraceEnd()	TraceVerbose
TraceError()	TraceError
TraceAssert()	TraceError
TraceMessage()	TraceInformation

> **NOTE**
>
> You might find it more natural to use a warning for TraceAssert(), but, in my opinion, it's definitely an error when an assertion is broken. I actually end the call sequence when that happens because the scenario is in an unsafe state.

Some of the trace methods will be executed automatically because TraceError() will be buried in the centralized method called when raising errors, and TraceAssert() in the method-checking assertions. `TraceBegin()` and `TraceEnd()` will get inserted automatically by the use of a template (see Chapter 5, "Architecture," for more information). It's only `TraceMessage()` that the developer has to insert manually, because the interesting places for that can't be decided automatically.

Standardized Information

Apart from the categorization, I also want the developer to add some specific information with every trace call:

- Source (such as method name or name of stored procedure)
- Specific message (for `TraceAssert()`, `TraceError()`, and `TraceMessage()` only)

  Apart from that, the tracing methods will automatically collect some more information, namely:

  - Time
  - Computer name
  - Name of EXE/DLL
  - Process ID
  - Thread ID
  - User ID (`DirectCallerName` for security-enabled serviced components and parameter for other components and for stored procedures, if one exists for the particular method and stored procedure)
  - In Tx (`InTransaction` for serviced components and `@@TRANCOUNT` for stored procedures)
  - Security (`IsSecurityEnabled` for serviced components, blank for stored procedures)

Format of a Trace Call

I decided to use a simple format for the trace calls that wouldn't incur much overhead. Each part is separated with a tab. This way, I can also consume the messages from another `OutputDebugString()` receiver and it will still be easy to read the output.

> **NOTE**
>
> There is a risk in using a common control character such as a tab if there is natively a tab in a string. To solve this problem, I could filter each string before adding it to the trace call, but I haven't experienced this problem in my applications so far.

Receiver

Finally, there will be some `OutputDebugString()` calls to catch. To do this, I use an `OutputDebugString()` receiver called `JnskTraceView.dll`, which is a COM component. It uses callbacks to send the `OutputDebugString()` calls to the consumer. The `OutputDebugString()` receiver is built as an ATL-component in Visual C++ 6 and it is easily consumed, as you can see in Listing 4.5 (VB6).

LISTING 4.5   VB6 Code Showing How My `OutputDebugString()` Receiver Can Be Used

```
Option Explicit
Implements JnskTraceView.ITraceEvent
Private m_TraceView As JnskTraceView.TraceView

Private Sub Form_Load()
  Set m_TraceView = New JnskTraceView.TraceView
  m_TraceView.SetCallback Me
End Sub

Private Sub ITraceEvent_DebugString _
(ByVal processID As Long, ByVal message As String)
  'Do whatever you want with the OutputDebugString()-call.
End Sub
```

I let `ITraceEvent_DebugString()` write to an array to have receiving done as fast as possible. A `Timer` is used to grab rows from the array and write them to the `ListView` every two seconds.

The receiver is used from the User Interface (UI) presented in Figure 4.1. The viewer UI is written in VB6 because consuming the receiver, which is a COM component, is probably more efficient from unmanaged code. (When version 1 of .NET has been released, I will publish a comparison of the receiver performance for a VB6 receiver compared to a receiver written in Visual Basic .NET at the book's Web site at www.samspublishing.com.)

Remote Receiver

I haven't actually built a remote receiver for a number of reasons:

- The UI shown in Figure 4.1 has the capability to import files from different machines so that the complete call stack can be analyzed afterward.
- Most often it's not the interaction between the different tiers that is the problem. When the tier with the problem is found, it can be analyzed in isolation.

- It's quite often the case that at least two tiers (such as the Web application and the COM+ components) physically execute at one machine. Sometimes (but less often), the SQL Server executes there too.

- It's increasingly common to find products for remote administration installed at the servers. I can then install my trace receiver at the server as usual, but sit and view that specific server from a remote computer.

NOTE

Unfortunately—in my tests—my trace receiver doesn't work in a Terminal Services session, but it works just fine with other products for remote administration.

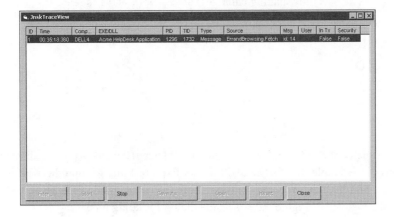

FIGURE 4.1
User Interface for showing trace calls.

Although I haven't had a use for it yet, I have planned how I can build a solution. A simple one would be to create a COM+ component that consumes my OutputDebugString() receiver at the remote server. That COM+ component will then send a callback (or perhaps a COM+ event) to another component living at the main receiver machine. (The calls would be buffered in this case, too, and sent only periodically.) The second COM+ component will replay the OutputDebugString() call locally, and then everything works out as normal.

What I consider the main problem is the time synchronization between computers. However, I could add an "exercise scenario," with numbered messages so that the solution can learn about the time difference between the computers and adjust for it.

4

NOTE

You should also check out the SysInternals[3] solution to receive OutputDebugString() calls remotely. They transfer the calls by TCP/IP.

Filtering

I want to be able to use filtering both at the sender and at the receiver. The motivation for having filtering available at the sender is to avoid expensive calls when they are not needed. This is even more important if you receive from a remote computer when the transport mechanism itself is expensive. Some of the available filtering possibilities are as follows:

- Category (such as only making calls to TraceError() and TraceAssert())
- Computer name
- EXE/DLL
- Process ID
- Thread ID
- Source
- User

It's also possible on the receiver's side to filter away OutputDebugString() calls from other applications (for example, MS Office and Internet Explorer) that would otherwise interfere with the view of your calls. You can configure both the receiver-side filter and the sender-side filter from the viewer UI. Figure 4.2 shows the dialog for doing this.

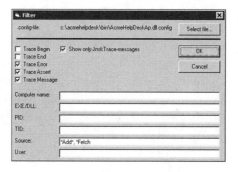

FIGURE 4.2

Filter dialog for configuring both the receiver and the sender(s).

Configuration

The configuration information, such as sender-side filtering and tracing activation, is stored in XML format in a couple of .config files. There will be one for the machine, one for every application, and one for the receiver UI itself (with the client filtering). The application .config file will be read first, and then the machine .config file will be read.

A great deal of configuration information other than tracing is also found in these files, such as the connection string and how often the configuration file should be checked for new information. Listing 4.6 shows an example of such a configuration file (but only with the tracing settings). Note the wildcards and multiple choices for filtering on the source method.

LISTING 4.6   Example of .config File

```
<configuration>
    <jnsk.instrumentation.trace active="1">
        <filtering>
            <add name="error" value="1"/>
            <add name="assert" value="1"/>
            <add name="message" value="1"/>
            <add name="source" value="*Add*, *Fetch"/>
        </filtering>
    </jnsk.instrumentation.trace>
</configuration>
```

The .config files will be administered by the filter dialog, as was shown in Figure 4.2, but they can also be administered manually.

Let's take a closer look at how centralization and categorization have been implemented for the different tiers. First, let's look at how I implemented it in the database tier.

Tracing in Stored Procedures

Let's start from the bottom, that is, from the database. As always, I call small helper routines for my tracing needs to avoid code bloat. The following is the collection of stored procedures used for tracing:

```
JnskTrace_Assert()
JnskTrace_Begin()
JnskTrace_End()
JnskTrace_Error()
JnskTrace_Message()
JnskTrace_Write()
```

Let's take a look at a few of those stored procedures and how they are called. The signature of the JnskTrace_Begin() procedure is shown in Listing 4.7.

LISTING 4.7   Signature for `JnskTrace_Begin()` Stored Procedure

```
CREATE PROCEDURE JnskTrace_Begin
(@source uddtSource
, @userId uddtUserId = '')
```

The only information that needs to be sent is the name of the stored procedure that was entered. Normally, I use a standardized code structure for my stored procedures too. I will discuss this in Chapter 5. For now, I'll just show a trace call in Listing 4.8 without a complete stored procedure.

LISTING 4.8   Making a Trace Call in a Stored Procedure

```
SET @theSource = OBJECT_NAME(@@PROCID)
EXEC JnskTrace_Begin @theSource
```

In Listing 4.8, you can see that I use `OBJECT_NAME()` instead of hard coding the name of the stored procedure. (I did this mainly for instructional reasons. I most often hard code the stored procedure name and `SET` it to the `@theSource` variable instead.) Then I send a `JnskTrace_Begin()` trace call. It's as simple as that. Of course, when you call `JnskTrace_Begin()`, for example, it's impossible to tell (and you shouldn't care) what mechanism is really used for sending the trace call. (Have I mentioned that I like information hiding?)

As you saw in Listing 4.8, I didn't provide an `@userId` parameter. This is because it is not always known. Typically, the real user isn't logged in to the SQL Server. To some stored procedures, a user identifier is provided as a parameter. If it is known in the stored procedure, it should be used when calling the trace methods.

NOTE

I will discuss users and authentication in more detail in Chapter 5.

The signature of the `JnskTrace_Message()` procedure is only slightly larger than for the `JnskTrace_Begin()` procedure (see Listing 4.9). Here, a parameter is added, which is most often used for inspecting a variable name and its value.

LISTING 4.9   Signature for JnskTrace_Message Stored Procedure

```
CREATE PROCEDURE JnskTrace_Message
(@source uddtSource
, @message VARCHAR(255)
, @userId uddtUserId = '')
```

The last stored procedure in the previous list, JnskTrace_Write(), could be used by all other trace procedures for centralizing the final call to OutputDebugString(). Yes, I know that I can't call the Win32 API directly from stored procedures, but there are other alternatives. Before I discuss the different alternatives for calling OutputDebugString(), I'd like to show an example of a call stack for when the tracing stored procedures are used. In Figure 4.3, you can see that the stored procedure Order_Insert() calls JnskTrace_Begin(), which in turn calls JnskTrace_Write().

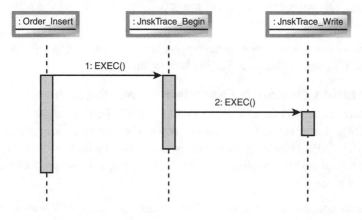

FIGURE 4.3
Example of call stack for the tracing solution.

If I want to call OutputDebugString() from my stored procedures, there are several ways to do this. I will discuss three of them in a little more detail.

Implementation Option 1: COM Automation

It's quite simple to wrap the OutputDebugString() call in a COM component and then use COM Automation (or OLE Automation, as SQL Server still calls it) from the stored procedures to instantiate the component and call a method. You should be careful because you will, of course, take away resources that SQL Server could have used instead. (In my case, I wrote the COM component in VB6 so there will be a couple of MBs of RAM occupied just for this small tool if it is the only VB6 application running on the SQL Server.)

You should also make sure you know that the source code is safe for the COM component. It will run in SQL Server's address space so it can bring down SQL Server and it can also be used for a hacker attack.

In my opinion, COM Automation in SQL Server is much more suitable when you have large granular calls that will take some time to run and that won't be called frequently. This is because there is quite a lot of overhead associated with the instantiation/method call/destroy mechanisms. Sending trace calls doesn't fit the description of large granular calls, because trace calls are the opposite. You will send plenty of them for a single request from the user, and each trace call will, in itself, do very little and it won't take much time.

Implementation Option 2: `xp_cmdshell()`

It would be easy to write an EXE that makes an `OutputDebugString()` call by using the command parameter. This EXE could be called from stored procedures with help from `xp_cmdshell()`. This will consume a lot of resources. Therefore, I find this solution leaves a lot to be desired.

Even so, there are certainly situations when `xp_cmdshell()` comes in handy. You will see this when I discuss my proposal for error logging later in this chapter.

Implementation Option 3: Extended Stored Procedure

SQL Server supports an API called Open Data Services (ODS). You can use it for writing your own external SQL Server resources in C, for example. The extensions are called extended stored procedures (XP). There are a lot of extensions included with SQL Server that Microsoft has built as extended stored procedures. In Visual C++ 6, there is a wizard for creating an extended stored procedure.

When I wrote an extended stored procedure for sending trace calls, with help from the wizard and a colleague, I found that if I sent strings longer than 255 characters, the strings were truncated. It took me quite some time to figure out that the wizard for Visual C++ used outdated functionality for receiving parameters. I needed to change the header and lib files for the ODS support that was delivered with Visual C++ 6. It didn't help to use the files from the latest Platform SDK, but using the samples from SQL Server's own installation CD-ROM and the header and lib files from the same place finally made it work. In addition, I had to export a function (the C way) that SQL Server 7 and 2000 call to see what version of the header files the extended stored procedure is using.[5]

When these problems are solved and the extended stored procedure is installed in the master database, it's very simple to use the extended store procedure from your stored procedures. Listing 4.10 shows an example of how the centralized stored procedure `JnskTrace_Write()` might look.

LISTING 4.10   Example of a Centralized Stored Procedure That Makes Trace Calls

```
CREATE PROCEDURE JnskTrace_Write
(@traceType INT
, @source uddtSource
, @message VARCHAR(255)
, @userId uddtUserId = '')
AS

  DECLARE @theDbName VARCHAR(30)
  SET @theDbName = DB_NAME()

  EXEC master..xp_jnsktracewrite @traceType
  , @source
  , @message, @userId
  , @@TRANCOUNT, @theDbName
```

Finally, to bring the whole tracing solution for stored procedures together, the
JnskTrace_Begin() stored procedure is shown in Listing 4.11.

LISTING 4.11   Code for the JnskTrace_Begin Stored Procedure

```
CREATE PROCEDURE JnskTrace_Begin
(@source uddtSource
, @userId uddtUserId = '')
AS
  EXEC JnskTrace_Write 2, @source, '', @userId
```

Several of the drawbacks of COM Automation apply to extended stored procedures too. I also
think it's much harder to build extended stored procedures than COM components, but that
depends on your background, of course. On the other hand, extended stored procedures have
several advantages, the most important of which is that they are faster than COM Automation,
especially when several small calls are needed, which is the case with tracing. I measured a
simple stored procedure that only completed a single update and had JnskTrace_Begin() and
JnskTrace_End() trace calls. When the trace calls were done with my extended stored procedure, I could execute the stored procedure almost twice as many times in a certain time frame
than when COM Automation was used instead.

Start and Stop Tracing During Production

I use .config files for determining whether trace calls should or should not be sent from my
components. The .config files are read at certain time intervals so that reading does not
become the bottleneck it would have become if I had read them before each trace call was
done.

4

ADDING
DEBUGGING
SUPPORT

At first, I thought I should read from the `.config` files in my stored procedures too because it would, of course, be easiest to control the tracing for all the tiers with the same mechanism. I could have used `xp_cmdshell()` for reading from the files, so it wouldn't have been difficult, but it would slow down the tracing. I couldn't come up with a really good cache solution for how to store the `.config` values for my stored procedures. Instead, I decided to let the developer/administrator go in directly and comment/uncomment code in the stored procedures, such as `JnskTrace_Begin()`, `JnskTrace_End()`, and so on, or only in `JnskTrace_Write()` if all calls are made through that one. This is not the perfect solution, but is the one I prefer.

I keep an instance of all the stored procedures mentioned in this section in every database. This way, I can start tracing in just one specific database and not have it started for all the databases of that particular SQL Server instance.

Sender Filtering of Trace Calls for Stored Procedures

If you let `JnskTrace_Begin()`, and so on, complete the trace calls directly, you have a simple way of filtering, such as only allowing trace calls of a certain type to be done. It will also give you a small performance gain because you skip calling the `JnskTrace_Write()` procedure. On the other hand, I find it easier to always use `JnskTrace_Write()`. It means I only have one place to add all sender filtering. This works, for example, if I am interested only in the trace calls from three specific stored procedures or concerned only about `"Message"` trace calls containing a certain variable, and so on. And, as I said earlier, when you don't want to have tracing activated, you just comment out the code in `JnskTrace_Write()` and optionally in `JnskTrace_Begin()`, and so on.

> **NOTE**
>
> It would be possible to control the server-side filtering for stored-procedure tracing from the User Interface I showed in Figure 4.2, but I haven't implemented this. I find it convenient to take care of it directly and manually in the `JnskTrace_Write()` stored procedure.

Tracing Needs in .NET Components

For my tracing needs in .NET components, I use a simpler solution than the built-in Base Class Library (BCL) tracing solution. I created a new class within my own namespace. Let's take a look at the class.

A New Class: `Jnsk.Instrumentation.Trace`

In this section, I propose that you use `Jnsk.Instrumentation.Trace` instead of `System.Diagnostics.Trace`. The classes are quite different. The first thing you'll notice is the selection of methods in my class. The only methods of the class are

`TraceBegin()`, `TraceEnd()`, `TraceMessage()`, `TraceError()`, and `TraceAssert()`.
Their signatures are all similar in that they all require the following parameters:

- *source*—It would be easy to add an overloaded version of each method that you can use
if you don't want to give the source yourself. Then, reflection will be used to decide
from where the call was made. Handing over a constant string is much faster, but less
productive. Another reason for explicitly handing over `source` as a `String` is that it does-
n't matter if the trace method has been wrapped within another method.

- *exeOrDllName*—Just as with `source`, reflection could be used to find out from what EXE
or DLL the call was made. Once again, it's faster to hand that information over to the
trace method and, in this case, all that is needed is a `Public Const` for the complete project.

Some of the methods (`TraceMessage()` and `TraceAssert()`) take a third parameter, namely:

- *message*—Here, the value of a certain variable can be inspected or an error message can
be shown.

`TraceError()` takes an exception as parameter instead of the message parameter. (More about
this in Chapter 9, "Error Handling and Concurrency Control.")

Different Signatures

To make the class as usable as possible, I decided to overload the methods. All methods can
also take one or both of the following parameters:

- *userId*—This is the user who is using the component right now, if it is known as a parameter or via `SecurityCallContext`.

- *transaction*—This indicates whether the instance is participating in a transaction.

To make it easy to use tracing with serviced components, I also created the
`Jnsk.Instrumentation.ServicedTrace` class, which inherits from
`Jnsk.Instrumentation.Trace`. Here, the trace methods grab a `ContextUtil` object
so that the required information (`userId` and `transaction`) can be taken from there.

To summarize the design, I have provided the class diagram in Figure 4.4. Here you can see
the classes I just discussed.

Forwarding the Call

Internally, the `Jnsk.Instrumentation.Trace` class could easily choose among
several different implementations. The two most typical to choose from are to call
`System.Diagnostics.Trace.WriteIf()` or to directly make `OutputDebugString()` calls via
P-Invoke. The former is ideal to use if you only want to listen to your managed code, while the
latter is what I will discuss most, because I like to collect trace information from different tiers
and processes on the system and present them in one list of messages.

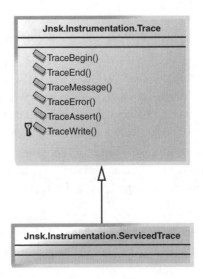

FIGURE 4.4
Class diagram for the tracing solution.

Format of the String

As I said earlier, I need a string in which the different parts are separated with tabs. Listing 4.12 shows an example in which `String.Format()` has been used to create a string.

LISTING 4.12   Example of How to Use `String.Format()`

```
Dim anTmp As String = String.Format("{0}|{1}|{2}", _
"Hello", "World", "Today")
```

Unfortunately, I haven't found out how to add `vbTab` to the template string (apart from having a placeholder such as {0} for it). In C#, \t is used for the control character tab. When I did a quick-and-dirty test comparing `String.Format()` and a `StringBuilder` object for building the trace message, the `StringBuilder` solution was much faster. Therefore, I decided to use `StringBuilder` instead. `StringBuilder` works very well, and the code is almost as readable as with `String.Format()`. (The real power of `Format()` is the capability to accept custom formats and `IFormatProvider` objects.)

Making an `OutputDebugString()` Call

Suppose that I want to make an `OutputDebugString()` call. The easiest solution is to use `System.Diagnostics.Trace.WriteIf` because the `DefaultTraceListener` will forward the message as an `OutputDebugString()` call. Still, I believe you get better throughput by using P-Invoke, and I have decided this is the solution to go for. Thanks to centralization, it's very simple to change if my guess proves wrong. (When version 1 of .NET has shipped, I will provide a performance comparison at the book's Web site at www.samspublishing.com.)

There are several ways to call Win32 functions via P-Invoke. In Listing 4.13, you see how I prepare for the `OutputDebugString()` call with the method I prefer. It's the most similar to VB6 of all of them.

LISTING 4.13   Using P-Invoke to Call `OutputDebugString()`

```
Private Declare Ansi Sub Ods Lib "kernel32" _
Alias "OutputDebugStringA" _
(ByVal message As String)
```

When you have the declaration in place, you just call `OutputDebugString()` like this:

```
Ods("Hello world")
```

Making a Trace Call with My Tracing Solution

Now that I have presented my tracing solution at length, I'm sure you're wondering what the code will look like. As I said before, there are two different classes to choose from when making a trace call—`Jnsk.Instrumentation.Trace` and `Jnsk.Instrumentation.ServicedTrace`. `ServicedTrace` inherits from `Trace` and is `System.EnterpriseServices` aware. Because of this, you don't have to explicitly give `userId` information, for example, but it can still be traced. Listing 4.14 shows what making a trace call (of `"Message"` type) from a serviced component might look like. As you can see, I am inspecting the value of a parameter called `id`.

LISTING 4.14   Making a Trace Call from a Serviced Component

```
Jnsk.Instrumentation.ServicedTrace. _
TraceMessage(AssemblyGlobal.exeOrDllName, theSource, "id: " _
& id.ToString())
```

The Implementation

I'm not going to show you all the code from the trace classes—because of all the overloaded methods, there is quite a lot of code. However, I'd like to give you a sample. (You can find all the code at www.samspublishing.com.) Listing 4.15 shows the `TraceMessage()` method that was called in Listing 4.14.

LISTING 4.15   An Example of a Public Trace Method (in This Case, `TraceMessage()`)

```
Public Overloads Shared Sub TraceMessage _
(ByVal exeOrDllName As String, _
ByVal source As String, ByVal message As String)
    Dim anUserId As String = ""
    Dim anIsSecurityEnabled As Boolean = False

    If EnterpriseServices.ContextUtil. _
    IsSecurityEnabled Then
        anUserId = EnterpriseServices. _
        SecurityCallContext.CurrentCall. _
        DirectCaller.AccountName.ToString()

        anIsSecurityEnabled = True
    End If

    TraceWrite(TraceType.TraceTypeMessage, _
    exeOrDllName, source, message, anUserId, _
    EnterPriseServices.ContextUtil. _
    IsInTransaction.ToString(), _
    anIsSecurityEnabled.ToString())
End Sub
```

> **NOTE**
>
> You should use `Try` and `Catch` in the code shown in Listing 4.15, while in the `Catch` block you most likely just log the problem. This is also true for the code in Listing 4.16. Of course, it's very important that you don't introduce problems in your code with your tracing solution.

All the different trace methods, both in `Trace` and `ServicedTrace`, will call `TraceWrite()` in the `Trace` class. Listing 4.16 shows the code for this method.

LISTING 4.16   The Protected Trace Method That All Public Trace Methods Call

```
Protected Shared Sub TraceWrite _
(ByVal traceType As TraceType, _
ByVal exeOrDllName As String, _
ByVal source As String, ByVal message As String, _
ByVal userId As String, _
```

LISTING 4.16   Continued

```vb
ByVal transactionInfo As String, _
ByVal securityInfo As String)

    Const aDelimiter As String = vbTab
    Dim aBuffer As New Text.StringBuilder()

    'Type of trace call.
    Select Case traceType
        Case TraceType.TraceTypeMessage
            aBuffer.Append(TraceTypeMessageText)
        Case TraceType.TraceTypeError
            aBuffer.Append(TraceTypeErrorText)
        Case TraceType.TraceTypeBegin
            aBuffer.Append(TraceTypeBeginText)
        Case TraceType.TraceTypeEnd
            aBuffer.Append(TraceTypeEndText)
        Case TraceType.TraceTypeAssert
            aBuffer.Append(TraceTypeAssertText)
        Case Else
            Throw New Exception("Programming error!")
    End Select
    aBuffer.Append(aDelimiter)

    'Current time.
    Dim theNow As DateTime = DateTime.Now()
    aBuffer.Append(theNow.ToLongTimeString)
    aBuffer.Append(".")
    aBuffer.Append(theNow.Millisecond)
    aBuffer.Append(aDelimiter)

    'Name of EXE/DLL.
    aBuffer.Append(exeOrDllName)
    aBuffer.Append(aDelimiter)

    'Source.
    aBuffer.Append(source)
    aBuffer.Append(aDelimiter)

    'Message.
    aBuffer.Append(message)
    aBuffer.Append(aDelimiter)

    'ThreadId.
    aBuffer.Append(AppDomain. _
```

4

ADDING
DEBUGGING
SUPPORT

LISTING 4.16   Continued

```
    GetCurrentThreadId.ToString())
    aBuffer.Append(aDelimiter)

    'Transaction information.
    aBuffer.Append(transactionInfo)
    aBuffer.Append(aDelimiter)

    'Security information.
    aBuffer.Append(securityInfo)
    aBuffer.Append(aDelimiter)

    'UserId.
    aBuffer.Append(userId)
    aBuffer.Append(aDelimiter)

    'ComputerName.
    aBuffer.Append(computerName)
    aBuffer.Append(aDelimiter)

    Ods(aBuffer.ToString())
End Sub
```

Note that in the TraceWrite() method shown in Listing 4.16, the name of the computer is kept in the following variable:

```
Private Shared Readonly computerName _
As String = GetComputerName()
```

Thanks to Shared and Readonly, the GetComputerName() method will be called as seldom as possible. Also worth mentioning is the fact that when I used Process.GetCurrentProcess.MachineName.ToString() to get the name of the machine, only a dot was the result. Although this is correct, it is not what I want, because I'd like to have the possibility to collect trace information from several machines in one list, so I need the real machine names. Therefore, I called GetComputerNameA() in kernel32 via P-Invoke instead. I learned later that Environment.MachineName works fine too.

Start and Stop Tracing During Production

When I discussed the basic tracing solution earlier, I mentioned that I wanted to use a .config file to start and stop tracing during execution. When I discussed the tracing solution for stored procedures, I also said that I had failed to come up with a good solution for using the .config file because of performance reasons. When it comes to the .NET components, I have success-fully used a .config file. You have to take care not to let the reading of the .config file kill performance, such as caching the values and only refreshing them at certain intervals (even the refresh rate is stated in the file).

> **NOTE**
>
> I will discuss dynamically adjusting to values in a `.config` file later in this chapter.

Sender-Filtering

It's important not to make unwanted trace calls, so even though my viewer application can filter trace calls and only show those that the user wants to see, it's sometimes better to filter at the sender-side. It's extra important when it comes to receiving over the network. The main drawback is that the client can't go back and bring the calls back again. That can be done for receiver filtering because the calls have been done and caught but just not shown in the UI. Even the sender-filtering solution depends on the configuration file and the tricks I mentioned in the previous section.

VB6 Components, Windows Forms, ASP, and ASP.NET

The complete tracing solution using `OutputDebugString()` works perfectly well for VB6 components too. I could reuse my .NET trace component, but to skip the overhead of interoperability, I make the call directly from a VB6 code module instead. (See the book's Web site, `www.samspublishing.com`, for the code.)

Although I am focusing on the data and middle tiers in this book, there is nothing to prevent you from using the tracing solution for the Consumer tier. In fact, I actually recommend you do, so that you can gather all the relevant information in one trace list. Once again, the centralization shines because you can easily shift to ASP.NET built-in tracing if you only want to trace the ASP.NET code.

Checking the Solution Against the Requirements

There is definitely a performance penalty with tracing. When no one is listening, it's quite low, and when it's also deactivated, it's very low, which is just the way I want it. I can accept that the performance penalty is high on the rare occasions when I am listening. When I listen, there is a good reason, and if the throughput suffers a bit for a few minutes, that is typically less of a problem than the one I'm trying to solve. The important thing to remember is to use trace calls in a smart way. Watch that you don't put them in a tight loop, for example. In the evaluation section at the end of this chapter, we will discuss performance in detail. To be honest, my proposed solution for remote receiving is primitive and will probably only work in some scenarios. If you need to use remote receiving, I would consider investigating a third-party solution instead.

In addition, the stored procedure solution is not really usable from user-defined functions (UDFs). In the current implementation of UDFs in SQL Server 2000, you can't call stored procedures. However, you can call extended stored procedures, so it's possible to use my trace solution, but you run into trouble with the configuration aspects. I could create two versions of the `xp_jnsktracewrite()`: one empty and one that does the trace call. It's then possible to register the correct one, depending on whether tracing should be activated, but now things are starting to get messy. There are just too many places to change before tracing can be started and, because the extended stored procedure is for the whole system, it won't be possible to decide to use tracing for some databases and not to use it for others. On the other hand, it wouldn't be such a good idea to send trace calls in a scalar UDF. Imagine having it operate on all rows in a resultset with 10,000 rows, for example.

There's a lot more to say about the tool. If you are curious, take a look at the code download on the book's Web site, but remember that it is not a commercial product but rather a quick hack, so use it for inspiration purposes only.

Error Logging

Let me tell you a story that happens often in my professional life and that you're sure to recognize yourself. The story starts when I go to see a customer to discuss a new project:

"Hi Jimmy! Nice to see you."

"Hi John Doe! Nice to see you too."

"Before we get started, one of the users had a problem last week with the other application."

"Oh, that's not good. What was the problem?"

"Hmm…, I don't remember. I think it was Sarah, or perhaps it was Ted…. There was an error message saying something about a problem."

What do you do in this situation? Sure, you can ask them to write down the specific error message in detail every time. But it isn't their responsibility to log information about errors—it's yours. The story ends with you saying, "No problem, I'll take a quick look in the error log and see what the problem was and probably what caused it too." (I love happy endings.)

> **NOTE**
>
> A friend of mine has trained his clients very well. Once, one of his clients gave him all the information found onscreen at the event of a "blue-screen," which was two handwritten pages full of hex codes. His client did what he had been told to do.

Tracing is good when you listen. Logging is good even when you haven't listened, after a problem has occurred, for example. I don't think of logging as seeing the execution paths, but rather as storing information about exceptional situations, such as errors and broken assertions. If I want to see the execution path, I use the tracing solution instead and set it in file mode, which means writing received trace calls to a file.

In this section, I'm going to show you a proposal for how to take care of the logging for both the stored procedures and the components. But before doing that, let me briefly describe how the built-in logging solution in .NET works.

> **NOTE**
>
> Although in this section I discuss logging only as it refers to error logging, you can extend the solution so that it applies to logging in general (to collect statistics, for example).

The Built-In Logging Solution in .NET

The built-in solution for logging in .NET is actually another subclass of the `TraceListener` class, called `EventLogTraceListener`. It can be used to listen for failed assertions and traced errors.

My Proposal for a Logging Solution

In earlier logging solutions I have used, I wrote information about problems to the event log. I thought about using the database, but my argument for not doing so was that the problem I wanted to log could be that the database server wasn't up and running. The two main problems with writing to event logs are

- You don't have a centralized log. One part of the total log could be stored in the event log at the SQL Server, one part at the application server, and the last part spread over all the workstations.

- Running statistics and drawing conclusions from the problems is not "at your fingertips." Let's face it, we use databases for solving business problems for our customers. Why not use this great technique for our own business problems? In Sweden, we have a saying that goes, "The shoemaker's child has the worst shoes." Would you try to convince your customer that using the event log is a great solution for storing his business data? Hopefully not.

I'd want my logging solution to use a more convenient storage vehicle than the event log. I also want my solution to "force" the developer to provide a standardized set of information.

The information is different depending on the tier, but the more relevant information, the better. In addition, I find logging is different from trace calls because it should be possible to listen to trace calls, but not obligatory. It should even be possible not to have them in the release version. It is just the opposite with logging. Logging is obligatory and should always be used. Nobody will listen to log calls in real time; they'll analyze them afterward.

Because of the problems discussed with both the built-in logging in .NET and my earlier attempts, I have designed a small solution of my own that I find better suited to my needs. Although the problem could certainly be that the database server is down, in reality, most often the database server is working just fine, week after week, month after month. Nowadays, I use a database table for my error logging. It will consume some resources and it will take some time to log a problem, but, on the other hand, you're usually not in a hurry when you have an unexpected error. You then have a more fundamental problem.

I also like the idea of using an ordinary file in the file system for the logging. The file system would probably have problems even less often than the database. It's also highly efficient in NT and Windows 2000 to write to a file. (On the other hand, writing to a share is not that fast, and remember that there will be several processes and threads that will write to the same file, which will lead to serialization effects.) Another advantage is that when the developer wants a log, the local administrator just has to attach the log to an email (if the developer doesn't have direct access). Anyway, personally I prefer the database solution.

> **NOTE**
>
> A powerful solution is to log on to Unicenter TNG, Microsoft Operations Manager 2000 (MOM), Tivoli, or a similar administration tool, if your organization/customer uses one of these. (Many of the administration tools support Windows Management Instrumentation, WMI.) You can also use an agent for the product at hand that can sniff the event log, for example. That way, you don't have to make specific calls in your code.

I usually pop an error one layer up (or just leave it) to the callee until I reach the root method. I have tried to have the problem logged in each layer, but I couldn't find a good solution to that when stored procedures call stored procedures. There are problems with T-SQL error handling, and the best way to escape them is to use RETURN() for returning the result to a calling stored procedure and RAISERROR() for returning information from each stored procedure back to a .NET component that can take care of the logging.

> **NOTE**
>
> You will find a lot more information about error handling in Chapter 9.

Let's take a look at the infrastructure for the logging solution. The database table for the logging solution is shown in Figure 4.5.

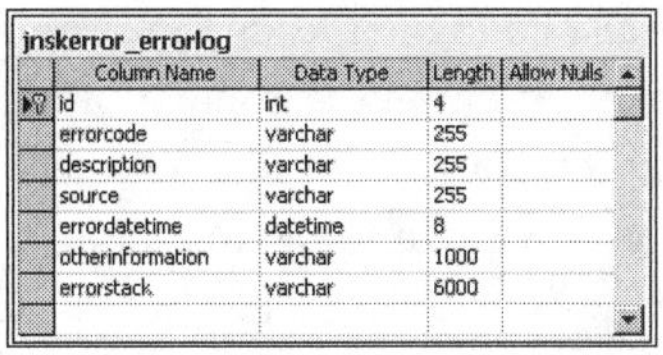

jnskerror_errorlog

Column Name	Data Type	Length	Allow Nulls
id	int	4	
errorcode	varchar	255	
description	varchar	255	
source	varchar	255	
errordatetime	datetime	8	
otherinformation	varchar	1000	
errorstack	varchar	6000	

FIGURE 4.5
Database table for the logging solution.

NOTE

Before .NET, I used an `INT` for errorcode; nowadays, I use a `VARCHAR` instead so that I can write the name of the exception instead of a `HRESULT`.

In the database table, you can also see that I decided not to provide a column for every possible piece of information. Instead, I decided to group most of the information together and write it to the `otherinformation` column, typically as an XML document. That is where I store information about the process ID, if there was an active transaction, and so on. In fact, I store everything that could prove useful when I try to understand the problem. Still, I use separate columns for the most basic information, such as `errorcode` for the name of the exception, `description` as usually used, `source` for the name of the method or stored procedure, `userId` as usually used, and `errordatetime` provides when the problem occurred.

You also see that there is a column called errorstack and that it is also in XML format. The log item is typically written from the "first" layer of .NET components, which I call the "Application layer." (Sten Sundblad and Per Sundblad[6] call it Facade, and Tim Ewald[7] calls it Process, to mention a few alternatives.) There, the complete error stack will be logged together with what was the `errorcode` and `description` in every layer and method where the error was raised. Finally, for the times when there actually is a problem with logging the error to the database, I will resort to writing to the event log.

Stored Procedures for the Logging Solution and Logging Errors in Stored Procedures

Because I store the error information in a table in the database, stored procedures are used for taking care of the writing. I will discuss these stored procedures in this section and how they are used from components later in the chapter.

General Stored Procedures

The actual work of writing to the jnskerror_errorlog table is taken care of by a group of stored procedures. At first, this seems straightforward, but the solution must be able to handle a situation in which an error that must be logged leads to rollback of the transaction. Most often we think of transactions as our friends, but in the context of logging an error, they actually create a problem for us. Assume that the component that will take care of the logging is transactional and that a problem needs to be written to the log table. Unfortunately, logged rows will get rolled back when COM+ decides to go for ROLLBACK instead of for COMMIT. For serviced components, we have a specific transaction attribute to use in this situation, namely RequiresNew transaction, but I think it's overkill to create a distributed transaction just because you are writing an item to the error log.

We could also have an outer object that is not transactional to take care of the logging. This would also solve the problem, but then we have created a solution where we can't change the transactional settings for the outer object without severely affecting the application. (In Chapter 6, "Transactions," I discuss why I want to be able to redeclare the attribute values for transactions.)

Yet another solution is to take care of the logging from a component that is marked with NotSupported transactions. That way, the work of the component will never happen inside a COM+ transaction. The drawback with this solution is that your component must be located in a context object of its own. (I will discuss location of objects in context objects a lot in Chapter 5.) The best solution I have come up with is to use xp_cmdshell to call osql, which, in turn, will execute the stored procedure that will write to the jnskerror_errorlog table. By using this trick, the logging will run in its own transaction, and the problem is solved. The solution is a bit of hack, but it works fine. To speed things up a bit, I only use this solution when I find an active transaction at logging time; otherwise, I skip this extra overhead and just call the stored procedure for logging directly. In Listing 4.17, you can see the code that decides how to write to the jnskerror_errorlog table. As you see, if there is an active transaction, a stored procedure is called; it will use xp_cmdshell as I described earlier. If there isn't an active transaction, another stored procedure will be called that will write to the jnskerror_errorlog table directly.

LISTING 4.17   The Stored Procedure That Is the Entry Point for Logging

```
CREATE PROCEDURE JnskError_Log (@source uddtSource
, @error VARCHAR(255), @description VARCHAR(255)
, @errorDateTime DATETIME
, @otherInformation VARCHAR(1000)
, @errorStack VARCHAR(6000)
```

LISTING 4.17   Continued

```
, @userId uddtUserId)
AS

  SET NOCOUNT ON

  IF @@TRANCOUNT > 0 BEGIN
    EXEC JnskError_LogWriteInNewTransaction
    @source, @error
    , @description, @errorDateTime, @otherInformation
    , @errorStack, @userId
  END
  ELSE BEGIN
    EXEC JnskError_LogWrite @source, @error
    , @description, @errorDateTime, @otherInformation
    , @errorStack, @userId
  END
```

Figure 4.6 shows an interaction diagram for the different call stacks used, depending on whether there is an active transaction.

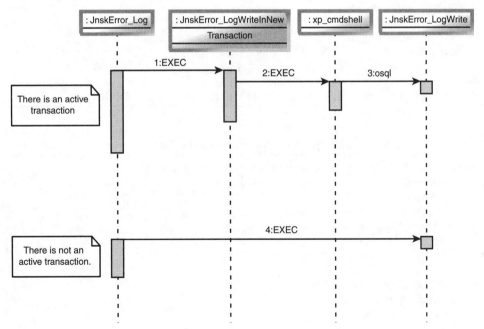

FIGURE 4.6

Interaction diagram for the different call stacks.

For completeness and to make it easier to understand the concept, I have shown the JnskError_LogWriteInNewTransaction() in Listing 4.18 and JnskError_LogWrite() in Listing 4.19. (Please note that I skipped to show the error-trapping code here.)

LISTING 4.18   The Stored Procedure That Creates a New Transaction Before Logging

```
CREATE PROCEDURE JnskError_LogWriteInNewTransaction
(@source uddtSource
, @error VARCHAR(255), @description VARCHAR(255)
, @errorDateTime DATETIME
, @otherInformation VARCHAR(1000)
, @errorStack VARCHAR(6000)
, @userId uddtUserId)
AS

    DECLARE @aTmp VARCHAR(8000)
    , @aReturnValue INT
    SET NOCOUNT ON

    SET @aTmp = 'osql -E -d' + DB_NAME() + ' -Q"JnskError_LogWrite '
    + '''' + @source + ''','''  + @error + ''''
    + ',''' + @description + ''','''
    + CONVERT(VARCHAR(30),
    @errorDateTime,113) + ''''
    + ',''' + @otherInformation + ''','''
    + @errorStack + ''','''  + @userId + ''''
    + '"'

    EXEC @aReturnValue = master..xp_cmdshell @aTmp
```

LISTING 4.19   The Stored Procedure That Writes to the Table

```
CREATE PROCEDURE JnskError_LogWrite (@source uddtSource
, @error VARCHAR(255), @description VARCHAR(255)
, @errorDateTime DATETIME
, @otherInformation VARCHAR(1000)
, @errorStack VARCHAR(6000)
, @userId uddtUserId)
AS

    DECLARE @anError INT
    , @aRowCount INT
    , @aTmp VARCHAR(8000)

    SET NOCOUNT ON
```

LISTING 4.19   Continued

```
INSERT INTO jnskerror_errorlog
(source, errorcode, description, errordatetime
, otherinformation, errorstack, userid)
VALUES
(@source, @error, @description, @errorDateTime
, @otherInformation, @errorStack, @userId)
```

Logging an Error in a Stored Procedure

Now that you have the error-logging stored procedures in place, how can you use them from your ordinary stored procedures? Once again, because of problems with error handling in T-SQL, I only log problems that are returning to the components. Otherwise, I would have several log rows for every problem.

> **NOTE**
>
> I talk more about the error-handling tips and tricks in Chapter 9, "Error Handling and Concurrency Control."

Logging an Error in a .NET Component

My proposal for taking care of logging in .NET components is pretty straightforward. In this section, I'm going to show you what the solution looks like and how it can be used from your .NET components.

Creating the Error Stack

With the help of reflection in .NET, it's easy to get the error stack from the components generated. Actually, using the ToString() method of an exception will give you that information, but you can also iterate the error stack manually to grab the information you want and format it the way you prefer.

> **NOTE**
>
> For this to work, the exceptions need to be chained with the help of innerException. I will discuss this further in Chapter 9.

The Log() Method Itself

In Listing 4.20, you can see one of the Log() methods in Jnsk.Instrumentation.Err. It gathers all the information and then sends it over to LogWrite(), which will save the information to the database.

> **NOTE**
>
> Once again, Try and Catch are left out in the code in Listing 4.20, but this is done intentionally. I will discuss this issue a great deal in the following chapters. That said, you definitely should use exception handling in the code in Listing 4.20. For some errors, you will log to the event log only, and for some errors, you will probably do nothing and just "eat" the exception.

LISTING 4.20   The Log() Method That Extracts All the Information to Log, and Then Calls the LogWrite() for Saving to the Database

```
Private Shared Sub Log(ByVal exeOrDllName As String, _
ByVal source As String, _
ByVal anException As Exception, _
ByVal userId As String)
    Dim anExceptionName As String = _
    anException.GetType.ToString
    Dim aDescription As String = _
    anException.Message
    Dim anErrorDateTime As DateTime = DateTime.Now

    'Build the ErrorStack.
    Dim anErrorStack As String = _
    BuildErrorStack(anException)

    'What other information to grab?
    'Only exeOrDllName for now.
    'Extend later on.
    Dim anOtherInformation As String = _
    BuildOtherInformation(exeOrDllName)

    'Write to the database.
    LogWrite(source, anExceptionName, _
    anDescription, anErrorDateTime, _
    anErrorStack, anOtherInformation, userId)
End Sub
```

`Jnsk.Instrumentation.ServicedErr` inherits from `Jnsk.Instrumentation.Err` to get the
same advantages as for the `Trace` and `ServicedTrace` classes. As you saw in Listing 4.20, I
didn't show the serviced version this time, but in the class diagram in Figure 4.7, you can see
both the classes with all their overloaded methods.

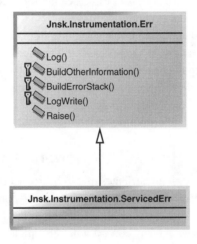

FIGURE 4.7
Class diagram showing the Err *and the* ServicedErr *classes.*

Call to the `Log()` Method: Hidden in Another Method

I centralize my code for raising errors in a method called
`Jnsk.Instrumentation.Err.Raise()` (and `Jnsk.Instrumentation.ServicedErr.Raise()`).
Here, I make my error trace call and I also log the problem, but I won't always log problems
with the `Raise()` method. I will discuss this in more detail in the next section. Note that it
could be interesting to be able to configure what types of errors to log, and how unexpected
errors are always logged, but broken business rules are not. I haven't implemented such a solution here, but the proposed solution can easily be extended to support this functionality.

> **NOTE**
>
> Throw() isn't recommended to be moved to a helper. Even so, I recommend you use a helper when raising exceptions. Skip the flaming e-mails until you have read about my solution in Chapter 9.

Reflection, Interception, and Attributes to Your Service

It's tedious to add specific code snippets over and over again to every method. It will also give you code that is harder to read because you "won't see the forest for the trees" due to all the noise. Because of this, I created a generator back in the VB6 days that made a copy of all the source code and then inserted code snippets at standardized places in the copy. For example, it added calls to TraceBegin() and TraceEnd() to all my methods. When it was time to work on the code again, I went back to the original source code without all the routine-used trace calls. When I started to play with .NET, it was my idea that I could combine attributes and reflection to have the calls generated for me. In the following sections, I will discuss several ways you can benefit from attributes and reflection in .NET.

Custom Attributes Helping to Generate Code

When I started to think about custom attributes in .NET, I thought they would come to the rescue and create code for me. Unfortunately, I'm not the compiler and therefore I don't have that opportunity. What I can do is to ask if a certain attribute is set and use that in an ordinary If clause. However, this won't save me any code, it will only add to it. It will also cost quite a bit of runtime overhead.

A possible solution to the problem could be to use interception. If your component inherits from ContextBoundObject, that could be usable.[8] In the case of serviced components, this is just the situation because ServicedComponent inherits from ContextBoundObject. Then it's also possible to investigate the actual values of the parameters. At first, I thought automatically caching the parameter values for my tracing solution was a very promising solution, but I prefer a more manual solution where I decide what parameter values to show. (What should I otherwise do with more complex parameters such as DataSets, for example?)

> **NOTE**
>
> It's possible, and easy, to trace parameter values for stored procedures called from components. You'll see how in Chapter 8, "Data Access."

I also prefer a more general solution that I can use for all components, no matter from where they are inherited. If I use raw-configured components (discussed in Chapter 5), I will also be unlucky with interception because instances of the raw-configured components will share the context of the first component and have no interception of their own. Finally, this solution consumes a lot of resources too.

Another solution would be to use the `ICorProfilerCallback` interface and create a profiler that will be notified when a method is entered and exited. This looks very exciting, but building a profiler just for adding trace calls seem to be overkill for me, and I haven't investigated it further.

Therefore, I decided to stay with the solution of manually adding a `TraceBegin()` and `TraceEnd()` to my methods. It's not that big a problem because I try to standardize my code structure and use templates anyway. (We'll examine standardized code structures more in Chapter 5.)

Still Benefiting from Custom Attributes

So, is there no way to benefit from custom attributes? There can only be one answer to that question, can't there? Of course there are situations when we can benefit a lot from custom attributes. One obvious situation is when I only want to log errors in my entry methods in the first layer of .NET components. In this case, I could define, for example, `Jnsk.Instrumentation.EntryMethodAttribute` for those methods. In my logging method, I could investigate if that attribute was defined in the calling method and then I would know whether I should make a log call.

Another possible solution would be to implement an empty interface and use that as a marker. This is not Microsoft's recommended approach, but in performance-sensitive code, it could be preferred.

Even faster, and perhaps the most obvious solution is to add a parameter to the `Raise()` method that says whether the error should be logged. That is the solution I am using. Not because of efficiency, because that is not that big a problem for error logging, but because of simplicity.

Putting Reflection to Good Use Once Again

Before the days of .NET, I sometimes wrote methods that could give the description for the value of an enumerator variable instead of just the numeric value. That was very helpful in some debugging situations. Nowadays, we don't have to do that. Instead, we can just use reflection to describe the values.

Suppose that you have an enumerator that looks like the one in Listing 4.21, where some possible aspects of a programmer are listed.

LISTING 4.21   An Enum with Possible Aspects of Programmers

```
Public Enum ProgrammerAspect
    Eager
    Geeky
    TopLevel
    Lazy
End Enum
```

If you want to trace not only the value of an Enum variable called aProgrammerAspect, but rather the description, the code shown in Listing 4.22 can be used.

LISTING 4.22   Get the Description of the Values of an Enum Variable

```
aProgrammerAspect.Format(aProgrammerAspect.GetType, _
aProgrammerAspect, "G")
```

The result of Listing 4.22 would then be, for instance, "Geeky." We would probably get a more useful Enum in this case by adding the Flags() attribute, because a programmer will most often have more than one of the given aspects. In Listing 4.23, the same Enum as in Listing 4.21 is shown, but this time with the Flags() attribute set.

LISTING 4.23   An Enum, Where the Flags() Attribute Has Been Set

```
<Flags()> Public Enum ProgrammerAspect
    Eager = 1
    Geeky = 2
    TopLevel = 4
    Lazy = 8
End Enum
```

Now, the result of Listing 4.22 could, for example, be Eager, Geeky, TopLevel because the variable this time has the first three bits set.

The Conditional Attribute

Yet another way to benefit from attributes is to use Conditional attributes. Even though I prefer to leave my trace calls in the release version, there are situations when I don't. As usual, you could use conditional compilation arguments around the body of the trace methods, but then the calls to the trace methods will still be done. If the trace methods are decorated with the `Conditional` attribute, the calls will not be in the executable, either. In Listing 4.24, you can see an example of a sub that has the `Conditional` attribute set.

LISTING 4.24   A Method with the `Conditional` Attribute

```
<Conditional("MyCustomConstant")> _
Public Sub MySub(ByVal message1 As String, ByVal message2 As String)
```

The `Conditional` attribute doesn't automatically delete the code for preparing the call, because building strings and such will not benefit from this solution, unless the building is done inline in the call itself. In Listing 4.25, the call to `MySub()` won't take place if `MyCustomConstant` hasn't been set to `True`. The same goes for the call to `BuildAnotherString()`. The call to `BuildTheString()` will execute in both cases.

LISTING 4.25   The Call Itself Will Also Be Deleted from the Intermediate Language (IL)

```
Dim aTmp As String = BuildTheString()
MySub(aTmp, BuildAnotherString())
```

Attributes and Reflection in Stored Procedures

As usual, the sophistication levels for .NET and T-SQL are light years apart, so it is not possible to use an attribute technique for stored procedures. On the other hand, you can script all the stored procedures and then run a similar generator to the one I used for my VB6 components on the script; I mean to insert the code at certain places.

I normally skip that and work on my stored procedures with all the routine code included. At least tools similar to the template functionality in SQL Query Analyzer for SQL Server 2000 makes it a no-task to write the routine code.

Configuration Data

Even though this is a chapter about how to add debugging support, I would like to discuss in more detail how you can deal with configuration data. I hope none of my readers are the "I don't create any bugs, so I don't have to read about debugging" types and have therefore skipped this chapter. As we all know, techniques for dealing with configuration data are clearly useful in many situations, not only for adding debugging support.

When I refer to configuration data, I'm talking about the kind of configuration data that you need to refresh on-the-fly (such as enabling/disabling tracing), as well as more static configuration data, such as connection strings. Before we look at how to deal with configuration data, I'd like to say a few more words about the data itself.

> **NOTE**
>
> It's not just possible to enable/disable tracing by changing configuration data. It is also easy, for example, to switch between different tracing implementations to be used by changing the content of the configuration data.

Different Types of Configuration Data

The following are the different types of configuration data:

- Fetched once, used many times
- Fetched every now and then, used many times
- Fetched each time it is used

I just mentioned connection strings, and this kind of configuration data is a typical example of "fetched once, used many times." When your server application is running, it's perfectly fine to say that for the application to refresh the connection string to work with another database server instead of the current one, you have to shut down the server application so that the next request will lead to the connection string being read again (and the new value is then found).

The second category, "Fetched every now and then, used many times," can be exemplified with settings for configuring tracing. You don't usually want to shut down the server application simply to change the filter for tracing or to activate tracing. Instead, reading the configuration data from persistent storage is often good enough, say, once a minute, and all requests for the configuration data are serviced with cached data in this time.

Finally, the third category, "Fetched each time it is used," is not actually a common type of configuration data (at least I can't think of an example). If you encounter this situation, it might be a good idea to think twice about whether this is really configuration data or session data, user data, or application data. Such data that must be fetched from persistent storage each time it will be used often enjoys living in the database.

There are several techniques to choose from when dealing with these different types of data. However, I'd like to start with a short discussion about how I solved the problem of dealing with configuration data in the old days of VB6.

Dealing with Configuration Data in VB6

When we wrote COM+ components in VB6, they were Single-Threaded Apartment (STA) components. This meant that in one specific STA, only one method could run at the same time. To get multitasking, several STAs were available at the same time for a process. In the case of the COM+ server application, there were approximately ten STAs multiplied by the number of processors in the machine. Assume that you were using a machine with two processors; your COM+ server application would then have had approximately 20 threads. Each thread would have had its own public data—that is, global variables, module-global variables, and static variables (but not member data). The public data was stored in Win 32's Thread Local Storage (TLS).

This implementation could be a major problem in some situations. Developers who didn't know that global variables were local to threads and shared between users created horrible, hard to find bugs, because several users were sharing the global data. Yet the global data wasn't completely shared; there were several (say, 20) instances of it.

On the other hand, global data per thread could sometimes also be a great benefit. Even though it was an implementation detail that could change "anytime," I actually based some solutions on this very situation. The typical example was purely configuration data. When the first request came in to a newly started COM+ server application, it was possible a connection string was needed. Then a global variable was investigated to see whether it had been initialized. If not, the connection string was read—for example, from the Registry—and the value was put in the global variable. The next time a request for that very thread made the same investigation, the connection string was found and there was no need to read the Registry again. The nice thing with the solution was that it never introduced any wait states, because each thread had its own data and didn't have to wait for any other thread, which was very efficient. (The main drawback was that you had the data loaded in several instances in memory, which could be a problem in a situation where you wanted to refresh the data for all the threads at the same time, without doing a shutdown of the COM+ application, or if the data was large. If so, you wasted memory.)

When you write COM+ components in .NET, you get free-threaded components, but there is a technique to get a similar solution to that in VB6. Before I start the discussion about how to deal with this in .NET, I'd quickly like to point out two important design decisions—the design perspective and centralization.

The Design Perspective

First, remember that in this book we are discussing writing serviced components, and it is from this perspective that I need the ability to refresh the values on-the-fly. For an EXE, this is not usually a problem; it's just a matter of restarting the EXE. However, restarting a COM+ server application will often affect many users.

NOTE

In Chapter 9, I point out that you should be prepared for the problem of when the COM+ application is shut down and discuss *how* to prepare for it.

4

Because I'm talking about serviced components, this also means that I have more options for how to deal with the configuration data. I'll discuss this more later in the chapter.

Centralization

You probably know by now that I'm very fond of centralizing code. I feel the same when it comes to accessing the configuration data. When a method needs configuration data, the method should just call another method, probably a `Shared` one, to find the needed data. The mechanism that is used should be completely transparent to the calling method.

Now that we've looked at these two important design decisions, let's get down to the nitty gritty. You'll see that I have divided the solution options I'm about to discuss into two parts. The first part discusses how to store the configuration data persistently, and the second part discusses how to access the configuration data from transient storage. I'll start with the first part—persistent storage.

Persistent Storage

There are many techniques from which to choose. The following is a list of a number of them, although the list is not exhaustive:

- Using the usual database
- Using the Registry
- Using Active Directory
- Using Object Construction (OC)
- Using a `.config` file

Let's discuss each of these techniques a little further. When you read this discussion, please keep in mind that it's not my intention that the persistent storage should be hit each time the configuration data is needed, but rather it should only be hit once or at least infrequently. (The second part of the solution, how to access the configuration data in transient storage, will further explain this.)

Using the Usual Database

The first technique, using the usual database for holding configuration data, might seem a bit strange, but this is often a really good idea. The good thing about it is that you have one centralized place for the stored configuration data, even if you have a cluster of application servers. You also have the protection of transactions if that is a requirement for you in this case.

One drawback could be that you waste some scarce resources when you have to hit the database for fetching configuration data too. This is not usually a problem, because you will rarely hit persistent storage for configuration data, but it's still something to think about.

I know, I know. Storing connection strings in the database is *not* a good solution, at least not if the connection strings describe how to reach the database.

Using the Registry

I have to confess that I used `.ini` files long after the Registry was introduced, but after a while I started to like the solution that the Registry represents. (Sure, I see the problems with it, too, but I still like it.) As you know, Microsoft has now more or less put the Registry on the legacy list and you're not supposed to use it anymore, mainly because it creates a more difficult deployment situation compared to using `.config` files instead, for example.

You will normally use the `Registry` class in the `Microsoft.Win32` namespace as the entry point when working with the Registry in .NET.

Using Active Directory

You can think of Active Directory as the "Registry," but it spans all the machines in your network and all the information found on all machines. For many developers, it has become a popular place for storing connection strings and similar items.

It was hard to work with Active Directory (or rather ADSI) from VB6, but it's now much easier in .NET. You start by using the `DirectoryEntry` class of the `System.DirectoryServices` namespace for finding information in the Active Directory.

Using Object Construction (OC)

COM+ 1.0 made it possible to store a string in the COM+ catalog for a specific component and then retrieve that value when an object of the component was activated. This is still a useful and viable solution for serviced components. As you will see in the next section, I see OC both as a solution for the persistent storage and also as an access mechanism. However, you can also use it just as a persistent storage mechanism so that when you find that you need to read the value from persistent storage, you instantiate an object of the component that is using OC, grab the value, and store it in transient storage.

Listing 4.26 shows code that illustrates how OC can be used for serviced components. As you can there, I override the `Construct()` method, and the parameter called `constructString` is the string that can be changed in the Component Services Explorer.

LISTING 4.26   Example Showing How to Use OC in a Serviced Component

```
Imports System.EnterpriseServices
<ConstructionEnabled _
(Default:="Hello world")> _
Public Class OcTest
    Inherits ServicedComponent
    Private m_Data As String

    Protected Overrides Sub Construct _
    (ByVal constructString As String)
        m_Data = constructString
    End Sub

    'And some more methods...

End Class
```

Using a `.config` File

`.config` files are files in XML format for holding configuration data. They were introduced in .NET as a solution for helping with XCOPY deployment. (With XCOPY deployment, a single XCOPY command deploys an application at another server. There are no Registry settings that have to be written, no registrations of DLLs, and so on.)

You have already seen examples of `.config` files in this chapter in Listing 4.4 and Listing 4.6. There you not only saw that `.config` files are used for configuring the built-in tracing solution in .NET, but also how I used it to configure my own tracing solution.

Unfortunately, `.config` files don't work so well with serviced components. `.config` files are for EXEs, rather than DLLs, and that is pretty natural. Consider a DLL that is shared by several EXEs. It should probably be possible to use different settings for each EXE. So far, so good. The problem is that COM+ server applications are executed by the surrogate EXE called Dllhost, and there is only one EXE for all COM+ applications, so it's problematic to use the settings for, say, built-in tracing in the `.config` file. It's also the case that Dllhost isn't written in managed code, and it doesn't know that it should load a `.config` at all. This is why it's also problematic to use the System.Configuration namespace. Finally, you will have to keep the `.config` file in the same directory as the Dllhost EXE, and it's located in your system32 directory. So much for XCOPY deployment.

> **NOTE**
>
> Yet another problem with using .config files is that the built-in tracing solution won't refresh the values found in the .config file. Instead, the .config file is read only once for the process. This is not a big problem for a Windows Forms application, but it might be a huge problem for a COM+ application.

Instead, I have decided to use a custom approach for reading .config files from COM+ applications. I use the format of .config files, but I give them the name of the DLL to which they belong (same value as for AssemblyGlobal.exeOrDllName constant). First I thought about having the .config files together with the DLLs, but the GAC creates a problem for this. Therefore, I decided that the .config files will then be stored in one specific directory. I have decided to use c:\complusapps. Then I use custom code for parsing the .config files, so this approach is quite easy after all.

> **NOTE**
>
> An interesting white paper that is not only related to adding support for debugging but also about configuration data is Amitabh Srivastava and Edward Jezierski's "Monitoring in .NET Distributed Application Design."[9] The paper discusses Windows Management Instrumentation (WMI) and how it can be used for updating .config files, which is just another advantage of the technique of .config files.

Access Mechanism (and Transient Storage)

You also need to think about how to access the configuration data. You can, of course, go to the persistent storage each and every time, but this is probably too costly if you need to go there often. Therefore, the following are a few techniques that I'd like to discuss for providing an access mechanism to transient storage. (Note that this list is not exhaustive.)

- Using the Shared Properties Manager (SPM)
- Using Object Construction (OC)
- Using a Shared (static) member
- Using the ThreadStatic attribute
- Using Object Pooling (OP)

> **NOTE**
>
> You can also read about server-side caching in Chapter 8, where I discuss Object
> Pooling in a context similar to this one.

Once again, let's look at each of these techniques in detail, starting with the SPM.

Using the Shared Properties Manager (SPM)

The Shared Properties Manager (SPM) is an old, faithful component service that is still around.
You can use it from your serviced components as a dictionary object to store keys and values,
similar to the Application object in ASP.NET. However, the SPM can group the keys in property groups.

The programming model of the SPM is a bit different from other dictionary objects, but it's
still quite simple. You can see a sample in Listing 4.27, where a value is read from the SPM (or
written if it wasn't found in the SPM).

LISTING 4.27   Reading a Value That Is Stored in the SPM

```vb
Imports System.EnterpriseServices
Public Class SpmTest
    Inherits ServicedComponent

    Public Function Test() As String
        Dim theExist As Boolean
        Dim aManager As New SharedPropertyGroupManager()

        Dim aGroup As SharedPropertyGroup = _
        aManager.CreatePropertyGroup("MyGroup", _
        PropertyLockMode.SetGet, _
        PropertyReleaseMode.Process, theExist)

        Dim aProperty As SharedProperty = _
        aGroup.CreateProperty("MyProperty", theExist)

        If Not theExist Then
            aProperty.Value = Now.ToString()
        End If
        Return aProperty.Value.ToString()

    End Function
End Class
```

Using Object Construction (OC)

In the previous section, I talked about OC as a mechanism for persistent storage, but it is also a mechanism for accessing transient storage. Refer to Listing 4.26 for a code sample.

Using a Shared (Static) Member

Using a Shared member variable is by no means specific to serviced components, of course. It's a simple and efficient mechanism. Its main problem is that you only have one single instance that is shared by all users and their components, which can lead to concurrency conflicts when the value isn't read-only. Because of this, you have to protect the value by writing thread-safe code. This will result in wait states in a highly stressed environment when the Shared member is to be used all the time. Most often, it won't cause you any problems, but in some situations—as I said, under extreme load—it might be a show-stopper.

To get a cheaper locking solution, you can implement a ReaderWriter lock instead. That means that there might be several readers at the same time, but only one writer. Do you get a déjà vu from the database area? You can find more information about how to implement a ReaderWriter lock in the .NET online help.

> **NOTE**
>
> Because this chapter is mostly about debugging, I must warn you against trying to write thread-safe code manually. If you do so, you might create a debugging nightmare for yourself, either now or in the future. Be careful and make sure you know what you're doing.

Using the ThreadStatic Attribute

It's possible to use TLS in .NET too, so that each thread will have it's own local data. It's easily achievable by just marking a Shared variable with the ThreadStatic attribute.

This will mean that you will have as many instances of the data as you have threads. There will be no blocking, because each thread will have the data it needs. This might also mean a problem for you because you waste memory, but that is most often not the case for configuration data.

Using Object Pooling (OP)

The final technique that I'd like to discuss for providing an access mechanism to transient storage is using Object Pooling (OP) in serviced components. If you still remember the technique of thread-specific global variables from the days of VB6 (and which I discussed earlier in this section about configuration data), OP is another technique that comes close to that solution.

Not that pooled objects are tied to a specific thread, but you will have a pool of n number of objects with OP, so that you can avoid the situation of several simultaneous requests of the same value leading to wait states. On the other hand, the larger the pool, the larger the amount of used memory, of course.

However, while it is an advantage that several instances minimize contention, it's a disadvantage if it's necessary for all instances to have the same values all the time. If it is necessary, you'd better use one single value instead (unless it's not a "fetch once, use many times" type of data).

> **NOTE**
>
> Both Object Construction and Object Pooling can be used, even when the object is located in the context of the caller, because neither of these services are built with interception.

Summary of Persistent Storage and Access Mechanisms

Not all access mechanisms can be used with all persistent storage mechanisms. Table 4.3 presents the possible combinations.

TABLE 4.3   Possible Combinations of Access Mechanisms and Persistent Storage Mechanisms

	SPM	OC	Shared Member	Thread Static	OP
Database server	OK	N/A	OK	OK	OK
Registry	OK	N/A	OK	OK	OK
Active Directory	OK	N/A	OK	OK	OK
OC	OK	OK	OK	OK	OK
.config file	OK	N/A	OK	OK	OK

As you see in Table 4.3, only OC is a bit inflexible as an access mechanism because it is so closely related to its storage. You *can* let the users affect OC as an access mechanism by using the Admin API for COM+ to change the stored value, but it is sort of a hack. At least, I don't think this was the way OC was supposed to be used.

How and When to Refresh the Cached Configuration Data

Finally, it might be a problem deciding when to refresh the cached configuration data. A simple approach is to encapsulate the data so that each time there is a request for the data, you can investigate whether a certain amount of time has elapsed since the last time the date was refreshed. If so, you go to persistent storage to read the data and remember when this happened.

If you use, for example, Object Pooling for caching the data, it might be a good idea to introduce a two-phase technique so that not every object in the object pool has to go to persistent storage. Instead, you have one single pooled object (of, say, class A) that is responsible for this, and every pooled object (of, say, class B) will only go to the object of class A when they find out that it's time to refresh their data. Class A uses a similar algorithm so that it doesn't go to persistent storage each time it is called by a B instance. If you use a schema like this, you have to remember that the maximum time for different instances to be out of sync is the sum of the refresh delay of the A object and the refresh delay of one B object.

Evaluation of Configuration Data Solution

For some types of configuration data, the data will be read extremely frequently. Flags for tracing is a good example of this. With these types of configuration data, probably the singlemost influential of the factors discussed in Chapter 2, "Factors to Consider in Choosing a Solution to a Problem," is performance. Because of this, I have decided not to print my evaluation in this book, because I will finish the book before .NET is available in version 1. For this reason, I consider it dangerous and misleading to run performance tests. Instead, you will find performance results and my recommendation regarding configuration data at the book's Web site at www.samspublishing.com. You will, of course, also find all the code there for the recommended solution.

> **NOTE**
>
> This is the only time in the book that I have ended a discussion without giving a recommendation, but as I said, this proposal is extremely performance dependent, and before V1 of .NET has been released, it's just too dangerous to decide on a winner.

These were a few words about the aspect of accessing configuration data. When it comes to persistently storing configuration data, I tend to find the .config solution is the best one. The second best is using the database server or Active Directory.

4

ADDING
DEBUGGING
SUPPORT

Evaluation of Proposals

It is time to evaluate my proposals again. This time, I will evaluate my tracing and logging proposals to see how they stand up to the criteria we discussed in Chapter 2.

Evaluation of the Tracing Proposal

I think my tracing solution is more "consumer type-friendly" than the built-in solution in .NET because it works well and in exactly the same way with ASP.NET too. It's also easy to collect trace information from several processes in one single list of trace calls.

It's extremely important that the tracing solution doesn't create a lot of overhead, especially when everything in the system is fine and nobody is listening. My proposal is at a high abstraction level because it is added directly in the source code. It's not without penalties to performance and scalability, but still I think that in real-world applications, the overhead is not too high.

You can find the results of several performance tests at the book's Web site at `www.samspub-lishing.com`. All the tests have been executed with V1 of .NET. Note that you should be prepared to see that the overhead is quite large for calling empty methods/stored procedures, but how often do you have the need for that? Not that often, I hope. You will also see by the results that the tracing solution doesn't add that much overhead to methods that do real work.

Almost all the "-abilities" I discussed in Chapter 2—maintainability, reusability, productivity, testability, and debuggability, but not reliability—will benefit from having tracing in the code. The productivity will degrade slightly because of the work involved in adding the calls, but, because debugging will be so much more effective, it will also help productivity in the long run. Reliability is hopefully not adversely affected either, but you should be aware that there is always a greater risk for problems purely because of extra code.

Coexistence and interoperability are also addressed by the proposal. For example, browsing a complete call stack from a VB6 component to a Visual Basic .NET component to a stored procedure and all the way back can be very helpful in certain situations.

When it comes to security, you must be cautious. When you add trace calls, you can end up opening up windows to sensitive information so that a skilled and interested person could listen to passwords and whatever information you send in the trace calls. You should discuss this with your customer up front so that you establish clear routines.

I have said it before, but I'd like to say again that the main focus of this chapter isn't the tracing tool itself, but rather the concept of using tracing in any form.

Evaluation of the Logging Proposal Evaluation

The logging solution I have proposed doesn't really consider the type of consumer. At the entry level that the consumer calls, the error will be logged no matter what the consumer type. Perhaps the consumer will log the error too, but then it will be from the perspective of the consumer. I think you should see your server-side application as a black box and let it log its errors, even if the consumer handles the errors as normal conditions.

Thanks to centralized storage in the database, it doesn't matter how many database servers and application servers are involved. All error information will be collected at one place.

Of course, scalability and performance will be affected negatively at an error because the proposed solution consumes a lot of resources. Hopefully, you won't have that many errors needing to be logged. Also, when you do have a problem, it's not that urgent to have the MsgBox() or an equivalent back to the user. A general rule of performance tuning is to make the common case fast. Hopefully, exceptions aren't the common case.

Maintainability, productivity, and debuggability benefit greatly from using a logging solution such as the one I have proposed. For debuggability especially, using a logging solution in production is not optional, it's obligatory! A minor problem with regard to reliability is that if it isn't possible to contact the database, it's of course impossible to log a problem there. Therefore, in this case, I write to the event log.

The logging solution can be used for .NET components, stored procedures, VB6 components, and so on. Still, there are certain rules that the code must adhere to for the protocol to work. This is a problem if you reuse components and stored procedures without being aware of the protocol. The reverse situation is also a problem because it's not possible for a consumer to have the logging solution to adapt to his or her solution. (This is a good example of a situation when the listening architecture that is used in .NET shines.)

Just as with the tracing, the logging can be a security problem in some applications. On the other hand, hopefully the database, which will hold the log, is secure, which reduces the risk.

What's Next?

.NET opens up a lot of new possibilities for you to design your system and its different parts. You have new flexibility, but that doesn't make it easier. Some architectural guidance or inspiration is needed for architects, team leaders, and developers. In the next chapter, I will discuss architectures, both in the broad perspective such as tiers and layers, and in the narrow perspective regarding code structures.

References

1. J. Robbins. *Debugging Applications*. Microsoft Press; 2000.

2. `http://msdn.microsoft.com/msdnmag/`; the "Bugslayer" column.

3. `http://www.sysinternals.com`; DebugView.

4. K. Beck. *Extreme Programming Explained: Embrace Change*. Addison-Wesley; 1999.

5. `http://msdn.microsoft.com/library/default.asp?url=/library/en-us/odssql/ods_6_con_01_22sz.asp`.

6. S. Sundblad and P. Sundblad. *Designing for Scalability with Microsoft Windows DNA*. Microsoft Press; 2000.

7. T. Ewald. *Transactional COM+: Building Scalable Applications*. Addison-Wesley; 2001.

8. `http://www.razorsoft.net` (see TraceHook.NET).

9. A. Jezierski and E. Jezierski. *Monitoring in .NET Distributed Application Design*. `http://msdn.microsoft.com/library/en-us/dnbda/html/monitordotnet.asp`.

Architecture

IN THIS CHAPTER

So far, we have discussed ways in which you can prevent problems by planning and testing in the beginning phases of a project. One example was to add support for tracing to your components and stored procedures early. However, the most important aspect of a project in terms of preparation is deciding on its architecture. In making such preparation, you should think in terms of scale. If your project has a small scale (such as only one or a few end users, a short application life expectancy, and only one developer), having a well–thought out architecture isn't all that important. On the other hand, if you know that the application will support many users or if you want to prepare for future growth in any way, a good architectural plan is crucial. And remember, a short life expectancy for a system can actually last a very long time, making it no fun to have a quick-and-dirty system to maintain for years. Meanwhile, .NET Component Services and SQL Server 2000 are also very much about scale. You would probably not consider using either of them if you are not expecting to build a large-scale application for numerous users.

In this chapter, we'll look at several different architectural styles—a database-independent and pure object-oriented architecture, a database-centric architecture, and the classic Windows DNA architecture. We'll also spend time looking at a sample application based on the Acme HelpDesk. I'll then present my own achitecture proposal, which, as in earlier chapters, I will evaluate based on the criteria established in Chapter 2, "Factors to Consider in Choosing a Solution to a Problem." In addition, we'll look at various architectural factors to consider, such as physical partitioning, and I'll present a second proposal, which deals with consistent code structures.

Three Examples of Architectures

As we all know, a vast number of architecture examples have been presented in literature and magazines over the last few years. To narrow the scope, in this chapter I will discuss only examples where relational databases are used because that is the most typical database technique for business applications. This section will look at three such examples, a database-independent and pure object-oriented architecture, a database-centric architecture, and the classic Windows DNA architecture.

Example 1: The Database-Independent and Pure Object-Oriented Architecture

Members of the pure object-orientation community believe that architectures should be completely database independent. In extreme cases, the application only touches the database at startup to read all the state and at termination to write back all the state. Although this style works well in some situations, it is not suitable for the typical multiuser business application. This is because there is too much data to keep in the memory, and the data can easily be lost. If the state is kept at the workstation, you won't see other users' changes until the next startup. If the state is kept at the server and is shared by all users, you will experience synchronization problems that you have to solve. Meanwhile, if the state is kept at the server with one object model per user, once again, you won't see other users' changes until the next startup, and it will eat up memory from the server.

The style of pure object-oriented design could be changed slightly so that at the start of a use case, everything needed is read from the database to a pure object model, the object model is worked on, and then the resulting object model is written back to the database. This is a common approach for business applications too. In this case, a large part of the work will consist of mapping between objects and relational data.

As you can see, in this approach, the database's capabilities are rarely taken advantage of. The developers are left to take care of such functions as transactions, concurrency control, querying, and traversing the data. Because most navigation is done in the object model, the join capabilities of the database, for example, are not used.

Let's look at another example of when an architecture like this is used. Suppose a user wants a list of all her customers whose last names start with the letter A, as well as their order histories. In this case, there should be one collection; let's call it `CustomerCollection`, containing `Customer` objects. Each `Customer` object has an instance of an `OrderCollection`, which, in its turn, contains several `Order` objects. Each `Order` has a collection called `OrderRowsCollection` that contains information about products for the order. This approach could easily end up with hundreds or thousands of objects for each `Customer`, all of which must travel over the wire between different tiers. Using objects over the wire can be very expensive; this is definitely true for VB6-created COM objects, for example, because only object references will travel then. If the objects are serialized to a flat structure, sending them over the network will be more efficient, but the serialization and deserialization will also take some time.

The most realistic and interesting proposal I have seen for a pure object-oriented architecture is the one Peter Heinckiens discusses in his book, *Building Scalable Database Applications*.[1] In his proposal, he uses the database capabilities to make data-near operations more efficient. Still, he doesn't discuss the multiuser aspects, transactions, server-based object models, nor the implications his proposal has for distributed systems. As you probably have guessed, I don't think this is a good enough architecture for the platform we are going to use.

Example 2: The Database-Centric Architecture

Some architects and developers—myself included—are deeply enamored with the processing capabilities, such as stored procedures, of modern relational databases. This was especially true with the second wave of client server, when some or most of the logic was moved from the client to the database server. Michael Stonebraker and Paul Brown discuss this in their book, *Object-Relational DBMSs: Tracking the Next Great Wave, Second Edition*.[2] They think of the database server as an application server as well. For example, the authors suggest that one database server can act as the application server, while another can be responsible for the data. One merit of this approach is that it's easy to repartition the logic, because it can be located at any of the database servers.

A more recent version of this approach to database-centric architecture was presented by Microsoft's code sample, Duwamish Online.[3] Here, Microsoft demonstrated how to create part of an e-commerce application by using only XML/XSL and the XML support in SQL Server 2000.[4] In doing so, they succeeded in getting very good performance. However, a disadvantage with the database-centric approaches is that at the end of the day, a great deal of logic must be located in the client, and this, in turn, causes several problems, including deployment, heavy client applications, and many round trips to the database server. Although this could be a good approach for simple applications, I don't see it as a really flexible architecture to suit several different classes of applications.

Example 3: The Classic Windows DNA Architecture

Microsoft's first attempt at giving architectural guidance was when they suggested using Windows DNA as a way to build n-tier applications. Compared to pure object-oriented architectures, this architecture paid more attention to physical aspects—for example, value types instead of references were sent over the network between tiers. The concept was targeted at using Microsoft products and technologies, such as ASP, COM+, and SQL Server. There have been thousands of applications built in this style. The approach is pretty much structured upon layers.[5] Figure 5.1 shows a picture you probably have seen more times than you can remember describing the different layers according to Windows DNA.

What is also typical of Windows DNA is that it is service focused rather than object focused. When I discussed the pure object-oriented architecture earlier, I gave an example of a user who wants to have a list of all her customers whose last names start with the letter A and their order histories. With Windows DNA, this information would typically be found by a method that returns a simple structure, for example, as an array or an ADO Recordset, with all the information.

In the most classic definition of Windows DNA, all business rules should be put in the Business Logic layer, and it should be possible to easily port an application to other databases similar to SQL Server. Sten Sundblad and Per Sundblad, in their book *Designing for Scalability with Microsoft Windows DNA*,[6] changed the recommendation slightly so that the database is responsible for at least some of the business rules. Some of the code sample applications provided by Microsoft (called Duwamish Online[3] and Fitch and Mather[7]) were much more eager to use stored procedures than classic Windows DNA. As you will find when I discuss my architecture proposal later in the chapter, I think Windows DNA has a lot of merits. Although my architecture proposal is different from Windows DNA, it is inspired by it.

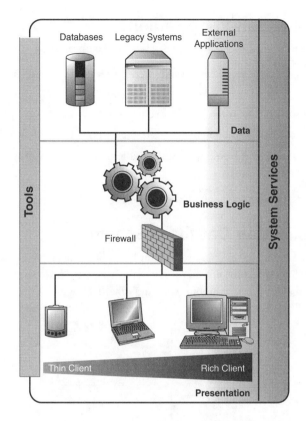

FIGURE 5.1
Classic Windows DNA tiers: Presentation, Business Logic, and Data.

Sample Application: Acme HelpDesk

Before I present my own architecture proposal, I'll briefly discuss the sample application that I'm going to use for the examples from now on.

Over the course of my career, I have built several different applications for errand handling for helpdesks, among other things. Chances are that you have built similar applications or have had some practical experience with one. In any case, it should be easy for you to quickly get an idea of the naive version of the sample application I'm going to present here. First, let's take a look at the sample application's requirements.

Sample Application Requirements

Some of the requirements for this simplified version of the application are as follows:

- Users should be able to report an errand, thereby revealing a lot of information about the problem in question.
- The problem solvers should be able to log all actions taken to solve the problem.
- The problem solvers should be able to route the responsibility of solving the problem.
- The user who reported the errand should be able to see how the problem has attempted to have been solved preciously.

Now let's move on to the database schema.

Sample Application Database Schema

Figure 5.2 shows the database schema of the sample application. As you can see, many columns, tables, and relationships are missing from this figure. However, the figure is meant to provide a simple database to show architecture and other techniques.

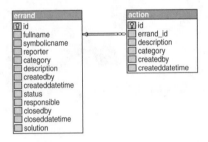

FIGURE 5.2

The simple database schema for the sample application Acme HelpDesk, showing the errand *and* action *tables.*

From this presentation of the sample application, you might think that I believe modeling should be done from the database up. This is not the case. I am showing it this way only to provide a background for discussing the architecture.

The two extreme—and quite popular—ideas for modeling are to

- Create the database model more or less automatically in accordance with how the components were created
- Create the components more or less automatically in accordance with how the database model was created

As always, I think the answer lies somewhere in between, and that goes for the modeling example as well. Database modeling is something of a parallel activity to object modeling.

Typical questions faced are: What methods are needed? What data is needed for this use case? What must this use case look like to support this data? and so on.

My Architecture Proposal: A .NET-Adjusted Version of DNA

As I write this book, there isn't much guidance on architecture in the .NET world. Given this dearth, I'd like to stick my neck out and present what is currently my preferred architecture proposal. In doing so, I will combine my experience with different architectures I have successfully implemented over the years with my knowledge of .NET. First, we'll discuss the key assumptions underlying my proposal, and then we'll look at the architecture proposal layer by layer, citing other important considerations.

My Proposal: Building Blocks

Before I explain my architecture proposal in detail, it's important that you understand a few of its key assumptions and components.

Serviced Components

Throughout this book, I will use serviced components to assist with enterprise infrastructure services. Examples of services that I will use in suitable situations are as follows:

- Object pooling
- Transactions and Just-In-Time (JIT) activation
- Synchronization

More or less automatically, I will also receive

- Resource pooling
- Administrative and production support

The choice to use serviced components will affect the architecture because serviced components set a number of rules for .NET components, such as stating that nondefault constructors and shared methods as entry points can't be used.

> **NOTE**
>
> When serviced components are used, .NET security must be opened up. On the other hand, it's quite common to be forced to trust server-side components. With or without .NET security, this can be a security risk.

Stored Procedures

I strongly believe that it is extremely important to use stored procedures. While there are drawbacks, such as lack of portability and a requirement for T-SQL skills, there are many more advantages in using stored procedures, including the following:

- They are typically the most efficient way to access the database.
- They can reduce network round trips.
- They are easy to change in deployed applications.
- They make it is easier to tune the performance of your data access code.
- They provide a better way to give out permissions rather than to give permissions out for base tables.
- They allow the database schema (and schema changes) to be hidden.
- They help to centralize all the data access code.

NOTE

Be careful if you use dynamic SQL with the help of EXEC('string') or SP_EXECUTESQL() within your stored procedures, because the user must be authorized to use the objects that are used—being authorized to use the stored procedure isn't enough. A good solution is to be very restrictive regarding the tables, but to use views/user-defined functions (UDFs) in the dynamic SQL, and then give out enough rights to the views/UDFs.

If all database access is done through your stored procedures, you get a controlled set of entry points. Why is this good?

- Auditing is easily solved.
- Disconnected pessimistic locking is easily solved.
- Data-close business rules can be put in stored procedures.
- There is no need for triggers, which is good for debuggability and maintainability.

NOTE

Instead of using the public stored procedures as entry points for auditing, you can use the transaction log itself in SQL Server. The log can't be used directly with ordinary SELECT statements or with an editor, but there are products that can help. One problem with this solution is if you want to audit SELECTs too. You have the same problem if you want to audit other nonlogged operations with this solution.

I'm not convinced that the use of stored procedures is only negative in the portability sense. When I have reviewed systems where stored procedures haven't been used because of portability reasons, they have had the SQL code spread all over the place, and the SQL code has been full of database-specific constructs. If you put all SQL in stored procedures, you have it at least at one place, and if you stay SQL 92–compliant when possible, a lot of the content of your stored procedures is portable.

In Chapter 7, "Business Rules," I will explain why I think stored procedures are a good and scalable place for evaluating some rules. Even so, a disadvantage is that the consequences are more serious when you write bad code in stored procedures than when you do so in the components. For example, add a loop in a stored procedure that goes through all rows in a table and repeat this several times. Then compare that to doing the same thing in the component, by looping the data in a DataSet. In the first case, you are severely affecting what is possibly the only database server. In the latter case, you can just add one more application server if throughput is bad.

Are Stored Procedures of Less Importance to Oracle?

I have gotten the impression several times from different sources that it is more important to use stored procedures with SQL Server than with, say, Oracle. Because I don't have current experience with Oracle, I asked my friend and experienced developer, Michael D. Long, about this. He told me that stored procedures are just as important for operations that will update a large number of rows. "Oracle DataBase Administrators (DBAs) will be of the opinion that stored procedures will improve overall scalability of the database server," Michael says, "but I have observed that the inefficiency of the client layer can have just as much impact."

In addition, during Michael's benchmarking of Oracle 7.3.4.x, 8.0.5.x, and 8i (8.1.5 and 8.1.7), he told me he observed that for operations involving a single row INSERT or UPDATE, a dynamic SQL statement used fewer resources and required less time than calling a stored procedure to perform the same activity. Michael says: "The characteristic is more a side effect of the client stack than the efficiency of Oracle Server. The chatter back and forth between the client and server is greater when setting up the stored procedure. The Lucent DBAs had noted strange SQL statements being executed; Oracle's Bug Diagnosis and Escalation team later found these were generated by the Microsoft data access layer."

ADO.NET and DataSets

There will most certainly be a lot of discussion regarding whether ADO.NET DataSets are the right medium for sending collections of data between layers and tiers, just as there was with ADO's RecordSets in VB6. In VB6, I actually preferred using ADO's RecordSets, even though they were a bit heavy and performance was not optimal. The main reasons were their ease of use and built-in metadata. I will continue that tradition in .NET, but I will use typed DataSets. If you're like me, Option Strict makes you jump for joy, as does the type safety you have when working with DataSets. In addition, thanks to DataSets, I can avoid my usual tricks for sending several RecordSets at once; DataSets has this built in with its DataTables, which simplifies my code a great deal. I do respect the opinion that developers don't want to be too dependent on ADO.NET because ADO changed often and caused a lot of problems because of this. This can be a reason for not sending around DataSets, but to build a custom structure instead.

If you don't like DataSets but want to build your own structure for sending the data, you can still use my proposed architecture. In this case, be sure to use DataReaders to grab the data out of the database instead when you move it to your custom structure.

> **NOTE**
>
> I will discuss ADO.NET and DataSets in more depth in Chapter 8, "Data Access."

My Architecture Proposal Tier-by-Tier and Layer-by-Layer

As I have said, my proposal is mostly inspired by Windows DNA. However, it is more database focused than is Windows DNA; that is, it is focused on solving all actions with one single round trip between tiers. In addition, I have adapted it to .NET. Figure 5.3 is an overview of my architecture proposal's different layers and their relationships. The figure also shows tier membership for the different layers.

The first impression you get might be one of overkill. Please remember that this architecture should be used as a starting point, and often several layers will be skipped (or merged together). It's extremely important that you adapt the architecture to your specific application and situation.

> **NOTE**
>
> Figure 5.3 shows only the layers (packages, in Unified Modeling Language [UML] parlance) regarding the main call stack for use cases. There will, of course, be several helper classes and packages as well. So far, you have been introduced to Jnsk.Instrumentation in Chapter 3, "Testing," and Chapter 4, "Adding Debugging Support."

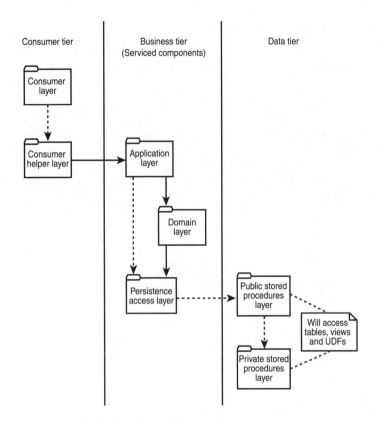

FIGURE 5.3

My architecture proposal's different tiers, layers, and their relationships.

Assembly and Layer

Layers are often implemented as separate assemblies, but I can think of putting the Consumer layer and Consumer Helper layer in one assembly (or exe) and the Domain layer and the Persistent Access layer in an assembly (or dll). This is especially the case for smaller systems and/or when it's not important to have the possibility to distribute and deploy changed layers in isolation. Even so, the default solution is to let each layer be an assembly of its own.

Proposal Used for Sample Application Acme HelpDesk

If I apply the conceptual architecture to the sample application Acme HelpDesk discussed earlier, it will appear as in Figure 5.4. As you can see, I have provided physical names in the packages. The namespaces (and names of assemblies with exe or dll as extension) will be

- `Acme.HelpDesk` (for the Consumer layer)
- `Acme.HelpDesk.ConsumerHelper` (for the Consumer Helper layer)

- `Acme.HelpDesk.Application` (for the Application layer)
- `Acme.HelpDesk.Domain` (for the Domain layer)
- `Acme.HelpDesk.PersistentAccess` (for the Persistent Access layer)

I will provide a thorough discussion about each layer shortly.

> **NOTE**
>
> I wish we had such a thing as namespaces for stored procedures too, but unfortunately we don't. I prefix my public stored procedures with a_ to categorize the stored procedures.

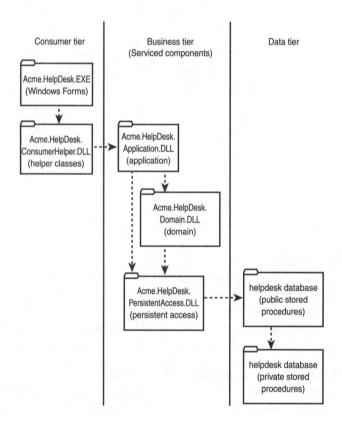

FIGURE 5.4

My architecture proposal applied to the sample application Acme HelpDesk.

Let's now delve deeper into the different tiers and layers of my architecture proposal. In this discussion, I will use an example in which the user wants to list all errands that have symbolic names such as "Printer*" or all errands for a specific reporter being reported between two dates. Then the user can select one of the errands in the list to see all the detailed information about that errand, including its actions.

Consumer Tier

The consumer tier can differ a lot, depending on which consumer type is used. For Windows Forms, it is typically one exe containing both the Consumer layer and the Consumer Helper layer. For Web Forms it will be a dll, once again containing both layers. As mentioned earlier, another typical solution is to let the Consumer Helper layer be in a separate dll.

Consumer Layer

Assuming the consumer is built with Windows Forms, the Consumer layer will be made up of Windows Forms classes. The purpose of the Consumer layer is to provide presentation services for the user in this case. I prefer to keep the Consumer layer as thin as possible and to delegate several responsibilities to the Consumer Helper layer.

Consumer Helper Layer

As the name implies, the main purpose of the Consumer Helper layer is to help the Consumer layer. This layer helps the Consumer layer mostly by hiding complexity, but also by providing services. The remainder of this section presents some of its typical tasks.

> **NOTE**
>
> The Consumer Helper layer is not a host for business rules! Even though it might be tempting, don't add any business rules to this layer. We will discuss business rules in greater depth in Chapter 7.

Hiding Factories

The Consumer Helper layer hides factories (or at least the use of factories), which can be very important because custom constructors aren't allowed for serviced components. Because custom constructors aren't allowed, serviced components will still have to use a two-step initialization to get instance-state from the client so that the client will first create the instance with New() and then call an Init() with the needed parameters to provide the state. Observe that the Consumer Helper layer class can have nondefault constructors because it is not a serviced component.

It's worth mentioning that often, all needed information from the client is sent over to the serviced component in every call instead. This is a must if the serviced component is using JIT

5

activation, because the state will be lost after the done-bit of the context object has been set and the method is exited. The consumer will not know that it has to provide the state again. I definitely prefer to design in such a way that I can change the attribute values regarding JIT activation or not, without breaking the code.

Factories have several other advantages (most of them due to code centralization), including the following:

- They easily take advantage of partitions (which is a new feature in COM+ 1.5).
- They can hide whether the serviced component is used as a queued component.
- They hide what class is providing the real implementation.

Hiding Communication over the Network

Remoting in .NET has several advantages over DCOM, but one drawback is that it is less transparent. Therefore, a good solution is to hide the chosen communication method in the Consumer Helper layer. This way, the Consumer Helper layer is the only layer that knows whether there will be a network call, whether DCOM or remoting will be used, what channel type to use for remoting, and so on.

The Consumer Helper layer can also help to make network round trips more efficient by only serializing rows in DataSets that have been changed.

Locating Presentation Logic and Helping with Input

Try to make the form classes as "thin" as possible and factor out logic. A good place to put the logic is in the Consumer Helper layer, because several forms can typically share one helper class. The Consumer Helper layer can also provide basic input help so that the end user has a smaller risk of giving incorrect data that will be caught by the business rules in "later" layers.

Hiding Consumer-Side Caching

In some situations, it's valuable to have consumer-side caching. If it is, the consumer layer shouldn't be aware of it or have to code appropriately for it. Instead, the Consumer Helper layer can hide consumer-side caching so that when the Consumer layer asks for a specific piece of data, the Consumer Helper layer provides it. If the Consumer Helper layer finds the data in the cache or asks the Application layer for it, it doesn't matter to the Consumer layer.

NOTE

In earlier attempts with consumer-side caching, I had a cache class that, for example, the User Interface (UI) form first checked to see if it was up to date. If it wasn't, the Application layer was contacted. In this case, the caching definitely wasn't transparent to the consumer. It was a main ingredient of the programming model. I consider this a mistake. Information hiding is preferable!

Translating Error Messages

The Consumer Helper layer can help translate error messages not only between languages, but also from programmer-friendly messages to end user–friendly messages.

Acting as Proxy, Hiding Stateless Business Tier

The Consumer Helper layer should be designed so that calls between the Consumer helper and the serviced component are few and efficient, because there will often be process-to-process communication between the Consumer tier and the Business tier. This requires the style of "one method call per use case," which is efficient but less intuitive than an ordinary object-based style where some properties are set and then some methods are called. The helper object will act as a proxy and can hide the "large" method calls and provide an ordinary, object-based style instead.

> **NOTE**
>
> You can read more about the Proxy design pattern in *Design Patterns: Elements of Reusable Object-Oriented Software* by Erich Gamma, Richard Helm, Ralph Johnson, and John Vlissides.[8]

Recovering from Problems

The Consumer Helper layer can discover and re-create an instance when the server-side instance is lost because the COM+ application has been shut down. The Consumer Helper layer can also help to recover from deadlocks.

> **NOTE**
>
> I will discuss further the problems with shutdown and deadlocks in Chapter 9, "Error Handling and Concurrency Control."

A typical Consumer Helper class could look as shown in Figure 5.5. There you can see the `ErrandBrowsingHelper` class. In this example, only three (of which two are overloaded) methods are shown for fetching a list of errands and fetching all details about a specific errand by ID.

As you can see in Figure 5.5, `ErrandBrowsingHelper` inherits from `Jnsk.Consumer.ConsumerHelper`. `Jnsk.Consumer.ConsumerHelper` implements `IDisposable`; that way, the amount of code for `ErrandBrowsingHelper` will be reduced and the pattern is similar to how the serviced components are built. It's also the case that the `Jnsk.Consumer.ConsumerHelper` uses the Template Method pattern[9] to force the subclass with the help of `MustOverride` to write a `Dispose()` method.

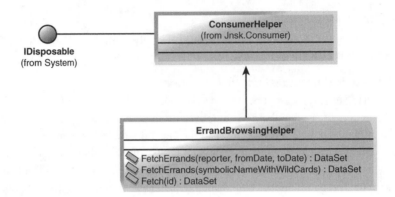

FIGURE 5.5
Example of a Consumer Helper class.

> **NOTE**
>
> I will come back to the Dispose() problem later in this chapter, where you will also find code for the entire solution.

The Consumer Helper class (such as ErrandBrowsingHelper) will often mirror the "parallel" class in the Application layer, but most often there will be more methods. Furthermore, as I said earlier, even though this isn't the case in Figure 5.5, it will be common to have properties that hide the fact that the Application layer is being operated on by "large" method calls where all state is provided in every call.

Business Tier

Now let's turn our attention to the Business tier, which will be built with serviced components and executed at an application server. This tier is made up of the following layers:

- Application layer
- Domain layer
- Persistent Access layer

The Consumer tier will only know about and interact with one of the layers in this tier, namely the Application layer.

Application Layer

The first layer in the Business tier is what I call the Application layer. It's very similar to what others call the Process layer,[9] the Facade layer,[6] the Workflow layer,[3] and so on. I call this layer the Application layer because it is the Application Programming Interface (API), as far as the consumer knows.

The purpose of the Application layer is to provide a class for each use case. When the system is modelled, the Application layer is the first Business layer to be modelled, typically along with the tables in the database. In addition, the Application layer will talk to the Domain layer and to the Persistent Access layer. A pure layered model would imply that all calls go to the Domain layer instead. The most important reason for sometimes skipping calling the Domain layer (even though you have decided that you need that layer in your application) is that reading from the database would otherwise typically only be a forwarding of the call through the Domain layer. The drawback is, of course, that the Persistent Access layer is visible to two layers.

It's important to note that the Application layer should be consumer independent. It should be possible to use the same layer from different consumer types at the same time. In Figure 5.6, you can see an example of a typical class in the Application layer. Here, the use case fetches a list of errands and collects all the information about a single one.

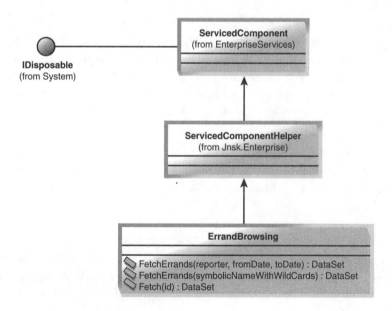

FIGURE 5.6

Example of a class in the Application layer.

As you can see in Figure 5.6, ErrandBrowsing is derived from ServicedComponentHelper, and ServicedComponentHelper is derived from ServicedComponent. ServicedComponent will provide the implementation for IDisposable. ServicedComponentHelper takes care of most of the Dispose() implementation for its subclasses. (The Template Method pattern is used.)

This layer is definitely a core layer and shouldn't be skipped in small systems. How you design this layer is crucial. This is because you will "blend" it into the Consumer tier because this layer will be the entry point for the Consumer tier. It's easier to change the style of the layers that come after the Application layer, so it's important you get this layer right.

Many use cases will use the same methods, such as FetchProblemSolvers(). I find it convenient to have that method in all the use cases that "want" it. The consumer programmer will find everything related to a use case in one class. Then the Application layer class will call a general method that will do the real work.

I often skip to using user-defined interfaces for classes in the Application layer mainly because all of the use cases and classes will look different from each other. But as you will see later in this chapter, if you like to prepare for having unmanaged consumers via interop, you should use user-defined interfaces to work with the classes in the Application layer too.

Domain Layer

Other authors and developers often call this layer the Entity layer or the Business layer. I prefer to call it the Domain layer because it deals with the concepts in the problem domain. The purpose of this layer is not only to validate rules, but also to provide core algorithms. Because most Domain classes will have similar interfaces, I use user-defined interfaces a lot in the Domain layer. Figure 5.7 shows an example of a Domain class that implements one user-defined interface.

As you see in Figure 5.7, I used a prefix do for the classname. I think that it doesn't have a big drawback because that name is internal to the Business tier. The advantage is to easily differentiate classes from different tiers. Classes in the Persistent Access layer will have pa as prefix.

NOTE

The examples in the previous sections from the descriptions of the Consumer layers and the Application layer dealt with browsing errands, which do not involve this layer. The Application layer will call directly to the Persistent Access layer instead.

Also as you see in Figure 5.7, I showed that the Domain classes inherit from ServicedComponentHelper just as the Application classes.

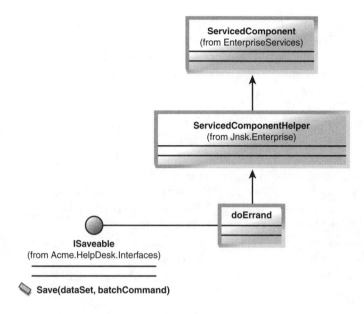

FIGURE 5.7
Example of a class in the Domain layer.

Another solution is to let the methods in the Domain classes be Shared. Then you won't instantiate the classes, and they won't inherit from ServicedComponent. Everything about Dispose() is gone; you don't have to think about COM+ contexts and the methods of the Shared class will be extremely fast to call. The drawback is less flexibility and that you hard-code the knowledge that the methods of the classes are Shared. You also have to avoid or at least take care with Shared variables because of multithreading aspects. You can't use user-defined interfaces either, and a Shared method can't be an entry point for remoting. Even so, I think this is often a very good solution for the Domain and Persistent Access layers. As a matter of fact, I most often prefer that solution.

In Figure 5.8, you can see the diagram of Figure 5.7 redrawn showing the use of Shared methods instead.

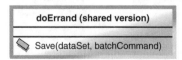

FIGURE 5.8
Example of a class in the Domain layer when Shared methods are used.

The classes in the Application layer are said to be *use case–specific*; that is, there is one class for each use case. The classes in the Domain level are used by several use cases (and that also goes for the later layers). In smaller systems, I have successfully skipped the Domain layer and have moved the responsibilities to stored procedures instead.

What Security "Style" Should I Use?

There are several different security "styles," or designs, to choose from, but the one I use most often is letting the end user be authenticated by the Application layer, which will use COM+ security at the component level. Then, the Domain and Persistent Access layers will *not* use COM+ security at the component level. It's not possible to use component level security for your COM+ application if you want to co-locate the objects within the context of their caller.

This gives the implication that if the Domain layer or "later" layers need information about the user, that must be provided from the Application layer as parameters to the following layers. For example, the Application layer can find the account name of the current user by calling EnterpriseServices.

```
SecurityCallContext.CurrentCall.DirectCaller. _
AccountName.ToString().
```

As you can see in Figure 5.7, I have simplified the method signatures somewhat and I haven't shown parameters for sending over user information.

If COM+ Role-Based Security (RBS) can't be used because .NET Remoting is needed, I still think that the Application layer is the place for checking authorization in your alternative solution.

When going to the next tier, namely the Data tier, I definitely prefer not to use accounts for personal users to log in to SQL Server. Instead, the COM+ application will use one dedicated user. Thanks to this, connection pooling will work as planned. Once again, the drawback is that user information must be sent as parameters.

Persistent Access Layer

The most common name for what I call the Persistent Access layer in other sources is the Data Access layer. This layer hides all details about how different stored procedures are called. It's kind of a helper for the Business tier, similar to the Consumer Helper layer discussed earlier.

NOTE

In earlier architectures I have used, I had the Persistent Access layer be responsible for transactions. I have now decided to transfer the responsibility to the Application layer instead. Because of this, there is no need to split the classes in the Persistent Access layer for writing and reading. Instead, both types of methods will be located in the same class. We will discuss this in Chapter 6, "Transactions."

Between the Persistent Access layer and the Public Stored Procedures layer, we often have machine-to-machine communication. Because the Public Stored Procedures layer is built with just stored procedures, that communication will normally be efficient. Unfortunately, without tricks, stored procedures can't take several rows as parameters. One of the reasons I create complete scripts at the business tier is that it will be sent in one call to the data tier to reduce the number of round trips between those tiers. Once again, I will discuss this in depth in Chapter 8.

Until it is time to investigate the inner workings of the classes in the Persistent Access layer, you can see an example of a class in Figure 5.9. As you see, it often implements several different interfaces.

NOTE

At first, the interfaces shown in Figure 5.7 and Figure 5.9 may look strange with regard to the parameters batchCommand, fetchType, and filter. This is because of the pattern I use for calling the stored procedures in the database. The Domain layer and the Persistent Access layer will build up an SQL script that the Application layer will act as a controller when building. The real call to the database will be delayed until the complete script has been built. This pattern will be discussed in Chapter 8.

Remember what I said about Shared classes in the section about the Domain layer. That goes for the Persistent Access layer too. In Figure 5.10 you can see a diagram similar to the one in Figure 5.9, but this time only Shared methods are used.

NOTE

As you may remember from Figure 5.2, there was a table called errand and also a Persistent Access class that reads from and writes to that table. However, please don't come to the conclusion that every table should have a class in the Persistent Access layer, because this is most often not the case. Lookup tables, for example, will usually only have one Persistent Access class. And there is nothing that stops me from letting paErrand call the sprocs for the action table too.

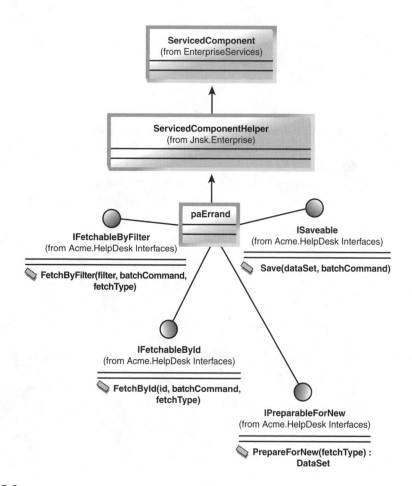

FIGURE 5.9

Example of a class in the Persistent Access layer.

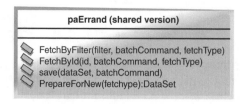

FIGURE 5.10

Example of a class in the Persistent Access layer, only with Shared *methods.*

SQL Server Authentication or Windows Authentication: Which One Is Recommended?

SQL Server 2000 can be run in two modes:

- SQL Server authentication and Windows authentication ("mixed mode")
- Windows authentication only

A common debate is over whether the SQL Server should be accessed using SQL Server authentication or by Windows authentication. SQL Server authentication means that the COM+ application can log in as sa (or, preferably, with a custom SQL Server account). With Windows authentication, users log into NT/Windows 2000, and this authentication is then used in SQL Server as well.

It's true that it is simple to use SQL Server authentication. Anybody can spell sa and remember a blank password. (OK, I am joking here, but someone presented statistics that said—if I remember correctly—that something like 30% of the world's SQL Servers in production use a blank password for sa.) Even with a password for sa, and when sa isn't used as the database user by the components, SQL Server authentication is less safe than Windows authentication.

If you use Windows authentication with a server-side application, you do not have to hardcode a password into the application (or keep the password elsewhere), and you can change the password without changing the application. NT/Windows 2000 passwords also have aging, which is yet another advantage.

Let's skip the server application scenario for a moment and consider a situation for when end users will log in to SQL Server. If users have to enter a password that is an SQL Server authentication password, I think it is more likely that that password will be shared with friends at the office than the user's own account for logging into the network.

Data Tier

Now that we've discussed the Consumer and Business tiers, let's move on to the Data tier. The Data tier is located at the database server and is made up of the Public and Private Stored Procedures layers, which access tables, views, and User-Defined Functions (UDFs).

Public Stored Procedures Layer

In the Public Stored Procedures layer, you find your small and controlled set of entry points to the database. There is no real distinction between public and private stored procedures, but with the help of discipline and a naming convention that says that public stored procedures should start with a_, only the public stored procedures will be called by the Persistent Access layer.

> **NOTE**
>
> I chose a_ as the prefix for public stored procedures so that these procedures will come first in an ordered list of all stored procedures. Even more important is that the stored procedures will be grouped in ordered listings.

Sometimes, the public stored procedures in this layer will do the real work on their own, but they will usually ask for help from private stored procedures. It's common to see a lot of duplicated code when it comes to stored procedures. This is because it is often much harder to call other stored procedures compared to calling subs/functions in Visual Basic .NET, for example, and T-SQL puts a lot of obstacles in the way. Still, the damage caused by duplicate code is as serious as in any type of programming. Make sure that you centralize code as usual, and do so by calling private stored procedures.

Figure 5.11 shows the three public stored procedures that will take care of the requests coming from the consumer. Note that the Unified Modeling Language (UML) used in Figure 5.11 isn't really for modelling stored procedures. Still, using it can help, even though it is cheating in a way.

FIGURE 5.11
Stored procedures in the Public Stored Procedures layer.

Private Stored Procedures Layer

The purpose of the Private Stored Procedures layer is to do the real work and access the tables, views, and UDFs. Because the layer is private, except for in the eye of the previous layer, you can change the interface of the private stored procedures without affecting more than the closest layer. This is one of the typical benefits of layering, but I'm mentioning it here anyway because layering is not that common for T-SQL programming.

In Figure 5.12, you find the three private stored procedures that do the real work in helping the public stored procedures. As you perhaps have guessed, the public stored procedures a_ErrandFetchBySymbolicName() and a_ErrandFetchByUserAndDates() are both solved with the Errand_FetchByFilter() stored procedure. And a_ErrandFetchById() calls both Errand_FetchById() and Action_FetchByErrand() to retrieve both the errand itself and all the actions for that errand.

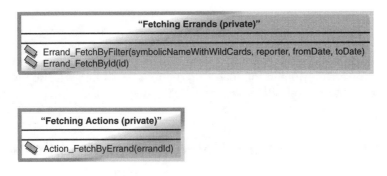

FIGURE 5.12
Stored procedure in the Private Stored Procedures layer.

The Private Stored Procedures layer is another layer that could be skipped, especially in small systems. In the examples shown in Figures 5.11 and 5.12, there is little reason to have a private layer. Instead, the public procedures could contain all the logic necessary to fulfill the requests. On the other hand, it is seldom as simple as just a single fetch of one row and nothing else in real systems. There is often a need for auditing, or perhaps the end user may only see his own errands, and so on. Add to this the fact that fetching an errand must be done from several different stored procedures, and that the private stored procedures can typically have more complicated parameter lists to be more general and usable from many public stored procedures, and voila—you have some good reasons for splitting the procedure into a public one and a private one.

Tables, Views, and User-Defined Functions

Sooner or later, we will access the tables in the database. If we wanted, we could add one more level in the form of views or UDFs. If you use single statement table-valued functions (one of the three types of UDFs), the code that will be executed will be the same as if a view had been used. However, I still think that UDFs have an advantage over views, namely the possibility of using parameters.

Because I use stored procedures as the only entry point to the database, views and UDFs are less of a must than in other systems. Still, they can be very helpful in the long run, for example, when (not if!) there is a need for schema change. A view or a UDF can often gracefully hide this change from the rest of the system. For simpler systems, I also skip views and UDFs, at least as something that should be used across the board. From time to time, there are problems that are solved elegantly with a view or a UDF in any system.

> **NOTE**
>
> Throughout all the layers, I used a very basic example. You will find more examples relating to the architecture in the following chapters, and there are also more code samples at the book's Web site at www.samspublishing.com.

Communication over the Network to the Application Layer

At the time work on this book began, a common question was how consumers would talk to serviced components over the network. With VB6, DCOM was most often used, but with .NET, there are several different methods from which to choose:

- XML Web services
- Remoting
- DCOM (as before)

Before we discuss these options a bit more, I'd like to give a schematic example of each one in the context of my proposed architecture.

> **NOTE**
>
> Unfortunately, the .NET component services won't travel over XML Web services and Remoting. (It still works when DCOM is used.) The main problem with this is that COM+ Role-Based Security (RBS) can't be used between machines. In my opinion, this is the most serious problem with the COM+ integration in .NET.

XML Web services is designed for situations when an external application isn't in our control. That is, a standardized way to build very loosely coupled systems. Figure 5.13 shows the appearance of the Business tier when it is deployed as an XML Web service. There are several ways to have the Business tier be deployed as an XML Web service, one being to use COM+ 1.5. Then the COM+ application can be deployed directly from the Component Services management console. IIS must be on the machine to provide a listener with the calls to the XML Web service.

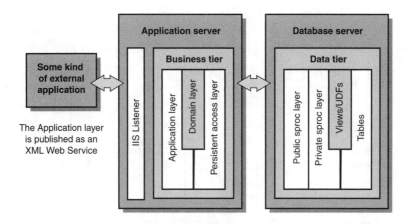

FIGURE 5.13

An XML Web service and my proposed architecture.

In the scenario shown in Figure 5.14, a Windows Forms application is talking to the Business tier. This is a more tightly coupled scenario than the one shown in Figure 5.13. In this case, good old DCOM could be used, or you could use Remoting. In Figure 5.14, you can see that DCOM and Remoting are similar schematically, but with DCOM, you get the proxy and the stub automatically. With Remoting, you have to write a listener on your own for some configurations, typically as a Windows Service.

NOTE

Of course, I could just as well have shown XML Web services as the way for the Windows Forms application to talk to the Business tier.

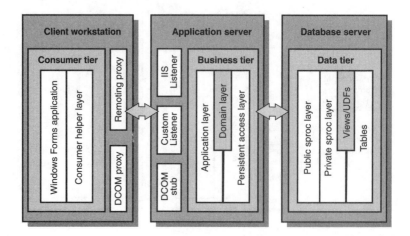

FIGURE 5.14

A Windows Forms application and the proposed architecture.

Another typical scenario is when a Web browser is used with an ASP.NET/Web Forms application, but then the Business tier is most often put at the same machine as the ASP.NET application. Otherwise, DCOM or Remoting will usually be the choice for communication, as in Figure 5.14. Figure 5.15 shows a scenario in which the ASP.NET application and the Business tier are put on the same machine.

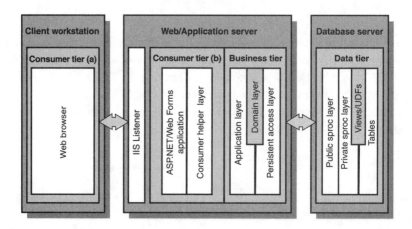

FIGURE 5.15

An ASP.NET application and the proposed architecture.

Although Remoting deserves a book to itself, I'd like to mention here that you can configure Remoting in .config files. In a way, this makes the Consumer Helper layer a little less important than it is if you decide to configure Remoting in code. Meanwhile, DCOM is connection-oriented, quite heavy, and has severe problems travelling through firewalls. These were the main reasons for building Remoting in .NET. Microsoft also tried hard to create Remoting as an extensible framework so that new channels, for example, can be added. (Out of the box, there is a TCP channel and an HTTP channel.)

As I said, one unfortunate problem with Remoting in the first version of .NET is related to serviced components. Component services won't flow over Remoting. Honestly, this isn't that much of a problem because you seldom have serviced components at two different machines talking to each other. (Component services will flow over DCOM as usual.) If you decide to go for DCOM between managed components, you will use interop, but this is a small performance penalty to pay compared to the network hop. (Remoting is not only to be used between machines, but also for calls between AppDomains.)

As you can see, there are several ways to take care of communications between tiers when placed at different servers, and no best practices have evolved yet. Only time will tell what the best choices for certain situations will be. Just to be sure, you should add a Consumer Helper layer that will hide most of the communication details for the Consumer layer.

Problems with My Architecture Proposal

Because there are several different scenarios that can be considered, this could potentially be a very lengthy section. As in other chapters, at the end of this chapter I will evaluate my proposal based on the criteria I established in Chapter 2. For now, let's take a quick look at some basic problems with my proposal:

- One size doesn't fit all—still, I find it convenient to use a flexible architecture as a starting point and to adjust it instead of starting from scratch. I have indicated in the previous sections what layers you may want to skip for small applications.

- Because of all the use of stored procedures and the amount of responsibility put on the stored procedures, it won't be easy to port the application to another database platform.

- All those layers may prohibit the use of custom exceptions. A consumer of a class must recognize an exception it receives. This means that if the consumed assembly uses another assembly with custom exceptions, the secondary assembly must be referenced by the consumer too. Otherwise, if the secondary raises an exception that the first assembly doesn't catch, the consumer can't catch the "real" exception.

New Concepts to Consider When Creating a New Architecture Today

As we all know, if you compare VB6 and Visual Basic .NET (or C#) code, you'll find many differences (when it comes to serviced components, for example). I will discuss some of these differences briefly in the following sections as well as COM+ contexts, some of the new features in SQL Server 2000, and some unusual design ideas. I will start with discussing Consumers.

New Concepts to Consider Regarding Consumers

There is one important concept that you have to grasp for building consumers for scarce resources. Serviced components are an example of such a resource, and the concept I am thinking about is `Dispose()`. Let's look at this in detail now.

Dispose()

It's not a must, but in my opinion, for the current version recommended that you use `Dispose()` when you are done with an object of a serviced component. This same recommendation applies to all scarce resources. I think this is ironic when you think that garbage collection should release us from the burden of `Set x = Nothing` as in VB6 and from `Release()` in C++. Instead, we have the new requirement of calling `Dispose()` in many situations.

Why Do We Have to Call `Dispose()`?

At first, the need to call `Dispose()` puzzled me. I thought that with object pooling it was natural to have to call `Dispose()` so that used objects were given back to the pool as fast as possible instead of waiting for the garbage collection. I didn't understand why it was preferable to use `Dispose()` for all other serviced components. When I discussed this with Microsoft, Egidio Sburlino, Developer Engineer Lead in the COM+ group, and Dave Driver, Developer Engineer in the COM+ group, explained it a bit more. They said, "In the case of JIT activation with `AutoComplete()` methods, we do know when to call `Dispose()`. But in all other cases, where you don't want to wait for the garbage collector to kick in to release your object's resources, you must call `Dispose()`." They also told me that currently, Object Pooling (without JIT activation and `AutoComplete()`) is the only feature where calling `Dispose()` is a *must*; when the garbage collector kicks in, it is too late to recycle the object because of the garbage collector nondeterministic behavior when it finalizes the objects; i.e., managed objects referenced by your object's data members may have already been finalized.

I would like to add that the consumer shouldn't and won't know if the consumed component is pooled or using JIT activation or whatever. Therefore, `Dispose()` should always be used if possible. (There are some cases where it is impossible for the clients to know when to call `Dispose()`. This is the situation when multiple clients reference

> the same object. In this case it is up to the component/system designer to decide to let the garbage collection kick in to release the resources when there are no more client references to the object or design the client in such a way that it is known who is responsible for calling Dispose(). For example, Singleton is such a pattern where multiple clients share the same object, without the clients having knowledge about each other.
>
> According to other sources at Microsoft, performance will be increased some, so it's mostly positive to have it as a rule to always use Dispose() for serviced components.

The Using() statement in C# is a good solution to the problem of objects at the method level, but we don't have Using() in Visual Basic .NET; the client has to remember to call Dispose() in the Finally block. Furthermore, when it comes to instance-level objects, Using() in C# is of no use if you want the object to live over several methods, because Using() has to be used at the method level. To conclude all this, nondeterministic finalization is a real problem in some situations, especially for those consumers over whom you have no control. The serviced components should be less of a problem because you have full control of these. Remember, too, that it's usually not a catastrophe if Dispose() isn't called, as sooner or later the garbage collector will kick in and clean up.

I will continue this discussion about Dispose() in the "Standardized Code Structure for Serviced Component" section later in the chapter where I show code structures for consumers and serviced components.

New Concepts to Consider Regarding Serviced Components

The requirement (or at least recommendation) for Dispose() we just discussed applies to serviced components. As I said before, what I see as the real problem is the responsibility put on the consumer programmer to call Dispose(). But there are other issues to consider regarding serviced components. We'll start by looking at overloading.

Overloading

The possibility of overloading in Visual Basic .NET is great. With its help, I can avoid some ugly tricks that I often used in VB6, such as sending empty parameters and to have different names for the "same" method when the methods just differ by the parameter lists. The possibility of overloading helps to create another layer of abstractions because you can talk about a method first, without thinking that much that there are really ten different signatures for that very method. You saw examples of that when I used overloading earlier in this chapter, such as in Figure 5.5.

Implementation Inheritance

We finally have implementation inheritance in Visual Basic .NET. Microsoft has attempted to lessen the problems with implementation inheritance (for example, with the help of shadowing), sometimes summarized by the term "the fragile base class scenario."[10]

Still, you can only use single inheritance, and it is often taken by the framework, so to say. One example of a situation in which you are forced to inherit from a specific class is serviced components. If, through your COM habits, you are accustomed to using user-defined interfaces instead of implementation inheritance, you're in luck, because that methodology fits perfectly well in the world of .NET too. There are situations when implementation inheritance can be your friend, but it's not a silver bullet. It is just one more important design tool that has been added to your toolbox. I typically use inheritance for generalized utilities and when I want to force a policy for a group of classes, not for application-specific code. (I mean, I don't use inheritance for building hierarchies such that `Customer` inherits from `Company` and similar constructs.) I will use inheritance so that I inherit from `ServicedComponent` to a class called `Jnsk.Enterprise.ServicedComponentHelper`. Then all my serviced components will inherit from the helper class instead. That way, most of the `Dispose()` problems will be handled for the ordinary serviced components. Thanks to the Template Method pattern,[8] the classes inheriting from `Jnsk.Enterprise.ServicedComponentHelper` will get help to implement a `Dispose()` method.

When I discussed implementation inheritance with Joe Long, the Group Manager for COM+ at Microsoft, he told me that another subtle problem with inheritance can show up with the usage of attributes. For example, he said, a base class is marked as "requires transactions," and the derived class is marked as "transactions disabled." If the implementation of a public method in the derived class calls on a public method in the base class, a transaction gets started up, which may not be obvious to clients given the attributes on the derived class. I don't use any COM+-related attributes on my `ServicedComponentHelper`.

Object Pooling

It has been possible to use object pooling with COM+ 1.0 for a long time now, but it wasn't possible for components written with VB6. Now that problem has disappeared, thanks to .NET, and we VB programmers can use object pooling too. You shouldn't use object pooling for all of your components, but if any of the following criteria apply, it can be a good solution:

- The component is expensive to create or destroy, for example, because it needs to grab some resources or clean up some resources.

- You want to multiplex many requests to a certain number of instances.

- You expect extreme load so even the memory manager will have a tough time doing its job.

I don't think it is a good idea to let the components in the Application layer use object pooling, mainly because calling `Dispose()` is a must with pooled objects and you can't be sure the consumer will behave well.

> **NOTE**
>
> We will discuss object pooling more in Chapter 8.

To JIT or Not to JIT?

When it comes to having the need for distributed transactions taken care of by the .NET component services, answering whether you should use JIT activation is easy. You must use JIT activation to use the transaction service. In most other situations, you should probably not use JIT activation. I ran into the trap of using it too often before, but as I see it today, it has little use in other situations. The following are a few examples of situations for which using JIT activation is not appropriate.

- For page-based consumers, such as ASP.NET, you will release the reference when the page is done. If you only use the reference once during the page, there is overhead because of JIT activation that you had no use for. If you use the reference several times during the page, there will be several activations/deactivations with no use. It's better to keep the reference for the life of the page.
- For Windows Forms consumers, you will normally not save any memory at the application server by using JIT activation. At least not if the JITed object is a small one that doesn't hold on to a lot of memory or other expensive resources. It's often better to keep the reference for the life of the form instance or maybe to instantiate the component each time you need it.

Whether you choose to keep the variable at instance level or method level is a matter of how many method calls you make. For example, if a form is to call an instance of a serviced component more than once, keeping the variable at instance level (and only instantiating it once during the lifetime of the container instance) is preferable for performance reasons. On the other hand, if there are minutes or more between calls, it is preferable for scalability that the method is declared at method level.

The reason for the performance benefit of JIT is that the proxy, the channel, the stub, and the context are kept alive between method calls. This is actually the case when you use the object as stateful too, but in that case, the object is also kept alive.

In his book, *Transactional COM+: Building Scalable Applications*, Tim Ewald[9] discusses another situation where JIT activation is useful with object pooling. Without JIT activation, a consumer may hold on to the object for too long, not releasing it back to the pool. I prefer not to let a component from the Consumer tier hold a pooled object directly, because the consumer component might behave badly. That is, I seldom use object pooling for the Application layer. For serviced components as consumers, I code so that the resource is disposed at the end of the method. If you use object pooling in the Application layer, it might be a good idea to use JIT.

I've also heard the motivation that JIT is good to move the responsibility of when an object should be deactivated from the consumer to the server. If you don't acquire expensive resources in the Application layer, this is not a valid reason, in my opinion, because the instance from the Application layer is probably not more expensive to hold on to than a JIT-enabled context. (If this is the case—that is, the object has a lot of data—you can always split the class in two so that one is held by the consumer and the second one has all the data and is pooled.)

Worth noting is that JIT provides deterministic finalization, but, as I've said here, you have to consider if it is worth the price.

Another and more subtle consideration regarding JIT activation is that using Microsoft's Component Load Balancing (CLB) in Application Center 2000 will have implications on load balancing. The load balancing will only take place when an instance is created, not activated. This means that when you activate your instance the second time, it's not at all sure that the server is the one with the most free capacity.

To conclude all this, watch that you don't overuse JIT activation, but make sure you test what is most efficient for your specific situation. Just as usual.

Contexts

One reason for trying to avoid JIT activation if possible is that it is interception based and requires the instance of a serviced component to live in a nondefault context. If you can skip JIT activation, you are one step closer to using co-location in the caller's context or using COM+ 1.5 to use the default context instead. Both settings will save you a lot of memory, instantiation time, and call overhead. In earlier tests I carried out, I had similar throughput when I compared unconfigured COM+ components and configured co-located COM+ components.

> ### Improved Context Activation Setting in COM+ 1.5
>
> COM+ 1.5 has a new context activation setting called "Must be activated in the default context." This means that there will be no "call" interception, and the object will be co-located with several other objects in the default context. The default context is a specific context for each apartment that will host all objects with this setting. It will also host all legacy unconfigured COM+ components.

Since COM+ 1.0, we have had the chance to use the setting "Must be activated in caller's context." That means that the object will be co-located in the caller's context and, therefore, it will not have interception on its own. The object will share the interceptors that its caller had. So, for example, I could be created in my caller's context, and then my caller hands an interface pointer to somebody else. I get called, my caller's context will be entered, and the properties will get the enter (and leave) events. There is also no extra context so memory is saved. To successfully co-locate your object in the caller's context, their settings must be compatible. Finally, observe that activation time services, such as object pooling and object constructor string, can still be used because they don't rely on interception.

At the time of writing, there was no source for further reading on "Must be activated in the default context," but Tim Ewald's book, *Transactional COM+: Building Scalable Applications*[9] is a good source for reading more about contexts.

Because of the context issues, I put the components of the Domain layer and Persistent Access layer in DLLs of their own. Those DLLs will then be configured in a separate COM+ library application. Basically, no services will be used for that application or its components. All services that require interception will be used for the components in the Application layer instead.

Finally, the rule of thumb is first to configure your components to use the services they need. Then, for resource saving and performance reasons, if you need interception, use a nondefault context (which is what you get automatically when you configure serviced components) for the root object and co-locate secondary objects in the root object's context (or let the methods of the secondary objects be Shared). If you don't need interception, use the default context for all objects.

NOTE

If you do some simple performance tests, you will find that instantiation time for a component that will co-locate in the caller's context is a fraction of a component whose instances live in contexts of their own. At first, I didn't think this should matter when real tasks are added to the components. However, a couple of months ago, I was invited to come up with ideas at a performance-tuning session where a specific use case was to be tuned. The single change of starting to use co-location in the caller's context increased the throughput of the real-world use case fourfold.

Once again, if you use Shared methods only for the Domain and Persistent Access layers, you don't have to worry about the context issues.

New Concepts to Consider Regarding the Database

So far, I have discussed a number of new design possibilities you have at your disposal thanks to .NET. Even though SQL Server 2000 isn't that new, there are some concepts that this version makes possible. In this section, I'll present these and a few other tips.

User Defined Functions (UDFs)

As I said earlier, UDFs can be useful. One example is the single-statement, table-valued functions which will be implemented as VIEWs behind the scenes, but with parameterization. You may wonder why I prefer to use stored procedures as entry points instead of UDFs. One reason is that there are many restrictions on what is allowed in a UDF. For example, you are not allowed to call a stored procedure.

XML Support

XML is a great technology in many situations. For example, it really shines when you don't have control of the consumer. Another situation when XML can be useful is when you are handing over much data in one single call to a stored procedure (which I will discuss further in Chapter 8, "Data Access").

Globally Unique Identifiers (GUIDs)

The possibility of natively using Globally Unique IDentifiers (GUIDs), or UNIQUE IDENTIFIERs as SQL Server calls them, came in version 7. I have used them in a couple of database designs for the primary keys, and I am more and more positive about using them. There are several reasons to use UNIQUE IDENTIFIERs for primary keys:

- There is "no" risk of outgrowing the size of the data type. That is actually a common problem with the 32-bit INT data type.

- You can reduce the number of round trips. The consumer can create the complete structure of several master rows and their detail rows and then immediately send over all that information to the application server for forwarding to the database server. There won't be any problems with duplicate keys. (There could be problems theoretically, but not practically.)

The most typical solution to creating a GUID is to use Guid.NewGuid() (or to use the Crypto API) in Visual Basic .NET code and to use NEWID() in T-SQL.

- A new GUID is not only unique per table, but, most often, it is also unique per database. In some situations and systems, this can be a real advantage.

- Having a GUID as the ID for all tables is consistent and makes the programming of the component layers easier. You will find that you can manage with fewer user-defined interfaces, for example.

- If you want to use merge replication in SQL Server 7/2000, you must have a UNIQUE IDENTIFIER in every table to be merge replicated. Then why not use it as the primary key because it's there anyway?

- A GUID will not mean anything at all to the users. An INTEGER can be read, understood, and remembered. It's common to see INTEGER keys in the UI.

- You know what a nightmare it can be, making a manual merge between two tables, both with INTEGERs as primary keys. Not only do you have to create a new sequence for the union of both tables, you must also change all the foreign keys for all the dependent tables. If GUIDs have been used, this sort of problem does not arise.

Obviously, there are also drawbacks to using UNIQUE IDENTIFIERs for primary keys:

- Because it is 16 bytes, the GUID is four times the size of the ordinary INT. For index trees, this can lead to much worse performance. On the other hand, the database doesn't have to maintain a sequence on its own.

- It's hopeless to work manually with GUIDs in the enterprise manager, for example, and to manually relate rows in different tables. By using SQL, this is not a problem.

- Relational database purists don't think it's a good idea to use synthetic keys. However, this is not a problem for GUIDs alone, more for the idea of having a key that is not value based.

> **NOTE**
>
> There are advantages and disadvantages with everything, but in the last few years I have grown more and more fond of using object identity style keys, or surrogate or synthetic keys—whatever you prefer to call them.

When version 1 of .NET has shipped, you will find the results of some performance tests regarding UNIQUE IDENTIFIERs as primary keys at the book's Web site, at www.samspublishing.com.

Databases as Components

For some time now, I have had what I thought was a wild idea—to think in terms of components regarding the database. That way, the database would be split into several databases. Let's look at an example of how this could be applied. A typical Enterprise Resource Planning (ERP) system contains a huge number of subsystems, such as orders, shipping, complaints, and so on. If you apply the component concept to these databases, there would be one database for each of those subsystems. When the system grows, it is easy to move one database to a separate server, which is scalable.

Just the other day I learned that perhaps this isn't such a wild idea after all. In fact, it is discussed a great deal in Peter Herzum and Oliver Sims's book, *Business Component Factory*.[11] Unfortunately, Herzum and Sims don't solve what I think of as the main problem, namely the problem with foreign keys between the databases because that can't be taken care of automatically with the built-in possibilities of declaring foreign keys in SQL Server.

Having databases as components is actually a way to provide physical partitioning of the database.

Physical Partitioning

In Figure 5.3, you saw that typical physical splitting is done between the Consumer Helper layer and the Application layer, and between the Persistent Access layer and the Public Stored Procedures layer. If the first tier is Web Forms, combining tier one and two is recommended. For small sites, it's common to combine tier 2 and 3 (regardless of whether the consumer type is Web Forms or whatever). But what if you want to have more than one machine for a tier? Let's investigate this, starting with the serviced components.

Physical Partitioning of Serviced Components

It's preferable to clone instead of physically partition your serviced components. This is especially true if the cloning or partitioning is to be done for performance or scalability reasons. If there are other reasons, for example, that some processing must be separate from the other for security reasons, you may not have a choice.

If partitioning is needed within a tier, between which layers should it be done? There is no standard answer to that question. I prefer to factor out what must be done at another server, and carefully tune the calls to minimize the number of round trips.

Physical Partitioning of the Database

Before version 2000 of SQL Server, it was not common to partition tables in On-Line Transaction Processing (OLTP) systems in that environment. When partitioning was used, it was mostly done for complete tables or for reasons other than load balancing. Here I'm going to discuss a new solution for partitioning an SQL Server 2000 database called Distributed Partitioned View (DPV). Afterwards, I will briefly discuss how you can build a similar solution on your own with any database product.

Distributed Partitioned Views (DPV)

DPV made it so that is was no longer difficult to scale out the database. Microsoft has proved with the TPC-C results the possibility of raw scalability thanks to DPV. Even so, it is pretty easy to get started using DPV. The main philosophy is to create the same table in several different databases (at different database servers), but with different mutually exclusive constraints. Then a view is created that uses UNION to combine the rows from each table into a virtual table at each server. To the consumer of the database, it is totally transparent at what server the data is really located. The consumer can talk to any of the database servers and get any of the rows.

Of course, it will be most efficient if the consumer hits the correct database server with his or her request. Therefore, a great tip is to use a routing trick in the Persistent Access layer to go to the right database, depending on the ID of the row to fetch, for example. If you want row 100200, you should go to server A because it has rows 1 to 200000. You can go to any database server, but it will be fastest to go to the correct one.

Unfortunately, the technology isn't mature yet and the administrative support is not strong. Other drawbacks are that you must have the SQL Server Enterprise Edition for each server, and that is not cheap. (On the other hand, in situations when we need DPV, the price for a few SQL Server Enterprise Edition licenses is usually not a real problem.) You will also have to make design preparations for using DPV. For example, you are not allowed to have columns of data type ROWVERSION (TIMESTAMP) in tables that will be partitioned.

Custom Solution

If you add a routing trick to your components, the next step is to build a DPV-like solution yourself. You can do most of it without SQL Server Enterprise Edition and without the design constraints. What you probably can't do is provide the transparency to database consumers, but if all requests are through the serviced components, that shouldn't be a problem.

> **NOTE**
>
> Please note that I am not recommending that you build a custom solution. Don't underestimate the work—now or in the future. My guess is that it will be much easier to administrate DPV in a coming version.

Proposals for Standardized Code Structures

Both the Visual Studio .NET IDE and SQL Server 2000's SQL Query Analyzer provide support for templates. These are great features that I use a lot to get starting points for my components and stored procedures. Why should standardized code structures be used?

- In my opinion, it's much easier to maintain a bunch of stored procedures that share a common structure than if each of them has a specific one. This goes for components too. Of course, you must be flexible to handle various situations, but it's good to have something to use as a rule of thumb and as a starting point.

- Some parts are quite difficult to code by hand, and inaccuracies will occur from time to time. A typical example of this is the error handling in the stored procedures.

- Some tasks should be done in every method and stored procedure to make the total architecture work. One example of this is using trace calls when entering and exiting the method/stored procedure. Another example is examining if there is an external transaction active before starting a new one in the stored procedures.

I'm going to show you my proposals for standardized code structures shortly. You don't have to like all of the code in my proposed code structures. I myself love looking at other developers' code because I get inspiration about how to refine my own. Perhaps you will get one or two such ideas yourself by looking at my code.

> **NOTE**
>
> I will discuss how to take care of transactions in more depth in Chapter 6.

Some developers would argue that it is better to think than to just copy and paste code. I totally agree, but some parts just don't have to be thought about each and every time a new method is needed. Another way of looking at it is that instead of thinking about matters from scratch, provide a starting point with a template and start the thinking at a higher level.

Of course, there are many factors to consider in how the typical code should look. I will walk you through one example for a consumer, one for a consumer helper and its super class, one for a serviced component, and one for a stored procedure. On the way, I will discuss a number of aspects.

Typical Code Structure for Consumer to Serviced Component

Instead of "Standardized Code Structure" I have written "Typical Code Structure" in this header. This differs from the sections where I discuss code structure for serviced component and stored procedure. The reason for this is that the book isn't focusing on the consumer. I just want to provide an example of typical code to give you a better feeling of the overall picture.

When you have some good code structures that you are happy with, you should save them to be used as templates, both for Visual Basic .NET and for T-SQL.

Just one more thing before we start. You will find that I decided to cut the code into pieces so that I comment piece by piece. If you want to browse all the code at once, download it from the book's Web site at www.samspublishing.com.

The Consumer

The consumer could be, for instance, a Web Form, an XML Web service, or a Windows Form. I have used a Windows Form here to show one specific point, namely that the consumer helper instance is held over a longer period of time. In the case of a Web Form, for example, the instance will only be kept for the life of the page generation.

The Consumer Code Section by Section

In Listing 5.1, you can see that I keep the consumer helper instance at instance level for the form.

LISTING 5.1 Instantiation of the Consumer Helper

```
Public Class frmErrandBrowsing
    Inherits System.Windows.Forms.Form

    Private m ErrandBrowsingHelper _
    As New Acme.HelpDesk.ConsumerHelper.ErrandBrowsingHelper()
```

It's important that the instance gets a Dispose() call when it's not going to be used any more. Of course, the garbage collector will clean up the instance, but it can take a long time before that happens and until then, resources at the server-side are occupied. In Listing 5.2, you can see that I call Dispose() in the OnClosed() event for the form. (I'm not showing the rest of the logic for the form, where the methods of the consumer helper are called because it is not important to our discussion.)

LISTING 5.2 The OnClosed Event for the Form

```
    Protected Overrides Sub OnClosed _
    (ByVal e As System.EventArgs)
        m_ErrandBrowsingHelper.Dispose()
    End Sub

    '...and a lot of presentation logic.

End Class
```

You can also register the object in the form with Components.Add(m_ErrandBrowsingHelper) so that the form will deal with calling Dispose().

Welcome to the World of Nondeterministic Finalization

My friend, Francesco Balena, author of *Programming Microsoft Visual Basic 6.0* and the upcoming *Programming Visual Basic .NET*, and I discussed the issue of building something similar to a smart pointer in .NET to help with automatically calling `Dispose()` when the smart pointer goes out of scope. He told me that as far as he knows, there is absolutely no way of implementing a smart pointer in .NET, regardless of the language. He said: "The `Using()` statement is nothing but a shortcut for enclosing an object creation in a `Try...End Try` block, and having the `Finally` block automatically call `Dispose()` if the object exposes the `IDisposable` interface. You can implement it manually in VB, but it doesn't solve the problem."

To recap, .NET programming requires a lot more collaboration with clients to work correctly—of course, you can always rely on `Finalize()`, but it isn't called *immediately* after the object is logically destroyed, and it also slows down performance because finalized objects require one more garbage collection to be reclaimed completely.

Finally, Francesco says, you can only state a few guidelines for programmers who use the object, such as

- Always bracket code inside a `Try` block, and call `Dispose()` from the `Finally` clause.
- Prefer class-level to procedure-level objects if possible, because the lifetime of the former can be controlled more easily.
- Implement `IDisposable` and call `GC.SuppressFinalize()` in the `Dispose()` method.
- Adhere to the programming guidelines that say that `Dispose()` should be callable multiple times without any error nor side-effect. (This can happen when multiple clients have a reference to the same object.)
- Implement `Finalize()` as a last resort.
- Manually run a `GC.Collect()` to force finalization of pending objects, but do it only when the application is idle (something rare in a server-side component).

The Consumer Helper

The consumer helper is much more interesting than the consumer itself, and this is by design. The more that can be taken care of by the helper, the better.

The Consumer Helper Code Section by Section

In Listing 5.3, you can see how the helper class is declared and that it inherits from `Jnsk.Consumer.ConsumerHelper`. Inheritance is great for forcing a protocol on the subclasses, such as when the Template Method pattern[8] is used. With the help of inheritance here, I get most of the help with `IDisposable` automatically.

LISTING 5.3   The Class Declaration, a Constant, and Some Variables

```
Public Class ErrandBrowsingHelper
    Inherits Jnsk.Consumer.ConsumerHelper

    Private Const theTypeName As String = "ErrandBrowsingHelper"

    Private m ErrandBrowsing _
    As New Acme.HelpDesk.Application.ErrandBrowsing()
```

In Listing 5.3, you can also see that I keep the name of the class in a hard-coded constant. I could use `TypeName(Me)` instead to get that information, but this is more efficient and it also helps me skip a couple of string variables, as you'll see soon. Then I instantiate the class in the Application layer and I keep the reference at instance level.

I said that I get most of the `IDisposable` logic automatically, thanks to deriving from `Jnsk.Consumer.ConsumerHelper`, but I have to provide a custom implementation of the `Dispose(Boolean)` method. The super class doesn't know what resources to dispose. In Listing 5.4, you can see the custom `Dispose()` method.

LISTING 5.4   The Custom Implementation of `Dispose(Boolean)`

```
    Protected Overloads Overrides Sub Dispose(ByVal disposing As Boolean)
        If disposing Then
            m_ErrandBrowsing.Dispose()
        Else

            'If this method was called from the finalizer,
            'that is an "error".
            Jnsk.Instrumentation.Assert.Assert _
            (False, "Not disposed.", _
            AssemblyGlobal.ExeOrDllName, _
            theTypeName, False)
        End If
    End Sub
```

If `Dispose()` has been called by a finalizer, the disposing parameter is `False`. On the other hand, if the consumer has called `Dispose()`, the disposing parameter is `True`. I use that information for adding an assertion so that I will notice if a consumer isn't taking care of `Dispose()` as planned. The broken assertion won't tell who the consumer is, but I have at least a notice that there is a faulty consumer and I will probably also get some more clues out of the broken assertions. If disposing is `False`, the consumer has a bug because it didn't call `Dispose()` explicitly. `Dispose()` will be called sooner or later automatically with the help of the garbage collection, but because I prefer sooner for consumers to serviced components, this is to be considered a bug.

Note that the last parameter to the `Assert()` method is `False` for `raiseException`. I don't want to raise an exception in this case. Raising an exception would be too violent.

Next, it's time for the `Fetch()` method, the first part of which is found in Listing 5.5. First, a constant is given the name for the class and the hard-coded name of the function. Then I check that I'm not trying to use an object that has been disposed of. If so, an exception should be raised.

LISTING 5.5   First Part of the `Fetch()` Method

```
Public Function Fetch(ByVal id As Guid) As DataSet
    Const theSource As String = _
    theTypeName & ".Fetch"

    If Disposed Then
        Throw New _
        ObjectDisposedException(theSource)
    End If
```

The `Fetch()` method continues in Listing 5.6 with making a trace call, which says that the method is starting. Then a `Try` block starts in which the Application layer will be called, and the result of that method will be returned.

NOTE

In the real version of this method, there are a couple of `Catch` blocks as well. I will discuss these in detail in Chapter 9, "Error Handling and Concurrency Control."

LISTING 5.6   Second Part of the `Fetch()` Method

```
Jnsk.Instrumentation.Trace.TraceBegin
(AssemblyGlobal.ExeOrDllName, theSource)

Try
    Return m_ErrandBrowsing.Fetch(id)

'I'll leave the discussion about Catch
'for chapter 9.
```

Finally (as you can see in Listing 5.7), the method ends with a `Finally` block where a new trace call is made. It's quite common to see a `Dispose()` call in the `Finally` block but, in this listing, I have kept the resource that should be disposed of at the instance level, not at the method level.

LISTING 5.7   Third Part of the `Fetch()` Method

```
        Finally
            Jnsk.Instrumentation.Trace.TraceEnd _
            (AssemblyGlobal.ExeOrDllName, theSource)
        End Try
    End Function
End Class
```

I'm sure you are wondering what the code for `ConsumerHelper` looks like, so let's take a look at that code too, before we move on to the serviced components.

In Listing 5.8, you can see that I use `MustInherit` because it's not interesting to instantiate the `ConsumerHelper` class. I also implement `IDisposable` in this class and I keep a flag indicating whether the instance has been disposed already.

LISTING 5.8   First Part of the `ConsumerHelper` Class

```
Namespace Jnsk.Consumer
    Public MustInherit Class ConsumerHelper
        Implements IDisposable
        Private m_Disposed As Boolean = False
Protected ReadOnly Property Disposed() As Bollean
    Get
        Return m_Disposed
    End Get
End Property
```

The implementation of the `IDisposable` interface is straightforward. The only part that is strange is that `Dispose(True)` is called. Thanks to that, the call will go to the subclass, which might be interested in disposing some resources, as shown in Listing 5.9.

LISTING 5.9   Second Part of the `ConsumerHelper` Class

```
        Public Sub Dispose() Implements IDisposable.Dispose
            If Not m_Disposed Then
                Dispose(True)
                m_Disposed = True
                GC.SuppressFinalize(Me)
            End If
        End Sub
        Protected MustOverride Sub _
        Dispose(ByVal disposing As Boolean)
```

Finally, the `Finalize()` is overridden too and, even in this case, `Dispose()` of the subclass is called, as shown in Listing 5.10.

LISTING 5.10   Third Part of the `ConsumerHelper` Class

```
    Protected Overrides Sub Finalize()
        If Not m_Disposed then
        Dispose(False)
        m_Disposed = True
        End If
    End Sub


    End Class
End Namespace
```

Standardized Code Structure for Serviced Component

The code for a typical serviced component is quite similar to that of the consumer helper. I will only point out the differences and not repeat what was said in the previous section.

Serviced Component Code Section by Section

In Listing 5.11, you can see that I use an `Imports` statement to save myself some work when writing all the `EnterpriseServices`-related attributes. Then, for the class, a whole bunch of attributes are set. (You only need to write an attribute when a service is needed. I have added more attributes here just for the sake of example.)

LISTING 5.11   Multiple `EnterpriseServices` Attributes for the Class

```
Imports System.EnterpriseServices                    .

Namespace Acme.HelpDesk.Application

    <Transaction(TransactionOption.Disabled), _
    JustInTimeActivation(False), _
    Synchronization(SynchronizationOption.Disabled), _
    ComponentAccessControl(True), _
    ConstructionEnabled(False), _
    InterfaceQueuing(False), _
    EventTrackingEnabled(True), _
    MustRunInClientContext(False)> _
```

The first three attributes shown in Listing 5.11 (`Transaction()`, `JustInTimeActivation()`, and `Synchronization()`) will be discussed in later chapters.

NOTE

Some attributes, such as size of the pool and value for the construction string, for serviced components will only provide default values that can be changed at deployment time. This is different from other attributes in .NET and means that an attribute setting found in the manifest isn't always correct. I've heard rumors that this will change in the future so that some of the values set in code won't be able to be changed by the administrator. That is a better approach and will save some runtime problems. Many COM+ long-timers can tell you a war story or two about the time a "smart" administrator changed an attribute for a couple of components to increase throughput.

Other attributes, such as `Transaction()` and `JustInTimeActivation()`, will not be affected if you change the values in the CSE tool. The metadata in the assembly will rule.

For the components in the Application layer, it's common to have `ComponentAccessControl()` on. This does prohibit you from locating the object with the caller's context but, because the caller is most often at another tier, it isn't a real problem.

I don't usually use `ConstructionEnabled()` and `InterfaceQueuing()`. If I use a COM+ Server application and for some reason can't locate my object in the caller's context (or use the Default context for COM+ 1.5), I set `EventTrackingEnabled()` on. That way, I can see how many consumers I have at any given point in time, for example. Finally, in this case (because of `ComponentAccessControl()`) I can't set `MustRunInClientContext()` on. This attribute is usually set on for components in the Domain and Persistent Access layers.

NOTE

Often, the assembly for the Application layer should have the `ApplicationActivation` attribute set to `ActivationOption.Server`. The assembly for the Domain and Persistent Access layers should have it set to `ActivationOption.Library`.

Some Attributes to Think About If You Are Using the Components from Unmanaged Code

In `System.Runtime.InteropServices`, there are some attributes I recommend you use with your classes and interfaces to prepare them for being used by VB6 consumers, say. The attributes I'm thinking about are `ClassInterface(ClassInterfaceType.None)` and `InterfaceTypeAttribute(ComInterfaceType.InterfaceIsIUnknown)`. You should also add ProgId and GUID attributes for your assemblies, interfaces, and classes.

`ClassInterface(ClassInterfaceType.None)` means that a managed class will be exposed only through its implemented user-defined interfaces. `InterfaceTypeAttribute(ComInterfaceType.InterfaceIsIUnknown)` means that your managed interface will be exposed as an `IUnknown`-based COM interface. If you treat your managed interfaces as immutable, this will version just fine for unmanaged clients too.

Unfortunately, `ClassInterface(ClassInterfaceType.AutoDual)` will give you versioning trouble because there is nothing to prevent you from adding methods to your class, for example, and that will break the early-bound unmanaged client. As a matter of fact, if you want to be able to call your Application layer from unmanaged clients, this versioning aspect is a good reason for giving each class in the Application layer a user-defined interface instead (even though I said earlier that I usually prefer not to do that) and use `None` instead of `AutoDual` for the `ClassInterface` attribute.

The class declaration (shown in Listing 5.12) starts in a similar way as the consumer helper (see Listing 5.13). The only real difference is that the serviced component inherits from `ServicedComponentHelper` and that this class doesn't hold another instance at the instance level.

LISTING 5.12   The Class Declaration and a Constant

```
Public Class ErrandBrowsing
    Inherits Jnsk.Enterprise.ServicedComponentHelper

    Private Const theTypeName As String = "ErrandBrowsing"
```

The similarity between the consumer helper and the serviced component continues for the custom implementation of `Dispose(Boolean)` as shown in Listing 5.13. There isn't anything new I need to add here.

LISTING 5.13   The Custom Implementation of `Dispose(Boolean)`

```
Protected Overloads Overrides Sub Dispose(ByVal disposing As Boolean)
    'Dispose resources here.
    'None in this example.

    If not disposing then
        'If this method was called from the finalizer,
        'that is an "error".
```

LISTING 5.13   Continued

```
        Jnsk.Instrumentation.ServicedAssert.Assert _
        (False, "Not disposed.", _
        AssemblyGlobal.ExeOrDllName, _
        theTypeName, False)
    End If
End Sub
```

In Listing 5.14, the first part of the `Fetch()` method is shown. Here, you can see that I set the `AutoComplete()` attribute off. (I will discuss that attribute a lot more in the next chapter.) I keep a constant with the name of the method as usual. This time I declare the variable at the method level and I declare the variable of an interface that the Persistent Access layer class implements. When you inherit from `ServicedComponent`, you don't need to check if an object has been disposed yet, because `ServicedComponent` will take care of that for you.

NOTE

If the methods in the Persistent Access layer are Shared, you won't declare them and instantiate them, but just call their methods directly.

LISTING 5.14   First Part of the `Fetch()` Method

```
    <AutoComplete(False)> _
    Public Function Fetch(ByVal id As Guid) As DataSet
        Const theSource As String = _
        theTypeName & ".Fetch"

        Dim aFetcher As Acme.HelpDesk.Interfaces.IFetchableById
```

After that, I start with a trace call, as you can see in the second part of the `Fetch()` method shown in Listing 5.15. This time the trace call is made to `Jnsk.Instrumentation.ServicedTrace` instead of to `Jnsk.Instrumentation.Trace`. Because of this, some more information (from `ContextUtil`, for instance) will be collected and used in the trace call. The method then continues with the instantiation of the component while the Persistent Access layer takes place. After that, there is a `Try` block in which the resource is used.

LISTING 5.15   Second Part of the `Fetch()` Method

```
Jnsk.Instrumentation. _
ServicedTrace.TraceBegin _
(AssemblyGlobal.ExeOrDllName, theSource)

aFetcher = New _
Acme.HelpDesk.PersistentAccess.paErrand()

Try
      'Call methods on the aFetcher instance
      'More about this in chapter 8.


      'I'll leave the discussion about Catch()
      'for chapter 9.
```

NOTE

The idea behind my use of structured exception handling is to use a `Try` block for when the resource is used. The `Dispose()` call for the resource will be made in the `Finally` block. If the instantiation fails, there is no resource to `Dispose()`. This nesting will be several levels for more complicated methods. (You can also add an outer `Try` block around the instantiation.)

When the `Using()` statement in C# is used, it is actually expanded to a `Try-Finally` construction, exactly as the one discussed here.

Finally, the method ends with a `Finally` block, as shown in Listing 5.16. Here, the resource is disposed with help from `DisposeHelper()`, which casts the object `IDisposable`. Then, another trace call is made here to signal that the method is ended.

LISTING 5.16   Third Part of the `Fetch()` Method

```
Finally
      Jnsk.Div.DisposeHelper(CType(aReader, Object))
      Jnsk.Instrumentation.ServicedTrace.TraceEnd _
      (AssemblyGlobal.ExeOrDllName, theSource)
   End Try
End Function

'The two other methods are not shown here.

   End Class
End Namespace
```

Using `IDisposable` Through `ServicedComponent`

Because `aReader` in Listing 5.13 is an instance of a class that is derived from `ServicedComponent` (which, in its turn, implements `IDisposable`), the cast to `IDisposable` is possible in `DisposeHelper()`. I could have made the cast to `ServicedComponent` instead of `IDisposable`. One reason I chose to do it like this is because there would be fewer changes if for some reason the object were not to be derived from `ServicedComponent` in the future.

I could let `IFetchableById` and all similar interfaces inherit from `IDisposable` to make it easier for the consumer of the interface, but I prefer to not do that because the instance already implements `IDisposable` and it feels like there are a lot of implications for such a short shortcut. (The `DisposeHelper()` makes this a no-task anyway.)

On the other hand, when I work with instances directly through their classes (without declaring the object as an interface), I don't have to do the cast. This was shown in Listing 5.4.

Finally, before we move over to discussing the code structure for stored procedures, I'd like to mention that the code for the `ServicedComponentHelper` is similar to the code for the `ConsumerHelper`. The key difference is that `ServicedComponentHelper` inherits from `ServicedComponent`.

Standardized Code Structure for Stored Procedures

In a way, it feels even more important to show a standardized code structure for stored procedures because little has been written about this and it is harder to get it right.

> **NOTE**
>
> Note that using a standardized code structure isn't that important for utilities! Therefore, you'll find that I often skip it in that kind of code. See, for example, `JnskAssert_Assert()` in Chapter 3.

Standardized Stored Procedure Code Section by Section

Let's look at a typical stored procedure. First, the name for the stored procedure and its parameters is given. You can see an example of that in Listing 5.14. As you can see, I use a "class or interface-method" style when I give the names of my stored procedures, which gives a useful categorization in the T-SQL tools. (For a small system, you often end up with hundreds of stored procedures. It can be a mess to navigate among them. In a large system, it's an even larger mess.)

You can also see that I often use user-defined data types (UDDTs) for domain-specific data. In doing this, it is easier for me to switch the length of all descriptions, say, or to change the integer type for a type of column, and so on. In the example in Listing 5.17, the uddtId is actually a UNIQUE IDENTIFIER.

LISTING 5.17   Name for Stored Procedure and Its Parameters

```
CREATE PROCEDURE a_Errand_FetchById
(@id uddtId)
AS
```

All stored procedures will be started with a section of standardized declarations and initializations, as shown in Listing 5.18. (It's not always so that all variables are needed, in which case, of course, they are not used.) After the declarations, I will use SET NOCOUNT ON because I don't need to send back to the client information about how many rows were affected for each statement in the stored procedure. (In the past, not using this clause also led to trouble with OLE DB drivers.)

The name of the stored procedure could be fetched with OBJECT_NAME(@@PROCID), but I hard-code it instead to save some resources. (Naturally, this change can also be done with a utility, before deployment.) Finally, there is a trace call, signaling that the stored procedure is starting.

LISTING 5.18   Standardized Declarations and Initializations

```
DECLARE @theSource uddtSource
, @anError INT
, @anErrorMessage uddtErrorMessage
, @aReturnValue INT
, @theTranCountAtEntry INT

SET NOCOUNT ON
SET @anError = 0
SET @anErrorMessage = ''
SET @theSource = 'a_Errand_FetchById'

EXEC JnskTrace_Begin @theSource

- - - - - - - - - - - - - - - - - - - - - - - - - - - - - - - - - - - - - - - - - - -
```

As you can see in Listing 5.19, there are no specific declarations or initializations in this example; otherwise, they would have been separate from the general ones found in Listing 5.18.

LISTING 5.19   Specific Declarations and Initializations

```
--Any specific declarations or initializations?
```

By now, I'm sure you know that I will be focusing on transactions in the next chapter. Therefore, I just ask you to be patient and I will explain the code in Listing 5.20 there.

LISTING 5.20   Decide Whether a Transaction Should Be Started

```
SET @theTranCountAtEntry = @@TRANCOUNT
IF @theTrancountAtEntry = 0 BEGIN
  SET TRANSACTION ISOLATION LEVEL SERIALIZABLE
  BEGIN TRAN
END
```

> **NOTE**
>
> As you know by now, I love to generalize code into small methods/procedures. Therefore, I have tried to do this with the code in Listing 5.20 and with the end of transaction block in Listing 5.22 as well. Unfortunately, generalizing this is not possible because SQL Server keeps track that @@TRANCOUNT has the same value when a stored procedure is started as it has when it has ended.

In Listing 5.21, you can see an example of when two secondary stored procedures are called. The first will fetch the errand and the second will fetch all the action rows for the errand.

LISTING 5.21   Fetching the Errand and Its Actions

```
EXEC @aReturnValue = Errand_FetchById @id
--Leave error handling for chapter 9.

EXEC @aReturnValue = Action_FetchByErrand @id
--Leave error handling for chapter 9.
```

After each statement that could lead to an error, there will be a clause investigating the result. If there is an error, a GOTO will be used for jumping to the ExitHandler similar to the one shown in Listing 5.22. The ExitHandler is also entered when the complete stored procedure executes normally. First, in the ExitHandler, the transaction will be taken care of (more about that in the next chapter), and then, if there was an error, this will be raised with RAISERROR() in JnskError_Raise(). (In that stored procedure, there will also be a JnskTrace_Error() being done.) Finally, there will be a JnskTrace_End(), and then the local @anError variable will be RETURNed to the caller.

5

LISTING 5.22   `ExitHandler` for Stored Procedure

```
ExitHandler:
  IF @theTranCountAtEntry = 0 AND @@TRANCOUNT > 0 BEGIN
    IF @anError = 0 BEGIN
      COMMIT TRAN
    END
    ELSE BEGIN
      ROLLBACK TRAN
    END
  END

  IF @anError <> 0 BEGIN
    EXEC JnskError_Raise   @theSource
    ,@anError, @anErrorMessage
  END

  EXEC JnskTrace_End @theSource

  RETURN @anError
```

> **NOTE**
>
> We will discuss finding and taking care of errors in depth in Chapter 9, "Error Handling and Concurrency Control."

Evaluation of Proposals

As in previous chapters, it's time for me to evaluate the proposals I have presented in this chapter—the architecture and standardized code proposals.

Evaluation of My Architecture Proposal

The architecture proposal that I discussed in depth earlier in this chapter is quite difficult to evaluate from the criteria set up in Chapter 2 because the architecture is created to be as friendly as possible regarding just those criteria. Still, let's take a look at how it does.

The architecture tries to be consumer independent for the Business and Data tiers. The first tier is consumer dependent (of course) because it is the Consumer tier, but attention has been paid to adapting different consumers as much as possible to the Business tier, with the help of consumer helpers.

The architecture optimizes calls between tiers because this will often mean process-to-process and machine-to-machine communication. Performance and scalability are also a focus. Still, the number of tiers and layers adds overhead even though the number of contexts will be reduced due to configuration settings or thanks to the use of Shared methods.

One of the main goals of the architecture is to provide a high degree of maintainability. The applications that I have built with similar architectures are most often a sheer joy in which to make changes. Productivity may suffer because of the complexity, but it may also benefit from it thanks to the opportunities for parallel work for developer teams that are made.

The business rules will be put in several layers instead of centralized to a single one. That means that it's harder to maintain them than if they are centralized to one location. (We'll discuss this more in Chapter 7.)

Not much has been said about security in this chapter. The architecture is expected to operate inside the intranet, so there should be a smaller risk of attacks. The sensitive parts of the application will typically be in the consumer; even so, there are potential security risks in the presented architecture. For example, a user ID will often be sent around between layers as an ordinary parameter, but it could be possible to catch and change that. Once again, don't forget that the application will most often be inside of the firewalls.

Evaluation of Standardized Code Structures Proposal

Earlier in this chapter, I gave you several proposals for code structures from the different layers. Performance and scalability are reduced because of the trace calls and such.

When version 1 of .NET has been released, you will find some test results at the book's Web site at www.samspublishing.com. In these tests, I show the overhead of the code structures presented in this chapter.

Productivity gains from the usage of metadata. Productivity also gains from having code structures to start from and from all the general methods/stored procedures to call to get tasks done. The same applies for maintainability, which also benefits from the common structure, as do debuggability and reusability. And finally, reliability benefits from the focus on error trapping.

What's Next

An important aspect of architectures, and something that has many implications for my proposed architecture, is transactions. In the next chapter, I will discuss such transactions—not much about what they are and how they work (as is dealt with in practically all books), but how to reason when choosing a certain style for taking care of transactions, and there will be several tips to use along the way.

5

ARCHITECTURE

References

1. P. Heinckiens. *Building Scalable Database Applications*. Addison-Wesley; 1998.

2. M. Stonebraker and P. Brown. *Object-Relational DBMSs: Tracking the Next Great Wave, Second Edition*. Morgan Kaufmann Publishers; 1999.

3. Introduction to the Duwamish Online Sample Application;
   `http://msdn.microsoft.com/library/default.asp?url=/library/en-us/dnduwon/html/d5dplywindna.asp`.

4. Duwamish Online SQL Server XML Catalog Browsing;
   `http://msdn.microsoft.com/library/default.asp?url=/library/en-us/dnduwon/html/d51ctlgbrowse.asp`.

5. F. Buschmann, R. Meunier, H. Rohnert, P. Sommerlad, and M. Stahl. *Pattern-Oriented Software Architecture: A System of Patterns*. Wiley; 1996.

6. Sten Sundblad and Per Sundblad. *Designing for Scalability with Microsoft Windows DNA*. Microsoft Press; 2000.

7. Fitch & Mather Stocks 2000: Introduction and Article List;
   `http://msdn.microsoft.com/library/default.asp?url=/library/en-us/dnfmstock/html/fm2kintro.asp`.

8. E. Gamma, R. Helm, R. Johnson, and J. Vlissides. *Design Patterns: Elements of Reusable Object-Oriented Software*. Addison-Wesley; 1995.

9. T. Ewald. *Transactional COM+: Building Scalable Applications*. Addison-Wesley; 2001.

10. C. Szyperski. *Component Software: Beyond Object-Oriented Programming*. Boston: Addison-Wesley; 1997.

11. P. Herzum and O. Sims. *Business Component Factory*. Wiley; 2000.

Transactions

IN THIS CHAPTER

Transactional design is crucial for a successful Online Transactions Processing (OLTP) application, and yet it is often totally "forgotten" in component-based applications. In this chapter, I discuss several different transaction techniques and recommend ways to choose between them. I then discuss transactions in the context of the proposed architecture of the previous chapter and show how you can design your application, making it easy to change transaction techniques if need be. Next, we look at the changes brought about by .NET concerning transactions and discuss tips on getting shorter transactions, lessening the risk of deadlocks, and avoiding traps with automatic transactions. Finally, I analyze my various transaction proposals based on the criteria established in Chapter 2, "Factors to Consider in Choosing a Solution to a Problem."

NOTE

This chapter discusses general solutions for transactions. In Chapter 8, "Data Access," I'll bind the solutions to my data access proposal and specifically to the architecture.

Locking and concurrency control are at the heart of transactions. We will touch on the subject in this chapter, but we'll also discuss locking and concurrency control in more detail in Chapter 9, "Error Handling and Concurrency Control."

Before we get started, it's important that you have a firm grasp of the following topics regarding general transaction theory and automatic transactions in .NET because I will not discuss them in detail in this chapter or anywhere in this book.

- Atomicity, Consistency, Isolation, and Durability (ACID)
- Shared and exclusive locks
- Transaction Isolation Levels (TIL)
- Two-Phase Commit (2PC)
- Doomed, done, and happy flags
- What the different transaction attribute values stand for

NOTE

If you feel you need to catch up on these topics, I recommend Tim Ewald's *Transactional COM+: Building Scalable Applications*[1] or Ted Pattison's *Programming Distributed Applications with COM+ and Visual Basic 6.0*.[2] To delve even deeper in general transaction theory, I recommend Jim Gray and Andreas Reuter's *Transaction Processing: Concepts and Techniques*[3] or Philip A. Bernstein and Eric Newcomer's *Principles of Transaction Processing*.[4]

Choosing a Transaction Technique

As you know, you can choose from several different techniques when dealing with transactions. In this section, I compare distributed transactions with local transactions and discuss the different approaches to working with those types of transactions, such as using transactional serviced components, ADO.NET, and stored procedures. First, let's start by looking at the main goal of any chosen transaction technique.

The Main Goal of Any Chosen Transaction Technique

As I mentioned in Chapter 2, the main goal of any chosen transaction technique is that it produces *correct* results when needed for certain scenarios. Keep this in mind when you read this chapter's discussions of performance, scalability, maintainability, and so on. Correctness is most important.

Although you may think that it is a given that correctness is extremely important, this notion goes one step further with transactions. Recall what I said in Chapter 1, "Introduction," about the new feature of COM+ 1.5 called process recycling. Although nobody likes a memory leak and we all try to avoid and/or try to find them, they're often not a large problem, even for critical Web sites—you just recycle the process once a day and nobody notices. However, if, at the very same Web sites, one transaction a day or a month produces an incorrect result leading to an inconsistent database, such leaks become disasters. The good news is that all the techniques I discuss in this chapter can be used to create correct transactions. Having said that, let's focus on issues of raw performance.

Description of the Selection of Transaction Techniques

It's possible to categorize transaction techniques in several ways. First, we can categorize them as being local (as are ordinary T-SQL transactions), being taken care of by one SQL Server instance, or as being distributed as 2PC transactions coordinated by Microsoft Distributed Transaction Coordinator (DTC). Transaction techniques can also be described as being automatic or manual. In automatic transactions, the desired transaction semantics are declared rather than programmed. In manual transactions, the transactions are controlled with explicit start and end statements.

> **NOTE**
>
> Don't confuse automatic and manual transaction techniques with the implicit and explicit transactions in, for example, T-SQL. As you probably know, when you do an UPDATE in SQL Server without first starting a transaction, the UPDATE will be wrapped inside an implicit transaction. If you begin and end your transaction on your own, you create an explicit transaction.

The final category is controller technology, such as ADO.NET (that wraps local T-SQL transactions) and the two wrappers for DTC transaction (namely, COM+ transactions and T-SQL distributed transactions). The last and very common transaction wrapper isn't really a wrapper. I'm referring to making pure T-SQL transactions. If we use the wrappers as categories, the situation shown in Table 6.1 occurs.

TABLE 6.1   Transaction Wrapper Techniques

Wrapper	*Manual/Automatic (Programmed/Declared)*	*Local/Distributed*
COM+ transactions	Automatic	Distributed
ADO.NET transactions	Manual	Local
Distributed T-SQL transactions	Manual	Distributed
Pure T-SQL transactions	Manual	Local

> **NOTE**
>
> In Table 6.1, you see that using COM+ transactions also means using distributed transactions. This is often overkill, especially if you have only one Resource Manager (RM) participating in the transaction. Even though a delegated commit will be used to optimize away some overhead from the 2PC protocol, this kind of transaction is expensive.

I haven't used distributed T-SQL transactions in any real-world applications, and I often find this to be a less commonly useful technique. Therefore, I will not discuss it in any detail now when describing wrappers. Instead, I'll briefly describe the different wrappers so that you understand what I mean when I use the different names. Note that I expect you to have a firm grasp of the techniques I present next so I will only describe them briefly.

COM+ Transactions

When COM+ controlled transactions are used, you get automatic and distributed transactions. COM+ asks Microsoft Distributed Transaction Coordinator (DTC) for help with the physical transaction, but COM+ will tell DTC when to start and when to end the transaction with the DTC-enabled RM(s). The transactional behavior is declared on the components with `transaction` attributes, and then COM+ uses interception to start and end transactions. If you use the `AutoComplete()` directive on the methods, you don't have to write any code to manage the transactions. You can see this in Listing 6.1, where a stored procedure is called and COM+ is starting and ending a transaction. Otherwise, you should use, for example, `ContextUtil.SetComplete()` and `ContextUtil.SetAbort()` to vote for the outcome.

NOTE

Although you obviously do not have to use stored procedures, I highly recommend it. In Chapter 5, "Architecture," I recommended that you always use stored procedures when components call the data tier. This presents a number of problems, but they are solvable. In Chapter 8, "Data Access," I present a few examples of such problems and offer suggestions for their solution.

LISTING 6.1   An Example of a COM+ Controlled Transaction

```
aCommand.ExecuteNonQuery()
```

NOTE

It's not only database engines that are RMs. Don't forget that Queued Components (QC) and MSMQ are other examples of RMs. In the future, I hope to see DTC-enabled RMs for Exchange's data storage, the Windows file system, and so on.

A major advantage with automatic transactions is that you can often reuse components without code changes, and they can directly participate in the transactions of the new consumers. One reason for this is that all the components participating in one transaction can open a connection of their own. The connections will auto-enlist in the transaction.

ADO.NET Transactions

ADO.NET transactions are conceptually really just a wrapper around ordinary T-SQL transactions. Listing 6.2 shows an example of how ADO.NET transactions can be used. In this case, there is a transaction around a call to a stored procedure. Of course, there is more to it than that—you have to make an aConnection.RollbackTrans() at the time of an exception.

LISTING 6.2   An Example of an ADO.NET Controlled Transaction

```
aTransaction = aConnection.BeginTransaction()
aCommand.Transaction = aTransaction
aCommand.ExecuteNonQuery()
aTransaction.Commit()
```

Pure T-SQL Transactions

Although T-SQL transactions are used by ADO.NET transactions, when I refer to "pure" T-SQL transactions, I'm referring to T-SQL transactions controlled by SQL scripts or by stored procedures. Listing 6.3 shows an example of how this might look. Once again, I have excluded the code for ROLLBACK TRAN and the complete code structure discussed in Chapter 5.

LISTING 6.3   Simplified Example of a Pure T-SQL Transaction

```
BEGIN TRANSACTION

UPDATE errand
SET closedby = @userId
, closeddatetime = GETDATE()
, solution = @solution
WHERE id = @id

INSERT INTO action
(id, errand_id
, description, createdby
, createddatetime, category)
VALUES
(@anActionId, @id
, @description, @userId
, GETDATE(), @aCategory)

COMMIT TRANSACTION
```

Why Care About Which Transaction Technique to Use?

There are huge differences between the different techniques when it comes to performance and scalability. The biggest difference is between local transactions and distributed transactions, because the 2PC protocol used by distributed transactions is pretty expensive as far as overhead is concerned. Table 6.2 presents a subjective overview of the advantages and disadvantages of each technique when you work with one RM. Note that the lower the value, the better.

TABLE 6.2   Comparison of the Transaction Techniques for One RM

Factor	COM+ Transactions	ADO Transactions	Pure T-SQL Transactions
Throughput	3	2	1
Participation in transactions together with other (unknown) components	1	3	3

TABLE 6.2   Continued

Factor	COM+ Transactions	ADO Transactions	Pure T-SQL Transactions
Getting portable code with regard to different database products	1	1	3
Fine-grained control of when to start and end transactions	3	2	1

ADO and Symmetric Multi-Processing Machines

A few years ago, I ran a test of COM+ transactions, ADO transactions (not ADO.NET), and pure T-SQL transactions with VB6 written components. I was puzzled when I saw that the COM+ controlled transactions had a higher throughput than the ADO controlled transactions. It took me a while to understand that it was only true on Symmetrical Multi-Processing (SMP) machines. When I turned off one of the two CPUs in my test application server, the throughput for the ADO controlled transactions actually increased and the resulting relation between ADO transactions and COM+ transactions turned out as expected. You will find the results from a test of the same techniques but in this new environment of .NET and ADO.NET on the book's Web site at www.samspublishing.com.

Reasons to Use Distributed Transactions

You may wonder why, given that they are so expensive, I am discussing distributed transactions at all. The reasons are simple:

- *There is more than one RM*—If you have more than one RM that must participate in the transactions, you should use distributed transactions.

- *Components that are "unaware" of each other coexist*—If you need to reuse a component that is out of your control or if you don't want to rewrite the component to fit into your architecture of local transactions, you can easily solve the problem with distributed transactions instead. This is also a useful technique for using legacy components in the .NET world.

Conclusion and Proposal: Choosing a Transaction Technique

My proposal for choosing a transaction technique is simple—use pure T-SQL transactions if you only have one RM; otherwise, use COM+ transactions. Also, use COM+ transactions if you need transactions to span unknown components that are not all within your control. This is another situation where COM+ transactions shine.

Transactions in the Proposed Architecture

Transaction design is extremely important and was a key factor I evaluated when creating the architecture I described in the last chapter. In this section, I'll discuss how the transactions fit in the architecture. But before we do this, let's review the proposed architecture.

Review of the Proposed Architecture

Figure 6.1 presents the architecture for the sample application Acme HelpDesk, which you first saw in Chapter 5. Keep this figure in mind in the following discussion of what I consider to be important information about an earlier attempt of an architecture I made. The figure applies to both my old and new attempt.

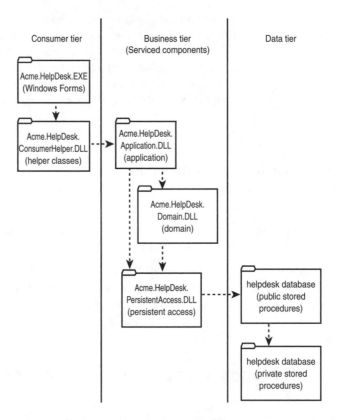

FIGURE 6.1

My architecture proposal applied to the sample application Acme HelpDesk.

Earlier Architecture Attempt

I've used several different architecture proposals over the years. One that I used a lot—let's call it the "old architecture"—looks exactly as shown in Figure 6.1, but there are a lot of differences to the current proposal. This old architecture isn't the last one I used before moving to .NET, but rather something that I used a few years ago. I'd like to discuss it here to show how my current architecture evolved.

When using automatic transactions in the old architecture, I only let the Persistent Access layer be transactional, so all the classes in the Application layer and the Domain layer had NotSupported for the Transaction attribute. (They could also have had Supported or Disabled, depending on what behavior was desired.) The idea was to get transactions as short as possible and not to let a transaction span more than one layer.

The main drawback was that using transactions only in the Persistent Access layer had a huge influence on design. All transactions had to reach one method in the Persistent Access layer in one call. Of course, this is possible, but it gave unintuitive code for the Application and Domain layers and it also made reusing the Domain and Persistent Access classes for different Application classes harder.

Another drawback when I used the architecture with manual transactions was that I relied on the stored procedures to control the transactions. The problem was when several stored procedures had to be called from a Persistent Access layer class to participate in one single transaction. In this situation, I let ADO control the transaction.

Yet another negative aspect about this proposal was that I split all the classes in the Persistent Access layer into two categories—one for fetching with the Transaction attribute set to Supported and one for writing with the Transaction attribute set to Required. Yet another drawback was that because I let the Persistent Access layer be transactional, I had interception and nondefault contexts for both the classes in the Application layer and the Persistent Access layer.

Transactions in the Current Proposal

When I use automatic transactions with the current proposal, I only declare transactional behavior on the classes in the Application layer by setting the Transaction attribute of the transactional classes to Required. (The classes in the other layers will have Disabled as the value of their Transaction attribute if they aren't Shared. If they are Shared, no Transaction attributes will be used, nor will inheritance from ServicedComponent.) Usually, the first contact with the database in a scenario will be deferred until the very end when the SQL script is to be executed. Consequently, the physical database transaction will not be longer by letting the Application layer be transactional.

Owing to this solution, the design will be less influenced by the transaction. The use case class in the Application layer can ask several Domain and Persistent Access classes for help by calling primitive methods, instead of having to move the control over to a Persistent Access class. The class residing in the Application layer will control the complete use case and, at the end, will send the SQL script to a helper class in the Persistent Access layer for execution.

Take a look at the interaction diagram in Figure 6.2 for an example of a call sequence. Here, you can see that the ErrandSaving class from the Application layer controls the scenario. First, it calls the doErrand class in the Domain layer to check whether the new errand is acceptable according to the defined rules. Then, it calls the paErrand class in the Persistent Access layer to receive the required rows to the SQL script. Finally, the SQL script is executed with the paHelper class and the public stored procedure a_Errand_Insert() is called. Finally, the private stored procedure Errand_Insert() will be called, and the INSERT statement will be executed there.

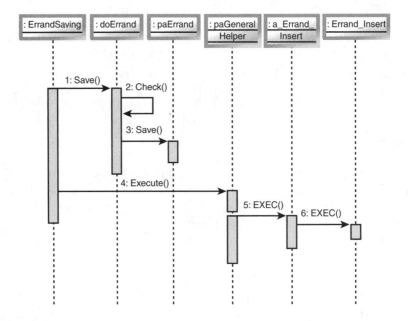

FIGURE 6.2
Interaction diagram, showing an example of a transaction.

Because an SQL Script is used, there is no need to use ADO.NET controlled transactions. Instead, the transaction can be started and ended in the SQL Script. There is no real reason for splitting the Persistent Access classes (paErrand in Figure 6.2) into two parts either.

The main drawback with the current proposal is that with automatic transactions, a method that does a fetch from the database and doesn't need a transaction will get a DTC transaction if it is located in a transactional Application layer class. When manual transactions are used, it isn't a problem to have a single class for both fetching and updating methods because I control exactly when to start and stop transactions. If it is a real problem with automatic transactions that fetching methods also starts DTC transactions, the classes in the Application layer have to be split. This is unfortunate because the use case then needs two different Application layer classes. Fortunately, the Consumer Helper layer can hide the fact that the class has been split from the Consumer layer.

A Flexible Transaction Design

If you follow the recommendation to use local transactions when you only have one RM, but want to prepare for a possible future change to distributed transactions and have as few programming changes as possible, there are a couple of things to think about.

Transaction Control

Assume you have followed the architecture that I have proposed. For simplicity's sake, we only have one root component in the Application layer that is called ErrandSolving in this scenario. It will use a component called paHelper in the Persistent Access layer. In turn, the paHelper will use a stored procedure called a_Errand_Close(). The stored procedure will UPDATE a row in the errand table and INSERT a row to the action table. Because there is only one RM involved in the transaction, I am using a local transaction in the stored procedure. Listing 6.4 shows how this may look, in a simplified version.

> **NOTE**
>
> I will discuss error trapping in greater depth in Chapter 9.

LISTING 6.4   Excerpt from Stored Procedure Showing a Simplified Pure T-SQL Transaction

```
BEGIN TRANSACTION

UPDATE errand
SET closedby = @userId
, closeddatetime = GETDATE()
, solution = @solution
WHERE id = @id
```

LISTING 6.4   Continued

```
INSERT INTO action
(id, errand_id, ...)
VALUES
(@actionId, @id, ...)

COMMIT TRANSACTION
```

Transaction Attribute Value

How should you declare the transaction-related attributes for the components in this situation when pure T-SQL transactions are used? There are several correct ways to do it. One possible proposal is to use the settings shown in Table 6.3.

> **NOTE**
>
> I assume here that paHelper isn't Shared. As you read in Chapter 5, it is preferable to use Shared whenever possible from a performance perspective.

TABLE 6.3   Transaction Settings: Proposal 1

Component	Transaction(TransactionOption)
ErrandSolving	Supported
paHelper	Supported

Because ErrandSolving is the root component for this scenario and uses Supported transactions, there will be no DTC transaction started. This is exactly the result I want. But did I achieve the result in the cheapest way? No, I can do better than this. A slight improvement would be to change paHelper to have Disabled instead of Supported. This makes it possible to save one context, but I'm still not satisfied. Let's investigate why not.

When Supported is used as the Transaction(TransactionOption) value, it means that you have to use just-in-time activation (JIT). As you recall from the discussion about JIT in Chapter 5, I prefer to use JIT only when I need COM+ transactions, so this isn't the perfect solution. Another way to see it is that because Supported requires interception, objects of this component can't go to the default context.

Before you say that you don't like this solution, remember that without any redeclarations, instances of both the components can participate in a COM+ transaction. If you really need the components to be able to participate in a COM+ transaction, this solution isn't so bad after all. (It's not all that it takes, but it's the first step.)

A more efficient declaration would be as shown in Table 6.4, in which the components can still participate in an outer COM+ transaction.

TABLE 6.4   Transaction Settings: Proposal 2

Component	Transaction(TransactionOption)
ErrandSolving	Disabled
paHelper	Disabled

Now there will be no interception (if no instances of those components will co-locate in a context that uses interception). There is also the possibility of co-location that I discussed in Chapter 5. Less memory will be used and there will be less overhead for creation and calling methods.

The good thing is that if you add a new component that required a transaction, say CustomizedErrandSolving, a created instance of ErrandSolving can participate in the transaction. This assumes that instances of ErrandSolving must co-locate in the context of instances of CustomizedErrandSolving. We then have the best of both worlds.

The drawback is that co-location is often a problem for instances in the Application layer because that layer often requires component-level security, and then co-location is impossible. This is also the case for root components. If the consumer is Windows Forms on another machine, there is no context to co-locate in for the Application Layer class. We should still use the settings from Table 6.4, but instances of a new and, today, unknown component can't start a transaction in which instances of ErrandSolving can participate. In any case, we have declared transaction attributes as being as efficient as possible for the current situation. And we haven't created any obstacles so far for easily changing the transaction technique to COM+ transactions.

Changing the Values for Transaction Attributes

At first I thought I'd recommend the solution that I'm now in the middle of describing as a means for administrators to change transaction techniques when they needed to. When I mentioned this idea to Joe Long at Microsoft, he strongly disagreed, and we had a long discussion on the matter. His main concern was that administrators can't know about the inner workings of the components and the assumptions the programmers made when they wrote the code. Even for well and strictly architected components with full documentation of supported transaction settings, there is a risk that the administrator may make a small mistake. And we all know what one mistake can do to the transactions. The reason for using declarative transactions isn't to make transaction semantics easier for administrators to maintain, easier for developers to program, or more efficient. The reason is correctness!

If we compare some of the EnterpriseServices attributes with other attributes in .NET, there is a fundamental difference. Some of the EnterpriseServices attributes can be changed from outside of the code. In the future, it will probably change, so we can lock the settings, but for the time being, it's very easy for someone to change the settings in the Component Services Explorer.

Another flaw with my original reason for my idea was that the administrator has little opportunity to make use of the flexibility I was about to propose. There are two basic situations when the transaction technique needs to be changed:

- The current components also need to hit another RM.
- The current components need to be used by other components, which in turn hit another RM, or they use another architecture for controlling transactions.

In the first case, it will usually be the developers who make that change anyway. In the second case, I think it's reasonable to contact the developers too.

Another reason—and certainly a big one—for not letting administrators change the settings in the Component Services Explorer for certain attributes is that the common language runtime won't look in the COM+ catalog, but rather in the meta data for the assembly to know how to deal with components regarding Object Pooling, for example. The only values that should be changed in the Component Services Explorer are deployment-related values, such as object construction strings, number of objects in the object pools, and similar deployment-related values—not the settings, for example, that enable object construction strings or object pooling.

So, Joe won the battle. I agree with him that setting the transaction attributes is a matter for the developers. Because of this, I have slightly changed the basic purpose of the proposal, and I'm now discussing it as a way for developers to prepare their design and code for a future change of transaction technique. They will carry out the change, but it will be easily done.

NOTE

It might sound strange to talk about the administrator as a person who would be thinking about using one of your components from another transactional component. However, it's very easy to publish XML Web services whose methods are transactional and that call your components. Meanwhile, BizTalk has been used to orchestrate a solution in which some of your components will participate. Think about this before you follow my recommendation of using Disabled for the transaction attribute. Are the implications reasonable in your situation?

Starting with Manual Transactions

Programming for a future change of transaction technique must start with coding for manual transactions and then move to automatic transactions, and not the other way around. Why? If everything works well for manual transactions, there is a good chance that it will work well for automatic transactions too.

On the other hand, if you start coding for automatic transactions, it's very common to use several connections in the same transaction so that participating components open their own connections. This works thanks to auto-enlist, so that all the connections will be enlisted in the automatic transaction. In a way, this is information hiding (which I normally appreciate) because the different components are more shielded from each other so they won't send around a connection object. On the other hand, this is less efficient than letting all instances that participate in the transaction share one connection. As you see, I prefer to let the instances share the connection because it's efficient and works with both automatic and manual transactions.

It's important to note that you shouldn't count on all RMs being able to successfully commit a transaction where several connections have been used in the same DTC transaction. This works well with SQL Server; however, at the time of writing it does not work so well with, for example, Ingres. (I've heard that a version of Ingres that is to be released soon—or has been released when you read this—will support transactions that span several connections, but it isn't documented as a requirement by Microsoft that "Tightly Coupled XA Threads" are a must for an RM to support DTC transactions.) A safe recommendation is to use only one connection in your DTC transactions too. On the other hand, be careful that you don't send a connection between processes or machines.

> **NOTE**
>
> You will see in Chapter 8 where I propose how to access the database, that only one method will hit the database for each scenario. The participating instances will just add logic to an SQL script that is executed against the database from a single method afterward.

There are two problems in starting with manual transactions and then expecting your components to work with automatic transactions without code changes. The first is that you have to remember that automatic transactions require JIT, so that the member state is lost when the transaction ends. What I mean is that you have to code your local transactions as if JIT were being used. That is definitely my intention with the architecture proposal.

The second problem is that you get slightly different transaction semantics in the two cases. You can delay transaction start with local transactions, and you will also, by default, work with another transaction isolation level (TIL). So watch out!

One Controlling Part

It's possible to use, say, BEGIN TRANSACTION and COMMIT TRANSACTION in your stored procedures, even if they are to be used from COM+ components. SQL Server will keep track of the current @@TRANCOUNT to determine whether COMMIT TRANSACTION really means a COMMIT or whether it is only subtracting one from @@TRANCOUNT. That's perfectly acceptable.

Nevertheless, there is at least one problem with this. ROLLBACK TRANSACTION won't just subtract 1 from @@TRANCOUNT; it will do a ROLLBACK of the complete transaction, which can create a problem for the components. In my opinion, it's much better to decide on just who is responsible for doing something, and then nobody else will interfere. (At least not as long as the first party does the job.) Therefore, I won't do a BEGIN TRANSACTION and COMMIT TRANSACTION/ROLLBACK TRANSACTION in my stored procedures if COM+ transactions are responsible for taking care of the transactions. However, this makes a real mess if the stored procedures are also to be used from other consumers that don't handle transactions on their own.

Moving from automatic to manual transactions for some scenarios will also take a lot of work. However, I use the solution to the problem shown in Listing 6.5. @@TRANCOUNT is stored in a local variable when the stored procedure is entered. When the stored procedure is about to start a transaction, it investigates whether there is already an active transaction. If there is, there won't be another BEGIN TRANSACTION. At COMMIT/ROLLBACK time, a similar technique is used. If there wasn't an active transaction when the stored procedure was entered, it should be COMMITted/ROLLedBACK now. You should also add to this the criteria that there must be an active transaction. (There can now be several COMMIT sections in the stored procedure without creating any problems.) Clean and simple.

LISTING 6.5 Excerpt from a Stored Procedure Showing How to Write Flexible Transaction Code

```
SET @theTranCountAtEntry = @@TRANCOUNT
IF @theTranCountAtEntry = 0 BEGIN
  SET TRANSACTION ISOLATION LEVEL SERIALIZABLE
  BEGIN TRAN
END

UPDATE...
```

LISTING 6.5   Continued

```
--Another DML-statement...
INSERT...

ExitHandler:
  IF @theTranCountAtEntry = 0 AND @@TRANCOUNT > 0 BEGIN
    IF @anError = 0 BEGIN
      COMMIT TRAN
    END
    ELSE BEGIN
      ROLLBACK TRAN
    END
  END
```

NOTE

Oracle, DB2, and even the SQL-99 standard do not support BEGIN TRANSACTION, but the first SQL command will start the transaction.

Something else you may need to add to this solution is handling the transactions that span over several stored procedures from your ADO.NET code. Then you can use ContextUtil.IsInTransaction() to determine whether you should start a new ADO.NET transaction. (You could also ask the database server for the @@TRANCOUNT value from your component, but that would lead to one more round trip, and you definitely don't want that.)

NOTE

Instead of starting transactions that must span several stored procedures from ADO.NET, I deal with this in the SQL script. This is at the heart of the data access pattern presented in Chapter 8.

Transaction Isolation Level (TIL)

If you use COM+ transactions, the Transaction Isolation Level (TIL) will be set for you. In the case of COM+ 1.5, you can configure the TIL you want to have. For COM+ 1.0, it will always be SERIALIZABLE. It's better to be safe than sorry.

> **NOTE**
>
> You can change the TIL within COM+ 1.0 transactions by using SET TRANSACTION
> ISOLATION LEVEL statements and optimizer hints. With SQL Server, this has a direct
> effect, but watch out because the behavior differs between different database
> products.

If you use manual transactions, you have to set the TIL on your own. (The default for MS SQL is READ COMMITTED.) I typically do this when I start the transaction seen in Listing 6.5. The problem is that, for instance, a public stored procedure doesn't know which TIL is needed by a used private stored procedure. It might then be the case that the public stored procedure SETs REPEATABLE READ, but the private stored procedure needs SERIALIZABLE. In this case, the private stored procedure must have its setting outside of the IF clause, so it executes even if the private stored procedure won't start the transaction. See Listing 6.6 for an example. When the code in Listing 6.6 executes, there is already an active transaction (@theTranCountAtEntry is not 0, so the BEGIN TRANSACTION won't execute), but the TIL will still be increased.

LISTING 6.6   Increasing the TIL Within a Transaction

```
SET TRANSACTION ISOLATION LEVEL SERIALIZABLE
IF @theTranCountAtEntry = 0 BEGIN
  BEGIN TRANSACTION
END
```

As you understand, it's very dangerous to change the TIL in code down the call stack, but as long as you only increase it, it's usually acceptable. How can you know that you have only increased the TIL? You can use DBCC USEROPTIONS and find an entry called isolation level that tells you the current TIL. If you don't find that entry, the TIL hasn't been changed and it has the default value. On the other hand, to avoid using this for my code, setting the TIL only to SERIALIZABLE can be done outside the IF-clause, as shown in Listing 6.6.

To summarize, I use the following rules for my stored procedures:

- If a transaction is needed, it will be started, but only if there isn't a current transaction.
- TIL is not SET if a transaction is already started, except if SERIALIZABLE is the needed level. That is, SERIALIZABLE will be SET, even if there is a current transaction.

I use the following rules when I generate the SQL script in the components:

- If the SQL script only calls one stored procedure, a transaction is not started from the SQL script. (The stored procedure starts a transaction if it is needed.)
- If the SQL script calls more than one stored procedure, the SQL script starts a transaction (if it is needed). Unfortunately, the only solution here is that the involved stored procedures must be investigated to decide whether a transaction is needed and should be started from the SQL script and what TIL is needed. This can be troublesome, but there is no shortcut.

As you know, I love to centralize code, so I tried to write helper stored procedures for my BEGIN TRANSACTION block and my block for ending transactions. This would have given me cleaner and smaller stored procedures, and I could also have hidden implementation details, such as that only SERIALIZABLE should be SET even if a transaction isn't to be started. Unfortunately, I failed because SQL Server monitors that the @@TRANCOUNT must have the same value when you exit a stored procedure as when you entered it. Otherwise, there will be an error.

> **NOTE**
>
> A colleague of mine once said that using a high (and correct) TIL is important if you work with bank applications, but you can cheat a bit and decrease it for simple administrative applications. This may sound like a dangerous viewpoint, but don't forget the context. In some applications, a high TIL may be very expensive and, at the same time, unnecessary. A typical example is applications that generate statistical information.
>
> If you are unsure about which TIL to use for a certain scenario, go for a higher one, presumably SERIALIZABLE. Of course, you could standardize on SERIALIZABLE for all scenarios in the application, but I prefer to use the lowest correct TIL for each scenario.

AutoComplete() Versus SetComplete()/SetAbort()

As you know, with COM+ transactions, you must vote on the outcome. Should it be COMMIT or ROLLBACK? Even in this case, you have to pay extra attention to support the flexibility pattern that I discuss in this section. You can check ContextUtil.IsInTransaction() before you do a SetComplete() and SetAbort() to determine whether there is a transaction for which outcome you may choose. If not, there's no need to vote, and remember that SetComplete() and

SetAbort() don't only vote, they also set the done bit to True, which will lead to a deactivation of the object. Because I only use JIT for classes that use COM+ transactions, I don't want the deactivation to occur in other situations.

Another solution to the problem of voting for what transaction outcome you want to have is to use the AutoComplete() attribute on the methods for the transactional classes instead. With AutoComplete(), a raised exception is understood as a SetAbort(), but you don't have to write any code for it. At the same time, a method that ends without a raised exception is thought of as being SetComplete().

A somewhat subtle positive effect of AutoComplete() is that you don't have to have a Catch block just to get a place for your SetAbort(), as shown in Listing 6.7. In this case, you can just skip the catch block because nothing is really happening except the SetAbort().

LISTING 6.7   Catch Block Only Due to Calling SetAbort()

```
Catch e As Exception
    ContextUtil.SetAbort()
    Throw(e)
```

A problem with AutoComplete() is that if you get an exception but want to make a compensating action in a method higher up in the call stack and still COMMIT the transaction, it is impossible if AutoComplete() has already voted for the secondary object and deactivated it. In this case, the transaction is doomed. (Of course, in this situation, SetAbort() in the secondary method would give exactly the same result. DisableCommit() should be used instead.) Anyway, I usually prefer to take the easy way. If there is a problem, the transaction should be rolled back, and, because of this, the problem doesn't exist with AutoComplete(). Furthermore, if your secondary object co-locates in the context of the root object, there is no problem in the first place because the doomed flag isn't set until the context is left. As a matter of fact, it's not a good idea at all to let your secondary co-located instances vote. It's better to only let one instance in the context be responsible for the voting, preferably the root.

New Possibilities to Consider with .NET

.NET brings us a flood of new possibilities, although not all of them are even close to optimal. In this section, I point out a few weaknesses that the marketing department in Redmond doesn't talk much about.

Transactions and XML Web Services

A method on an XML Web service can use an automatic transaction (owing to a parameter of the WebMethod attribute). That transaction can span several .NET objects, but it cannot span several XML Web services. The transaction won't flow. At first this may seem like a great limitation, but it makes sense because of the following reasons:

- Round trips between computers are always expensive. When XML Web services are used, it is not because they are the most performance efficient way of communicating, it is because of other reasons. What I mean is that transactions spanning several calls to XML Web services would be longer than with other communication mechanisms, and you don't want to have long transactions.

- Typical protocols for distributed transactions, such as OLE transactions (as are used by DTC), are inherently connection oriented. XML Web services are not.

- You don't know what technique is "hiding" behind that other XML Web service. Is it one that understands OLE transactions, for example? There is nothing in the XML Web services standard regarding transaction support.

- Several XML Web services publishers would certainly be very reluctant to let the consumers decide on the length of the transactions.

> **NOTE**
>
> Of course, you should pay a lot of attention to ensuring all the necessary information is given to the XML Web service in one method call so that it can take care of the complete transaction the normal way. This is a "must" for all root components in the Application layer, even if they aren't to be published as an XML Web service.

For the moment, the way to proceed to get transaction semantics over several XML Web services is to use a compensating mechanism instead. It won't be possible to fulfill the ACID properties, but this is the best you can do. Unfortunately, the Compensating Resource Manager (CRM) won't help you in this situation, even though its name suggests that it will. You have to roll your own solution instead.

The Compensating Resource Manager (CRM)

The Compensating Resource Manager (CRM) is relatively unknown, even though it has been around since COM+ 1.0 first saw the light of day. CRM helps to write a transactional resource dispenser of a resource that isn't DTC-transactional. CRM is to be considered as yet another RM. Typical examples of resources that the CRM are useful for dealing with are the file system and Microsoft Exchange. CRM won't perform magic and create a truly transactional resource dispenser for you, but with the help of compensating actions, you can go a long way.[5, 6]

> **NOTE**
>
> There is more and more interest in using sagas for transactions. A *saga* is a logical transaction aggregated from a sequence of physical transactions that must all succeed or be undone. One reason for the new interest in sagas is the interest in XML Web services. It is not within the scope of this book to discuss sagas further. For more information about sagas, see *Transaction Processing: Concepts and Techniques*[3] and *Principles of Transaction Processing.*[4]

Flow of Services Through Remoting

As you recall from Chapter 5, component services won't flow through XML Web services nor through Remoting. Actually, the lack of flow of component services through XML Web services is usually not as large a problem as it may seem at first. Most often, for reasons of efficiency, you have all the serviced components that are to talk to each other at the same application server (and in the same AppDomain). There is then no need for flow of component services over Remoting.

On the other hand, if you do need to let component services flow between machines, you can always rely on good old DCOM for that. Yes, DCOM is a nightmare through firewalls, but why would you have a firewall between your serviced components? If you do have a firewall between your serviced components, ask yourself again if this is the correct design to use.

Tips on Making Transactions as Short as Possible

The length of transactions affects scalability. Each transaction holds on to resources, such as locks in the database. If you can shorten your transactions, you can service more users (and transactions) with the same hardware. The following are tips I think are important in making transactions as short as possible.

Avoiding Large Updates

If you have to update several rows in a transaction, the transaction will take longer than if only a few rows are to be updated. No rocket science here. Even so, it is worth thinking about because, for example, this may affect your batch processes, which often update thousands of rows in each transaction. It is increasingly so that you don't have any downtime when you can run batch processes like this without interfering with other transactions. Therefore, it may be important to use a strategy other than using huge transactions. For example, you could use a compensating solution instead so that if you have to update 100,000 rows, you can update them in chunks of, say, 1,000 in each transaction. If one transaction fails, you will see that the total operation isn't atomic. As a result, you will have to compensate for this. For example, try again with those transactions that weren't updated the last time, or undo the result of the transactions that were updated before. Watch out—these can be dangerous design changes to make, and you have to make careful evaluations before moving along.

> **NOTE**
>
> Note that batch processes don't go well with COM+ transactions. First we have the timeout, saying that the complete transaction may not take more than x seconds. (Normally in production, x is set to 5 or lower.) Then we have the JIT behavior that leads to longer execution time, without any real use in this situation. Distributed transactions are also a drawback because they will be more resource consuming, which is not wanted if you don't need distributed transactions.

Another typical situation arising from too large updates is when you haven't used a high enough normal form. It then might be the case that a certain value is located in thousands of rows and, when the value has to be updated, you have a very large transaction to deal with. The solution to this is simple—use a high enough normal form for your database design, usually the third normal form or higher.

Avoiding Slow Updates

For all tasks, there are a number of different approaches to use. For relational databases, the correct way to proceed is usually to use a set technique instead of a row technique. Let's take a simple example. If you are going to increase the price of all products for a certain category in a stored procedure, you can do this by opening a CURSOR with a SELECT that fetches all the rows to UPDATE. Then you iterate the CURSOR and UPDATE row by row. It works, but it will be much slower than a simple UPDATE that updates all the rows in one statement. This might be obvious, but you should think in this way more often and for less obvious scenarios too. Think twice if there is a loop in your T-SQL code—check that it isn't a design bug.

Loops

Although you want to avoid loops, you may sometimes need to use a loop after all. Typical reasons for this are

- You need to update a large number of rows and you don't want to fill the transaction log, or you don't want to lock out all other users from the table.

- You need to use a very tricky algorithm that can't be solved or that can't be solved efficiently with set techniques. (However, don't give up too fast.)

- You need to call a stored procedure for each row in a resultset.

Even though you need a loop, you don't have to use a CURSOR. As a matter of fact, I recommend that you use a WHILE loop instead. It's as fast as or faster than a CURSOR in almost all situations. (If the used key is a composite of more than two parts, a CURSOR is slightly faster.) The code is also simpler and cleaner with a WHILE loop, and there is less chance of making mistakes, but once again, if the key is a composite, the WHILE code is more complicated than the CURSOR code.

Let's look at an example of what a WHILE loop looks like in action. I will solve the same example that I just used (increasing the price of all products), but this time I will update all the products with a WHILE loop, and I will update them category by category. The products are split into ten different categories.

In Listing 6.8, you can see that I first SELECT what is the smallest category from the product table. If I found a category, the WHILE loop is started. I UPDATE all the products for the particular category, and I investigate that the UPDATE went all right as usual.

LISTING 6.8 WHILE Example: Part 1

```
SELECT @aCategory = MIN(category)
FROM product
WHILE @aCategory IS NOT NULL BEGIN
  UPDATE product
  SET price = price + @add
  WHERE category = @aCategory

  SELECT @anError = @@ERROR, @aRowcount = @@ROWCOUNT
  IF @anError <> 0 OR @aRowcount = 0 BEGIN
    SET @anErrorMessage = 'Problem with...'
    IF @anError = 0 BEGIN
      SET @anError = 81001   --An example...
    END
    GOTO ExitHandler
  END
END
```

In Listing 6.9, you can see that I save the last processed category in an old variable, and then I search for the smallest category larger than the last processed.

LISTING 6.9 WHILE Example: Part 2

```
  SET @aCategoryOld = @aCategory

  SELECT @aCategory = MIN(category)
  FROM product
  WHERE category > @aCategoryOld
END
```

> **NOTE**
>
> Several years ago when I was porting an application that I built for SQL Server 4.21 to SQL Server 6, I decided to rewrite a WHILE loop to a CURSOR solution. I guess I was tricked by all the hype about server-side CURSORs that was taking place at the time. It was probably not a good idea, especially because the WHILE loop worked just fine and there weren't any problems with it. (Well, there weren't any problems with the CURSOR either, but it was probably a worse solution.) Since then, I've learned not to make transitions like these without having a real purpose and without examining whether such transitions will have a positive effect.

Avoiding Pure Object-Oriented Design

As you recall from Chapter 5, I stress in this book that object orientation is great, but it has to be used wisely. I've seen pure object-oriented design used often for COM+ applications, and the result has typically been scalability that's too low. (I've not only seen it used, I've been contacted by e-mail and in person several times and asked what to do in these situations. My answer has always been "Redesign.")

> **NOTE**
>
> When I say pure object-oriented design, I mean classic object orientation, for example, with many properties. Each row and column from the database has lead to instantiated objects, and methods have been primitive so that to accomplish a task, several method calls must be made.

One of the reasons that pure object-oriented design doesn't scale is that the transactions will start too early, and because several objects will participate in the transaction and each one of them will talk to the database, there is also a lot of overhead for round trips. Usually, stored procedures are not used in those applications, and if they are used, it's only for primitive operations such as one SELECT, one UPDATE, one INSERT, or one DELETE.

It might seem compelling to have all the code in the components and not let the database and transactions affect the design at all. Unfortunately, it doesn't work well in large-scale situations. I've heard war stories about applications built this way not scaling beyond five to ten users.

Avoiding Pessimistic Concurrency Control Schemas

Another typical reason for having long transactions is the need to use pessimistic concurrency control schemas. Try to avoid pessimistic concurrency control schemas and you will get shorter transactions. Of course, the disadvantage is that you don't know whether your transaction will be able to run when you use an optimistic schema instead, but most often this is the way to go.

With Web-based applications, it's not usual to keep a connection for a user between page renderings. It's the same for all COM+ applications where the connection is closed and the result is disconnected from the database and sent back to the user. Because of this, a built-in pessimistic concurrency control schema can't be used. In any case, you never want a user to decide the length of a transaction by asking the user for an answer between start of the transaction and COMMIT.

> **NOTE**
>
> In Chapter 9, I will show you an alternative to the built-in pessimistic concurrency control schema that works in disconnected scenarios and doesn't create long transactions.

Using an Efficient Pattern for Data Access

I won't go into detail about my pattern for data access until Chapter 8, but it is crucial that you have an effective pattern for data access. As you can guess, I think my pattern is a very efficient one. I defer all access to the database until the end of a scenario. Until then, an SQL script is built with all the calls to different stored procedures. A transaction won't be started until it's needed in the SQL script. When the SQL script has started to run, there are no other round trips and no operations other than the calls to stored procedures until the transaction is to be ended.

Starting Transactions Late and Ending Them Early

Suppose that you have five tasks to accomplish. Quite often, only two of these need to be done inside the transaction, so you should program in this way, of course. Don't do anything in the transaction that you don't have to do. Prepare the transaction before it starts by getting NEWID()s, if you need to INSERT a row that has a UNIQUE IDENTIFIER as the key, for example. Listing 6.10 shows an example of a simplified stored procedure for reporting a new errand and, at the same time, writing an action because the reporter also made a first attempt to solve the problem that failed.

LISTING 6.10 A Simplified Version of a Stored Procedure for Inserting an Errand and a First Action

```
CREATE PROCEDURE a_Errand_Insert
(@userId uddtUserId, @errandDescription uddtDescription
, @actionDescription uddtDescription)
AS

  DECLARE @anErrandId UNIQUEIDENTIFIER
  , @anActionId UNIQUEIDENTIFIER
  , @aCategory UNIQUEIDENTIFIER

  SET @anErrandId = NEWID()
  SET @anActionId = NEWID()

  SELECT @aCategory
  FROM category
  WHERE description = 'report'

  BEGIN TRANSACTION

  INSERT INTO errand
  (id, description, createdby, ...)
  VALUES
  (@anErrandId, @errandDescription, @userId, ...)

  INSERT INTO action
  (id, errand_id
  , description, createdby
  , createddatetime, category)
  VALUES
  (@anActionId, @anErrandId
  , @actionDescription, @userId
  , GETDATE(), @aCategory)

  COMMIT TRANSACTION
```

NOTE

I have cut out the error trapping code from Listing 6.10. I will focus on error trapping in Chapter 9.

As you see in Listing 6.10, I waited until I had created the two GUIDs and I read the category GUID before I started the transaction. The difference isn't huge, but it's the principle I like to push. However, what happens if this stored procedure is called together with other stored procedures? There is a great chance that you will need to create an outer transaction, and then my recommendation here is of no use. Even if it won't matter in some cases, it will in others. This is also an indication that it might be better to let the components prepare as much as possible before starting the database transaction. In the example in Listing 6.10, this would mean that the GUIDs will be given as parameters instead. It might result in a little more network traffic because more data will be sent over the network, but it's usually worth it.

That was the usual recommendation. Just be careful that you don't overuse it so that you fetch rows from the database that will not keep their shared lock during the complete transaction because you had the fetch before the transaction started.

Using Correct TIL

Be careful that you use the correct TIL. Overusing SERIALIZABLE can definitely affect scalability. I can't tell you how many times I've heard developers at COM+ newsgroups ask why there is so much blocking in the database when they start using COM+. They aren't doing anything unusual. If you only execute a SELECT COUNT(*) FROM mytable, other transactions will not be allowed to INSERT rows INTO mytable until the first transaction is done. COM+ 1.0 always uses SERIALIZABLE for automatic transactions with SQL Server. You can configure the TIL for COM+ transactions in COM+ 1.5.

When you use pure T-SQL transactions, you should sometimes use SERIALIZABLE, sometimes not—you have to decide from case to case. You could go for SERIALIZABLE all the time, but then your transactions will be longer and you will also affect concurrency much more than if you use a lower TIL.

> **NOTE**
>
> For a good discussion on how to think about the TIL, see Tim Ewald's *Transactional COM+: Building Scalable Applications*.[1]

Avoiding 2PC with the Help of Replication

If you are going to use more than one RM in your transactions, you have to use distributed transactions if you like to have transaction semantics over the RMs. Distributed transactions will operate with the 2PC protocol, which is very expensive when it comes to performance compared to local transactions. An alternate solution is to only UPDATE one of the RMs and then let the UPDATE affect the other RM with the help of replication. You won't get full transaction semantics, but often the consistency is good enough. In addition, the difference in throughput can be very big. This will also increase the reliability because if one of the participants in a 2PC transaction is down, the transaction can't be fulfilled. With replication, the transactions will still take place, even if one of the database servers is not operating at the time. The faulty server will get the UPDATEs when it comes back to life again.

Tips on Decreasing the Risk of Deadlocks

For local transactions, the RM will quickly find deadlocks itself. In this case, the RM will decide which transaction should lose, and it is interrupted so the other transaction can continue. Unfortunately, you can't catch a deadlock error in your stored procedures because they are interrupted, and even the batch that calls the stored procedure is interrupted. The error will always have to be caught in your components instead.

For distributed transaction, the Transaction Manager (TM) will, in most industrial implementations, not really try to detect a deadlock but will rather use a timeout. If the transaction takes more than x seconds, the TM decides that there is a deadlock and the transaction is interrupted. The case with distributed transactions is worse because it will often take longer to detect the presumable deadlock situation and, meanwhile, several transactions are blocked. It's also common that more than one transaction will be affected by the timeout and therefore be terminated.

In any case, deadlocks are bad for our health, both with local and distributed transactions. We can't avoid deadlocks completely, but we can make them less likely to appear. Using short transactions is extremely important for reducing the deadlock risk. The shorter the time you hold the locks, the smaller the risk that somebody else acquires the locks in a way that conflicts with yours. The following are other tips I recommend for decreasing the risk of deadlocks.

Taking UPDLOCK When Reading Before Writing

Another common reason for a deadlock is that two transactions first acquire shared locks on one and the same row and then both of them try to escalate their locks to exclusive locks. None of the transactions succeeds until one of the transactions is interrupted. The solution is simple—when you know you need an exclusive lock, acquire it immediately instead of starting with a shared lock that you later escalate to an exclusive lock. You can do that with the UPDLOCK optimizer hint in SQL Server, as shown in Listing 6.11.

LISTING 6.11   Example of How to Acquire an Exclusive Lock with a SELECT

```
SELECT description
FROM errand (UPDLOCK)
WHERE id = @id
```

Working with Tables in the Same Order for All Transactions

One simple tip is to always work with your tables in the same order in all transactions. In Listing 6.10, you see that one row is inserted into errand and then one row is inserted into action. That order should be used for all transactions. I usually say that the master table should be used before the detail table. You don't have a choice when it comes to INSERTs as in Listing 6.10 because of FOREIGN KEY constraints. When this rule doesn't help because there are no relationships between the tables, use alphabetical order for the table names instead.

Unfortunately, DELETE has to happen in the opposite order of master and detail, once again because of FOREIGN KEY constraints. The problem is easily solved by first taking an UPDLOCK on the master row, and then DELETE the detail rows followed by a DELETE of the master row.

Obscure Declarative Transaction Design Traps

Using COM+ transactions is often thought of as being simple because the system will deal with the transactions for you, deciding when to COMMIT and when to ROLLBACK. Even so, it's important to understand how COM+ transactions work and how your settings will affect the outcome.

All three traps that follow are taken from situations where my proposed architecture was not used. Even so, I want to point out a few "gotchas" so you don't fall into these traps if you decide to use another architecture.

Example 1: Incorrect Error Trapping

There are several examples of how error trapping might go wrong, some obvious and some not so obvious. The result might be that SetAbort() isn't called at all and that the transaction will therefore be COMMITed. It's probably obvious why the example in Listing 6.12 isn't one you want to have in your code. When the Throw() statement executes in Listing 6.12, the method will stop executing (except for one or more possible Finally and/or Catch blocks on an outer level).

LISTING 6.12 Incorrect Example of Error Trapping

```
Catch e As Exception
    Throw(e)
    ContextUtil.SetAbort()
```

Example 2: Incorrect Use of `NotSupported`

In this example, we will let a root component control a transaction and ask for help from two secondary components for doing subtasks. Assume you have the components listed in Table 6.5.

TABLE 6.5 Example 2: Instances, Components, and Transaction Attributes

Instances and Components	Transaction *Attribute*
aRoot (instance of component A)	TransactionOption.Required
aSecondary (instance of component B)	TransactionOption.Required
anotherSecondary (instance of component C)	TransactionOption.NotSupported

Assume that aRoot calls aSecondary and aSecondary UPDATEs a specific errand. (Recall the sample application Acme HelpDesk introduced in Chapter 5.) Then aRoot calls anotherSecondary that SELECTs the same errand, or at least anotherSecondary tries to. Because component C is marked with NotSupported, its instances will not execute in the same transaction that is still going on for aRoot and aSecondary. Instead, the SELECT in component C will be wrapped in an implicit transaction and put in a wait state waiting for the row in the errand table to be released. Now we're stuck in a wait state until the timeout for the transaction helps us. Unfortunately it won't; it will kill us.

The typical solution to this problem would be to use Supported or Disabled for component C. (Disabled only works if C instances can co-locate in the contexts of A instances.) It could also be the case that a redesign needs to take place. Perhaps the SELECT isn't really needed because there may be no UPDATE TRIGGER for the table.

Example 3: Incorrect Use of `RequiresNew`

The third example is perhaps a bit strange, but is still possible. This time, we also have three instances and components. You can see how they are configured in Table 6.6.

TABLE 6.6 Example 3: Instances, Components, and Transaction Attributes

Instances and Components	Transaction Attribute
aRoot (instance of component A)	TransactionOption.Required
aSecondary (instance of component B)	TransactionOption.Supported
anotherSecondary (instance of component C)	TransactionOption.RequiresNew

This time, aRoot calls aSecondary and aSecondary SELECTs a specific errand. Because of the information in the errand, aRoot understands that the errand must be updated; therefore, it calls anotherSecondary so that it can deal with the UPDATE. No matter what happens afterwards in the activity, the UPDATE must take place and therefore it is put in a separate transaction. The result is the same as for the second example; anotherSecondary grinds to a halt and waits for the timeout.

As a matter of fact, I have never used RequiresNew in any of the systems I have built. The only time I have even thought about it was for my error-logging component, but as I said in Chapter 4, "Adding Debugging Support," I use another trick instead for having the error logged in a separate transaction. The solution to this problem must be a redesign, but first we have to ask ourselves whether it is correct at all that C should run in a transaction of its own. The scenario I presented here was, as I said, a bit strange.

Traps Summary

All three examples of traps that I selected and discussed here were problems arising when several components interacted. None of the problems would have existed if all the code had been put in a single method instead. But that is *not* the moral of this story. That would lead to code bloat. Instead, what I'm saying is that you must understand how different settings affect your transactions and be very careful with error trapping. As usual, COM+ transactions don't change that.

Evaluation of Proposals

As in previous chapters, it's time for me to evaluate the proposals I have presented in this chapter against the criteria I established in Chapter 2.

Evaluation of Transaction Technique Proposal

As I said earlier, the transaction technique to favor is to control transactions in the stored procedures—that is, when you only have one RM. It's a very good idea to let the transactions be controlled in stored procedures when you have a slow network between the components and the database. As a matter of fact, this is most often the solution that gives the best performance and scalability. When version 1 of .NET has been released, you will find my results of a test in which stored procedure controlled transactions are compared to ADO.NET controlled transactions and COM+ controlled transactions at the book's Web site at www.samspublishing.com.

Productivity might be better if you go for automatic transactions instead, because you don't have to code the transactions yourself. In reality, I find the difference in productivity between automatic transactions and local transactions to be small.

Maintainability, reusability, and interoperability may be negatively affected if you don't also prepare for moving to automatic transactions when you need to. Therefore, you should also consider using the proposal I evaluate in the next section.

Evaluation of Transactions in the Architecture Proposal

My proposal of how to deal with transactions in the new architecture is totally independent of the type of consumer, at least as long as you let the consumer stay out of the transaction, which is definitely how it should be. The exception to this is when the consumer is a component that uses automatic transactions, but that is more a matter of interoperability. You should note that the transaction design in the architecture has interoperability as one of its major design goals.

When using pure T-SQL transactions, the most efficient solution for transactions is implemented. This is especially apparent when there is a slow network between the application server and the database server.

Both the performance and the scalability factors are targeted well by the proposal. The main problem is that methods at the Application layer classes that don't need transactions may also have automatic transactions started. There is an easy solution to this (splitting the classes into two parts), but it is not good for maintainability and productivity.

Apart from the drawback just mentioned, I think that the architecture proposal is good for maintainability, reusability, debuggability, and interoperability. To a large extent, this is because of the data access pattern that will be discussed in Chapter 8.

By getting shorter transactions, which is one of the results of the architecture proposal, the reliability will also increase because the risk for deadlocks will decrease.

Evaluation of the Flexible Transaction Design Proposal

The main reason for the flexible transaction design is to increase maintainability. Because of that, reusability and interoperability are improved as well. In the short run, it might be the case that productivity is decreased, but in the long run, it wins.

If you want your components to work well both with automatic and manual transactions, you have to test both situations thoroughly. The proposed design will increase testability because it is easy to just change the settings for some attributes and test again.

What's Next

There has been a lot of talk about business rules in the last few years, but relatively few concrete recommendations for how to handle them have been shown. In the next chapter, I will discuss several different proposals for how to take care of business rules, both in serviced components and in stored procedures.

References

1. T. Ewald. *Transactional COM+: Building Scalable Applications*. Addison-Wesley; 2001.

2. T. Pattison. *Programming Distributed Applications with COM+ and Visual Basic 6.0*. Microsoft Press; 2000.

3. J. Gray and A. Reuter. *Transaction Processing: Concepts and Techniques*. Morgan Kaufmann; 1993.

4. P. Bernstein and E. Newcomer. *Principles of Transaction Processing*. Morgan Kaufmann; 1997.

5. G. Brill. *Applying COM+*. New Riders; 2000.

6. D. Platt. *Understanding COM+*. Microsoft Press; 1999.

Business Rules

IN THIS CHAPTER

Most published architectures, such as Windows DNA, recommend having a tier for business logic, or business rules, and using a component layer to handle this business logic. Yet rarely do you find recommendations for *how* to handle business rules.

Centralizing all business rules to a single layer in the Business tier has its merits, such as having all the rules in one location, but, as always, it's a matter of give and take. While this may be beneficial for maintainability, it can be counter to scalability. Meanwhile, certain rules make more sense in the database from a performance, scalability, and productivity perspective.

Object-orientation is concerned with information hiding, which is good for placing and maintaining business rules during the life span of the system and for quickly and easily distributing and putting a new business rule into operation. My main concerns about business rules are structure and architecture.

In the previous chapter, I said that transactions drive the architecture I use. You can also think of transactions as a form of a business rule. Due to the importance of transactions, as well as other types of business rules, business rules have a major influence on how the architecture is designed. I have now touched briefly on where business rules should be located. In the rest of this chapter, I will discuss the location of business rules in depth and what my proposal is, namely to locate business rules in the Business or Data tier, depending on what makes most sense on a case-by-case basis. I will also look at different ways of constructing the rules, depending on the chosen tier. After that, I will discuss the location and implementation of a set of different examples of business rules. Finally, I will discuss how business rules might be dealt with in the future. Before I do all this, I'd like to start with a short introduction to business rules.

A Short Introduction to Business Rules

What do I mean by *business rules*? The term can be a little misleading. When I refer to business rules, I am referring not only to validations of rules—validations are an important part—but also to ordinary logic, such as core algorithms, transformations, compensations, calculations, and authorizations. Perhaps you prefer the term "business logic" or just "logic." Either way, the term isn't important; it's what the term refers to that matters.

Business rules apply not just to business systems, of course. Business rules can be found in technical systems as well (although developers of technical systems often refer to "domain" and "domain rules" instead). One example of a technical system with a set of business rules is a control system for an elevator. In this example, the business rules may dictate that the closest available elevator should answer any given request. Thus, when the control system is notified that someone on the first floor wants to go up, it sends the elevator waiting at the third floor instead of the one at the ninth floor to answer the request.

No matter the capacity, finding and defining business rules is an activity for both the client and the developer. Hopefully, as the developer you can get the client to consider real-world rules, leaving you to focus on technical rules, such as uniqueness and transactions, that the client probably won't think about. Thinking about business rules is a major step in the analysis and design activities for building a system.

> **NOTE**
>
> Although it is often useful to break down complex topics into categories, I am not going to categorize the business rules in this chapter because it would be too abstract. There are many classifications to be inspired by, and no de-facto standard as I understand it. Instead, I will give several practical examples of different kinds of business rules. For more information about categorizations, see Ronald G. Ross's *The Business Rule Book, Second Edition*,[1] the chapter on business rules in James Martin and James J. Odell's *Object-Oriented Methods*,[2] or the chapters on constraints in Terry Halpin's *Information Modeling and Relational Databases*.[3]

Now that you know what I mean when I refer to business rules, it's time to get down to the nitty-gritty of how and where to deal with them.

Location and Solutions of Business Rules

As you recall from Chapter 5, "Architecture," I use the tiers and layers shown in Figure 7.1 in my architecture proposal as a starting point for many applications.

```
Consumer tier
        Consumer layer
        Consumer Helper layer
Business tier
        Application layer
        Domain layer
        Persistent Access layer
Data tier
        Public Stored Procedures layer
        Private Stored Procedures layer
```

FIGURE 7.1
Tiers and layers in my proposed architecture.

Let's take a closer look at the different tiers we can choose among for locating the business rules.

Locating the Business Rules in the Consumer Tier

Where can I locate my business rules in this architecture? Let's decide that the Consumer tier is not a suitable place for business rules. Why not, you may ask? There are several reasons:

- *User Interface (UI) trends*—There is a new UI trend every year, and many organizations often adjust to these new trends. Because of that, they have to rebuild the UI (and the Consumer tier) or build yet another UI.

- *UI applications*—There are often several different UI applications for a specific set of components. The same rules must apply for all the UI applications.

- *Decentralized consumers*—Some types of consumers will be decentralized (for example, Windows Forms applications) and it might be difficult to force an update to take place for every consumer at the same time.

- *Not in our control*—It's common that another group of developers will develop the consumer(s), and this group will not be the same as the group that will develop the Business and Data tiers.

However, although it's not a good idea to locate business rules in the Consumer tier, it is a good idea to carry out early tests—such as required fields, formats, and so on—in the Consumer tier for scalability reasons so that useless, expensive, and resource-consuming round trips can be skipped. Still, this might mean more maintainability work. Later in the chapter, I will discuss an approach that allows you to have your cake and eat it too.

Locating the Business Rules in the Business Tier

Turning to the Business tier, the basic idea of the Domain layer is simply that it should take care of generic business rules. Doing this is possible in the Application layer instead, but the more rules that can be dealt with in the Domain layer, the better, because several different Application layer classes will use the same Domain layer classes. As I said in Chapter 5, the classes in the Application layer are modeled from the use cases. The classes in the Domain layer model concepts, and those concepts will be used by several use cases. The only rules that should be constructed in the Application layer are those specific to certain use cases only, as well as rules for authorizing business function use.

As you might recall from Chapter 5, I let the Application layer call the Persistent Access layer directly for fetch methods, but I call the Domain layer (which in turn calls the Persistent Access layer) for write methods. Business rules lie at the center of this decision. There are most often no business rules for the specific fetch operations, so a call to the Domain layer would tend to result in just a pass through to the Persistent Access layer. The only value in doing this would be to simplify the Application layer and make it more consistent so that it is only aware of the Domain layer. Still, this advantage doesn't make up for the drawbacks that come from more and "dumb" code.

As I said, when the Application layer requests a write method, the call will go to the Domain layer and the Domain layer then calls the Persistent Access layer. Of course, it would be possible to let the Application layer still call the Persistent Access layer after the Domain layer call has been executed, but I find my proposal is cleaner. In addition, sometimes the Domain layer needs to call the database to fetch data before evaluating the rule. The Domain layer might also know more about what is needed from the database in a specific scenario than the Application layer does. With this design, the Domain layer might also decide to go to the database or to just add rows to the script that will be sent to the database at the end of the scenario, which is completely transparent to the Application layer.

But we have one more layer in the Business tier. Why not let the Persistent Access layer handle the business rules? Well, it could, but it has another well-defined purpose, namely to encapsulate the access of the persistence mechanism, such as SQL Server. In my opinion, we should keep this layer free from business rules.

7

BUSINESS RULES

> **NOTE**
>
> Even though I use SQL scripts that are built by calling the Persistent Access layer and executed in the Data tier, I think of those rules as being located in the Application layer and the Domain layer because those layers are the driving forces and are the layers that define the rules.

Locating the Business Rules in the Data Tier

The next tier is the Data tier, which also is an appropriate tier for several business rules. First of all, you should deal with as many static rules as possible (which the application user shouldn't be able to affect by changing data in the database) using constraints (check constraints, primary keys, and foreign keys) and defaults. The two stored procedure layers are then very suitable for other rules. Thus, the Private Stored Procedure layer is better than the Public Stored Procedure layer as a location for business rules for the same reason as the Domain layer is better than the Application layer. That is, the Private Stored Procedure layer and the Domain layer will be reused more. As a result, there will be more generic code in the Private Stored Procedures layer and in the Domain layer.

It's extremely important to remember that if you decide to put any rules in the Domain layer, you don't let anybody reuse the Persistent Access layer or any lower layer because they will bypass the business rules. In addition, the users shouldn't be granted rights for direct access to tables in the database nor to stored procedures if they don't specifically have to have them. It's best to think of the Application layer as the entry point for users, even if you put *all* rules in the database from day one. You might need to add rules in other layers closer to the consumer in the application's lifetime.

> **NOTE**
>
> There is always a risk that an administrator will update the database tables directly without using the components or the stored procedures. The risk that he or she is violating the business rules is hopefully not that great, but it's still there. By using constraints, the risk is gone.

Assuming that we decide that the two main places for programmed business rules are the Domain layer and the Private Stored Procedures layer, let's take a closer look at the advantages for each approach and how the rules can be constructed.

Locating the Business Rules in the Domain Layer

For generic, concept-oriented business rules, the Domain layer is often a very fitting location. Even though there are numerous possibilities, let's take a look at how the rules can be implemented here.

How Business Rules Can Be Implemented in the Domain Layer

Let's review the architecture in Chapter 5 to see how the classes in the Domain Layer appear. In Figure 5.10 in Chapter 5, you can see the doErrand class and the ISaveable interface that the Application layer uses when calling the class.

Location and Call Mechanism

Having said that, I'd like to start the discussion by looking at where the rules check is located and how it can be accessed. An obvious solution for where to locate business rules is to let the doErrand.Save() method hide a call to a private Check() method. This is to ensure that the provided DataSet is checked according to those rules the class is responsible for checking.

> **NOTE**
>
> Be careful that you don't miss the fact that the data carrier (for example, a DataSet) has been changed with scrolling before you start checking the rules against the DataSet. Also, be careful that you don't touch the state of the data carrier because there is other code expecting the data carrier to be in a particular state. Using Clone() is often a good idea.

Another way to check the rules is through a public interface, for example `ICheckable`, to be used between classes in the Domain layer. The situation that should be solved here is when a Domain class needs another Domain class to check rules on behalf of the first class. I used this second approach a lot in my old architecture (which I discussed in Chapter 5 and Chapter 6, "Transactions"). In the new architecture, it is less useful, because it is totally acceptable for the Application layer to make several calls to the Domain layer within the same transaction.

Processing

When you have decided on the location and call mechanism for your business rules in the Domain layer, it's time to think about how they should be processed. As usual, there are several options:

- *Use ordinary VB code and check rule by rule*—No rocket science here. This is the most typical and the preferred way to go for rules in the Domain layer.

- *Add rows to the SQL script with the help of the Persistent Access layer*—By doing this, you actually delay the execution of the checks until the complete script is executed against the database. It is also the database itself that does the real checking of the rules.

- *Create another SQL script for retrieving data from the database (with the help of the Persistent Access layer, as usual) and use those values to check rule by rule with ordinary VB code*—Note that this solution partly defeats one of the main purposes of the SQL script solution because there will be several round trips to the database. Additionally, if you keep locks at the read rows, you may severely affect throughput.

NOTE

I will discuss the pattern of using SQL scripts for accessing the database in depth in Chapter 8, "Data Access."

Motivation for Using the Domain Layer for Most Business Rules

As you have probably understood by now, or certainly will understand as you read on, I don't think the Domain layer is the only suitable layer to locate business rules, but it certainly has its merits:

- *Certain rules are much easier to write in Visual Basic .NET than in T-SQL*—Among other things, the sophistication, productivity, comprehensiveness, powerfulness, flexibility, and extensibility are much better for Visual Basic .NET as a language compared to T-SQL.

- *Relational databases are very good at set-based processing, but not at row-by-row procedural processing*—Still, procedural rules are not that uncommon after all.

- *The processing will take place at a tier that is easy to scale out*—I have mentioned it before, but it's worth mentioning again—the database is harder to scale out than the application server. Be careful that you don't use too many resources from the database because of this. In the case of static checks, when data doesn't have to be fetched from the database for checking the rules, the Domain layer is a very efficient and suitable location for rules.

> **NOTE**
>
> In Chapter 5, I mentioned that for "small" systems and "simple" systems, it's possible to skip the Domain layer. I also said that this applied to the Private Stored Procedures layer, but I'm less inclined to skip the Private Stored Procedures layer. In any case, think twice before you skip either of these layers. Prepare for future growth by thinking large but initially building small.

Locating the Business Rules in the Private Stored Procedures Layer

Certain rules fit very well in the Private Stored Procedures layer, but before arguing the case for why they do, I will start with a discussion on how they can be implemented.

How Business Rules Can Be Implemented in the Private Stored Procedures Layer

As usual, I prefer to factor out the rules in specific stored procedures to make the code more maintainable. I typically add a Check suffix as the naming convention; thus, a typical stored procedure name for rules that apply only for UPDATE would be Errand_UpdateCheck().

I use two different styles for business rules in stored procedures that perform checks. Assume that an UPDATE is to be done. You can either let the UPDATE take place and read from the database and check the rules before the end of the transaction, or check parameters and read data from the database to check the rules before making the UPDATE.

Listing 7.1 shows sample code in a stored procedure in which the UPDATE takes place and then the data is read back from the database. In Listing 7.2, the second strategy is shown; that is, the data is checked when it comes as parameters to the stored procedure. In both cases, the rule is that the responsible problem solver cannot have more than 10 open problems.

LISTING 7.1 Simplified Example of When the First Strategy Is Used for Checking a Business Rule in a Private Stored Procedure

```
BEGIN TRANSACTION

UPDATE errand
SET responsible = @responsible, ...
WHERE id = @id
--Error trapping goes here.

IF @status = 1 BEGIN

  IF (SELECT COUNT(*)
  FROM errand
  WHERE responsible = @responsible
  AND status = 1) > 10 BEGIN
    SET @anError = 82121
    SET @anErrorMessage =
    'Too many open errands for this problem solver'
    GOTO ExitHandler
  END
END

COMMIT TRANSACTION
```

LISTING 7.2 Simplified Example of When the Second Strategy Is Used for Checking a Business Rule in a Private Stored Procedure

```
IF @status = 1 BEGIN
  IF (SELECT COUNT(*)
  FROM errand
  WHERE responsible = @responsible
  AND status = 1) > 9 BEGIN
    SET @anError = 82121
    SET @anErrorMessage =
    'Too many open errands for this problem solver'
    GOTO ExitHandler
  END
END

BEGIN TRANSACTION

UPDATE errand
SET responsible = @responsible, ...
WHERE id = @id

--Error trapping goes here.
COMMIT TRANSACTION
```

> **NOTE**
>
> As you see in Listings 7.1 and 7.2, I didn't show *real* transaction code and error trapping. You will find a lot more about this topic in Chapter 9, "Error Handling and Concurrency Control."

As you guessed it, both styles have their merits. The advantage to letting the UPDATE take place is that it is simpler and more productive to program because you don't have to send around a lot of parameters between stored procedures with the only purpose of evaluating rules. If you use triggers (I don't), another advantage is that you check the rules after triggers have done their job, which could be good because the triggers might have changed the data.

The advantage of checking parameters before starting the UPDATE is a matter of efficiency. You don't do an UPDATE that has to be ROLLedBACK directly after. Another, more important, efficiency aspect is that you get shorter transactions as well. It is also easier and more natural to evaluate rules at transitions with this approach. If you first perform the UPDATE, you don't know what the "before" value was when you go to see whether the transition was a correct one, and there is also a chance that you will reduce the length of the transaction and the locking time.

> **NOTE**
>
> We could have a similar discussion for the .NET components. Should only the data container (a DataSet for example) be sent over to the validation method, or should just the values needed be sent over as parameters? In this case, I'm more inclined to skip fine-grained parameters.

Why I Don't Use Triggers Anymore

In the past, I used triggers a lot—too much really. I liked the idea of triggers and wrote very complicated ones. However, when the time came to make changes, it was a real mess. In addition, it's difficult to test triggers completely, to follow execution sequences, and to write complicated triggers correctly. Writing set-safe triggers can also lead to slow execution. (There are other problems associated with triggers, too, but I'll stop here.)

Because the only way to call the database in my applications is through stored procedures, I don't really need triggers. As a result, I have stopped using them completely.

Motivation for Using the Private Stored Procedures Layer for Most Business Rules

Earlier I said that an advantage of locating business rules in the Domain layer is that it is harder to scale out the database. As always, advantages can become disadvantages. Due to it being more difficult to scale out, the database is more centralized than the application server because the database will be scaled out less often. That was a subtle advantage. Let's take a look at some other more obvious advantages to locating business rules in the Private Stored Procedures layer:

- *There are more reuse levels*—If you want to, you can reuse all layers in both the Business tier and the Data tier if you place all your business rules in the Private Stored Procedures layer. If you place some rules in the Domain layer, you can only reuse the Domain layer and the Application layer.

- *It is easier to work with data*—Business rules are often about data. Databases are good at working with data.

- *It is more efficient for certain rules*—For example, this is true when you need to read data first from the database. This way, you reduce round trips between the application server and database server. You also reduce the amount of data that is sent over the network. (However, my data access solution makes this less of an advantage.)

- *Redeployment is easy*—It is easy to redeploy a stored procedure when a rule has changed.

The biggest drawback to putting the rules in the Private Stored Procedures layer is the lack of portability between different database products. As I said in the Preface, you must decide what your first priority is—whether it is to create an application that is portable between different operating systems, types of machines, and database products, or whether it is to use the chosen platform as effectively as possible. You can't have both. I have decided to opt for the latter in this book.

Proposal for Where to Locate Different Business Rules

We have now discussed two typical locations for business rules—the Domain layer and the Private Stored Procedures layer—as well as their advantages and disadvantages. So, which one should you choose? As always, the answer to the question depends on many factors. Furthermore, I have already recommended that you locate certain rules in the Application layer, the Public Stored Procedures layer, or on the base tables (for example, with the help of constraints). To give you a feeling for how I choose where to place business rules, I will describe some typical rules in the next section and then explain where I would locate and how I would implement those rules.

Location of Business Rules in Classic Windows DNA

In my opinion, Classic Windows DNA prefers to put the business rules in the components rather than in the database. Sten Sundblad and Per Sundblad, in their book *Designing for Scalability with Microsoft Windows DNA,*[4] recommend placing business rules in both locations. The authors discuss a few business rules and recommend that those that can easily be dealt with by declarations in the database be handled that way. An example is uniqueness requirements that can easily be dealt with by a PRIMARY KEY, UNIQUE CONSTRAINT, or UNIQUE INDEX. I agree with this approach. However, when it comes to more complex business rules, Sundblad and Sundblad are more pro-components instead of pro-stored procedures than I am.

As I said, the easy answer to where to place the business rules for the examples I will show in the next section is that it depends. Is there a slow network between components and database? Are there already 10 application servers in place? Will there only be 15 simultaneous users? These are the kind of questions you must ask yourself as you make your decision. When I discuss my main proposals for my examples, I will assume a basic situation in which there is one database server and one application server, and that the network between the database server and the application server is fast. I will also assume that there are 50 concurrent users with, say, one minute of thinking time. I will also keep in mind that there may be more users in the future.

> **NOTE**
>
> This was, of course, a loose definition of the situation. As you know, it's possible to kill almost any configuration with five users, while the same configuration may also be able to handle hundreds of users. It depends on the tasks that have to be done and how they are accomplished.

Please note that you should consider my discussion that follows only as a selection of *examples*—it's not exhaustive by any means. Having said that, let's review the database model shown in Figure 5.2 in Chapter 5 for the Acme HelpDesk sample application. As you see in that figure, there are two tables named errand and action. In errand, the problem is described, and in action, the attempts to solve the problem are described. Now let's look at the first business rule example.

Business Rule Example 1: When an Errand Is Deleted, All Its Actions Should Be Deleted Too

Often I prefer not to delete rows from the database but instead to mark them as disabled to not lose the log, so to say. Sometimes you need to delete rows. If this is the case for the master rows, you also want to delete the detail rows, if any, so referential integrity isn't violated.

Because SQL Server 2000 supports declarative cascading delete for foreign keys, it is a candidate technique for handling this business rule. However, I prefer to program the rule in the Private Stored Procedure layer instead because you may also want to "intercept" the DELETE of the detail rows and perform something else before the DELETE takes place. My proposal is to use the Private Stored Procedures layer for this rule.

Business Rule Example 2: It Should Be Impossible to Report an Errand with an Unknown Category

As you will see, I am not going to include an example of a business rule where uniqueness is required. I think it's obvious that a constraint should be used in the database. You may find it obvious that a declarative foreign key should be used for Example 2 too—that is, it shouldn't be possible to report an errand with an unknown category. However, I'm still using it as an example because I'd like to point out the need to save incomplete rows to the database without breaking foreign keys constraints. To solve this problem, I often give default values to the foreign keys so that they point to a dummy row in their parent table. Simple, but efficient, and for wide tables where the user has to enter a lot of information, this is an especially good solution.

Business Rule Example 3: The Price Calculation of the Errand Should Depend on a Complex and Dynamic Discount Model

Assume that the customer who reports an errand must pay for the work on the errand. If the user has had a certain amount of errands in the last month, he or she gets a specific discount. There are several intervals with different discounts. Different customers also have different discount agreements, and different errand categories also give different prices. (These were just a few examples of the factors used for calculating the price.)

In this situation, I prefer to have the calculation in the Private Stored Procedure layer because a lot of data must be read from the database before the calculation can be executed. Another good approach could be to have the calculation in the Domain layer, especially if all the necessary data for making the calculation could be cached. However, there are drawbacks with this type of caching that make me reluctant to say that this is my basic recommendation.

> **NOTE**
>
> I will discuss the merits and problems of server-side caching in Chapter 8.

It's quite common that you want the consumer to do a precalculation without making a round trip to the Application layer. For example, assume that a user is placing an order, adding one article after another. He or she would probably find it useful to see how much the price is after each article is added. For most situations, the same result must be reached in both the ongoing and final calculations; otherwise, the user will get upset.

How should you deal with this? The simple solution is *not* to deal with it, but to allow there to be a round trip. (In the case of classic Web applications, this is not a problem because you, as a user, normally expect a round trip to the server for the calculation to take place.) If this solution is not good enough, you can let the consumer reuse the same component. Even better, you can let a calculation component serialize itself from the Business tier to the Consumer tier with .NET.

> **NOTE**
>
> At the time of writing, letting a calculation component serialize itself from the Business tier to the Consumer tier in .NET is a technique I haven't explored.

Business Rule Example 4: An Errand Must Be of a Correct State

Status codes are extremely common in workflow applications. The rule that an errand must be of a correct state could mean several different things, mainly depending on how the state is marked. If it is a single column, it is simple to check that the column has a valid value, for example, with the help of a foreign key to a lookup table or—more typically because this is system information rather than user information—as a check constraint in the database.

The state could also be understood from the values of several different columns. For example, if a couple of columns have had values, the state of the errand is, at any rate, "reported." If the closedby column has a value, the errand is, at any rate, "closed," and so on. In this case, the rule will be to determine the state of a specific errand rather than to check that it is a correct state. Because several static rules differ between different statuses, using a column to mark the status of a row makes other rules easier to implement.

Business Rule Example 5: An Errand May Only Transform from One State to a Specific Set of Other States

Let's assume that there is a way to easily determine the current state of an errand, such as a status column in the table. If there is, it's quite easy to check what the current value is and what the new value is. If you use DataSets for holding data, you have both the new and the original value there all the time. In the case of stored procedures, you can read the old value from the database and check the new value as a parameter before you save.

I have a hard time deciding on where this kind of rule should be located. The last time I built a system with a rule like this I had the rule located in a stored procedure. The advantages of the Domain layer solution is that you don't disturb the database when there is no use in doing so, and you don't make a read from the table. The advantage of the solution of putting the rule in the Private Stored Procedures layer is that the rule is closer to the database so you get more possible reuse layers. I prefer to have the rule in the Domain layer.

Business Rule Example 6: Only Users of Specific Groups May Use a Specific Business Function

When you want only users of specific groups to use a specific business function, COM+ role-based security (RBS) is one way to go. You can build a similar mechanism with common language runtime code access security, but I think the COM+ variant is easier to use and automatically more in accordance with its basic purpose. No matter which version you choose, I prefer to have this business rule implemented in the Business tier instead of in the Data tier. This makes for one less task (and a pretty large one too) for the database to handle. This recommendation is especially clear if the alternative is to let the end users log in to the database with personal accounts. That approach is a scalability trap because connection pooling won't be able to reuse connections between users.

But even if the user won't use a personal logon to the database, the stored procedures aren't business related. The granularity is much smaller if you compare the stored procedures to the Application layer classes, and there is no natural mapping between use cases and stored procedures.

> **NOTE**
>
> Unfortunately, in version 1 of .NET, COM+ RBS doesn't work over .NET Remoting, only over DCOM. In my opinion, this is the most important caveat regarding the .NET integration of COM+.

Business Rule Example 7: You May Only Read Your Own Errands

This rule is security related. I just said that I like COM+ role-based security to move out the security issues from the database so the user doesn't have to log on to the database with a personal account. Thanks to this, security checks can be defined in accordance with a flexible and prebuilt model.

However, COM+ role-based security on its own can't solve users being able to read only their own errands. In this particular case, I actually prefer to have the check in the stored procedure instead. I don't want to send the rows from the database to the Business tier for no reason if the user tries to read a row that he or she doesn't own. A drawback with the approach of having this check in the stored procedure is that you have to send the userId as a parameter to the stored procedure.

> **NOTE**
>
> For the solution of sending a userId as a parameter to the stored procedure to work at all, each row has to be marked with the owner in a column. This is true no matter where you decide to place the rule.

Business Rule Example 8: Every Action Must Be "Stamped" with Date, Time, and UserId for the Reporter

This is a simple yet common rule. In my opinion, the most typical place to handle this is in the Private Stored Procedures layer. You can use a DEFAULT in the table definition for the date and time by using the GETDATE() function; for the createdby, you have to provide a parameter to the stored procedure instead.

Business Rule Example 9: When an Errand Is Closed, an Action Should Be Created

This rule is an example of a compensating rule. "If this happens, this should also happen." You may wonder what the reason in the real application is for a rule like this. Assume that it is possible to reopen an errand that was incorrectly closed. Then it is very interesting to have the action row as a log to see that the errand had been closed earlier.

In my opinion, this example is a typical one for when to handle business rules in the Private Stored Procedures layer. The drawback is that you might have to provide a few more parameters (some of which might seem unrelated to the only task you think you are doing as a consumer of the stored procedure).

Business Rule Example 10: Every Errand Must Be Marked with a Unique Running Value

It is very common that you need a running value of some kind, such as:

```
1, 2, 3, 4, 5...
```

or

```
N20011031-0001, N20011031-0002, N20011031-0003, N20011101-0001...
```

The first example is a common incrementing numeric series, while the second example is a series using a prefix and the date with an incrementing numeric series. The first example might be the primary key of the table, but I prefer not to use the second example for that purpose. In any case, if the series is used for letting users associate to a certain row, I prefer not to have it as the primary key but only as an alternate key. (Nowadays, my favorite primary key data type is the UNIQUE IDENTIFIER, as I told you in Chapter 5.)

To create the first series, you can use an IDENTITY to get that functionality automatically, or you can roll your own solution, typically in a stored procedure. For the second example, you have to build it on your own. Because I have to consider earlier values, for scalability reasons and for shortening locks, I prefer to deal with this task in the Private Stored Procedures layer.

Why Scalability Won't Suffer If You Execute Logic in the Database

I've heard it said many times—particularly from Oracle experts—that the database shouldn't be used for logic, at least not if a scalable application is required. The main argument is that it is difficult and expensive to scale out the database, so it should do as little as possible to avoid becoming a bottleneck.

In my opinion, there is one problem with their reasoning. If the data has to be fetched anyway for evaluating a simple rule, it won't hurt scalability to stay in the database and evaluate the rule there instead of transporting the data to the components and then evaluating the rule in the components. As a matter of fact, it will often be better for scalability. The same work must be done in both cases for the database. In one case, the data must be transported to the components, and in the other case, there will be a single IF clause. You will typically also get shorter transactions if rules like these are evaluated in the database because you often have to hold a lock between the check and the writing to the database. If you have to transport the data to the Business tier, that lock will be kept longer and throughput might suffer.

They are right that the database will become a bottleneck faster if the rule is evaluated in the database, but that is just because more users can be serviced with one application server and one database server. If the database does nothing else than perform pure SELECT, UPDATE, INSERT, and DELETE statements, there will probably be much more round trip utilization so that the round trips can be the first bottleneck. Alternatively, the application server must be cloned to be able to stress the database enough to make the database become the bottleneck. When the database finally becomes the bottleneck in this case, you have perhaps four application servers (but it might also be so that there is another bottleneck before the database becomes one in this case too). The only problem is that the number of serviced users is the same as with one application and one database server when the database is executing logic too and not only pure SELECT, UPDATE, INSERT, and DELETE statements. Which solution do you find more scalable?

Business Rule Example 11: The Date for Closing May Not Be Earlier Than the Report Date

This is an example of a relationship rule between properties. It is a typical example of a rule that I think should be dealt with as a check constraint, but using the Domain layer here is also a good solution.

> **NOTE**
>
> One drawback with the declarative approach for checking rules is that it is harder to determine what the problem is. You get a generic error code from the database, and you have to parse the error description if you want to find out more about what the exact problem is. This is actually a reason why handling the task in stored procedures could be better than a constraint.

Business Rule Example 12: Those Responsible for Solving Errands May Not Have More Than Ten Open Errands

This example is similar to the previous one, but this time the rule is not to be evaluated within a certain row, but rather between rows. Even in this case, I prefer to deal with the rule as a check constraint (or possibly with a private stored procedure). Remember, more data must be read.

To solve the problem as a check constraint, you can use a scalar user-defined function. See Listing 7.3 for an example of a solution and Listing 7.4 for an example of the constraint.

LISTING 7.3   Scalar UDF for Solving Example 12

```
CREATE FUNCTION OpenErrandsForProblemSolver
(@problemSolverId UNIQUEIDENTIFIER)
RETURNS INTEGER AS
BEGIN
   DECLARE @theReturn INT

   SELECT @theReturn = COUNT(*)
   FROM errand
   WHERE responsible = @problemSolverId
   AND status = 1

   RETURN @theReturn
END
```

LISTING 7.4   Constraint for Solving Example 12

```
([dbo].[OpenErrandsForProblemSolver]([responsible]) < 11)
```

Business Rule Example 13: Only Solve an Errand If the Reporter Has Paid His or Her Membership

Once again, you have to read information from the database to decide whether this rule has been met or not. As usual, when this is the case, I prefer to deal with the rule in the Data tier, if possible as a check constraint, or otherwise in the Private Stored Procedures layer.

Business Rule Example 14: Closing Date May Not Be Later Than Today

In a way, this is a static rule to check. Today's date is not static, but no user needs to adjust it at intervals. The date is well known, so to say. In this case, I think the Domain layer is the best place for the rule, but a check constraint or the Private Stored Procedures layer works well too.

When it is a matter of time instead of dates, it is important to see that you have your machines time-synchronized. Of course you don't always have control of the client machines, which is a problem worth thinking more about. You can easily check that the client hasn't cheated with the time if you let the client set the time. On the other hand, if you do this, there is no real point to letting the client set the time in the first place. Yet another related problem is that of the different time zones. It's often a good idea to store all times in Greenwich Mean Time (GMT)/ Universal Time Coordinate (UTC) format.

Business Rule Example 15: It Should Be Impossible to Categorize Too High a Level of "Seriousness" Depending on the Customer Contract

I just discussed a static rule, but this example is dependent on dynamic information that the end users have the option of changing. Yes, you've guessed right: I think this rule belongs in the database, ideally in the Private Stored Procedures layer.

Business Rule Example 16: It Should Be Possible to Create a Halfway-Solved Errand Because of an Automatic Alarm

This is an example of when I create an instance out of a dynamic template. When the alarm sounded, a couple of actions were done automatically by the system and those should be logged as actions in the database. The template could be kept in a table in the database, and it will be most efficient to deal with this rule in the Private Stored Procedures layer. There is then no need to send a lot of data from the Business tier to the Data tier.

NOTE

Although this example is a bit strange, the concept is common in real-world applications.

You may think that I'm too fond of putting rules in the Data tier. Therefore, I will end this section by giving you a typical example of a rule that I don't think belongs in the database.

Business Rule Example 17: Calculate Priority of Errand in Accordance with Complex but Static Rules

I have already indicated so, but here I go again. It is better to have complex algorithms that don't need more information from the database to execute in the Domain layer than in the Private Stored Procedures layer. I'm very adamant about this. It's just so much easier to write this kind of code in Visual Basic .NET, for example, than in T-SQL.

Summary of Business Rules Examples and Solutions

Table 7.1 summarizes the examples we just discussed and the solutions I recommended. Keep in mind that when it is necessary for the user to dynamically update the values against which the rules will be checked, the database is the best place for the rules. In addition, for static values, the Domain layer or constraints in the database are the best options. Finally, of course, I may have chosen examples that are more database-centric than is common for your applications. In any case, I think these examples paint a clear picture of my reasoning when I decide where to put a rule.

TABLE 7.1   Business Rule Examples and Recommendations

Business Rule Number	Description	Recommended Location for the Most Typical Situation
1	When an errand is deleted, all its actions should be deleted too.	Private Stored Procedures layer
2	It should be impossible to report an errand with an unknown category.	Database constraint
3	The price calculation of the errand depends upon a complex and dynamic discount model.	Private Stored Procedures layer
4	An errand must be of a correct state.	Database constraint

TABLE 7.1   Continued

Business Rule Number	Description	Recommended Location for the Most Typical Situation
5	An errand may only transform from one state to a specific set of other states.	Domain layer
6	Only users of specific groups may use a specific business function.	Application layer
7	You may only read your own errands.	Private Stored Procedures layer
8	Every action must be "stamped" with date, time, and userId for the Reporter.	Private Stored Procedures layer
9	When an errand is closed, an action should be created.	Private Stored Procedures layer
10	Every errand shall be marked with a unique running value.	Private Stored Procedures layer
11	The date for closing may not be earlier than the report date.	Database constraint
12	Those responsible for solving errands may not have more than ten open errands.	Database constraint
13	Only start to solve an errand if the reporter has paid his or her membership.	Database constraint
14	Closing date may not be later than today.	Domain layer
15	It should be impossible to categorize too high a level of "seriousness" depending on the customer contract.	Private Stored Procedures layer
16	It should be possible to create a halfway solved errand because of an automatic alarm.	Private Stored Procedures layer
17	Calculate priority of errand in accordance with complex, but static rules.	Domain layer

Business Rule Tips

In this section, I will share with you some miscellaneous and disparate tips I have collected related to business rules.

Tip 1: Define Once, Execute at Several Tiers

The most important place to have your data checked for consistency is at the Data tier, so that integrity of the data is protected no matter what. Several tests are easily added with constraints in the database; even so, it would often be beneficial to check the same rules in earlier layers as well. If we start duplicating the rules for different tiers by hand, we are creating a maintainability nightmare.

At the time of writing, I haven't experimented much with this idea, but I think it could be wise to drag out information from the database about the business rules there, create Intermediate Language (IL) code on-the-fly, and execute it with the help of Emit() in .NET. (I have previously thought about solutions other than Emit(), such as using VBScript or JavaScript, but I now think Emit() of IL is the most promising solution.) The code could execute in the Business tier, saving some useless round trips to the database. Even better, let the code also execute in the Consumer tier, and skip even more useless round trips, and the user will get a snappier usability experience. You should, of course, not re-create the IL at every call, but rather periodically, for example, once a day.

At first, the simple rules, such as those found as constraints, can be dragged out from the database. You can then also drag out the rules put in stored procedures, but that probably requires quite a lot of work, as well as a lot of discipline and coding conventions when you write the stored procedures in the first place. Finally, you could, of course, also drag out data from the database that is used for evaluating against.

This sounds pretty cool, doesn't it? And it's great for scalability, but once again, make sure you have your business rules firmly implemented at one place first before you even start thinking about this idea.

In a way, DataSets sort of provides you with this effect, because it is here you can state that relationships between master and detail rows (in the form of DataTables), and the DataSet will evaluate those rules for you. (Assume a DataSet contains information about dogs and owners. If a rule is that a dog must have an owner, such a rule can be "told" to the DataSet so it's not possible to add dogs to the DataSet without having correct owners for those dogs. That is, the referential integrity check can execute at the Consumer tier too, as an early test.)

XML Schema Definitions (XSD) is a technique that you can use manually, so to speak, to easily have some rules evaluated at several tiers. The built-in option to use regular expressions in

.NET could also be helpful if you want to write a generic rule engine for which the rules can be moved between tiers.

Tip 2: Deal with Warnings Only

If you like to just give a warning back to the user, it can be a bit tricky—that is, raising an exception with `Throw()` isn't the right mechanism for warnings only. For example, just think about what warning exceptions would do to transactional classes that use the `AutoComplete()` attribute. A better approach is to use a custom method to signal the warning to the user.

Tip 3: Report Several Problems at Once

Have you ever filled in forms at the Web and had an error message, taken care of the problem, had another error message, and so on? I'll bet you have. I'm also sure you hated this. Sometimes, it is nice for users if they are given information about all the errors they have made in one message. For that to work, you can't stop checking rules just because you find a problem. Instead, you have to go through all the rules. For rules in stored procedures, you can make a `RAISERROR()` for every problem, have the components then iterate the errors collected, and produce one exception to send back to the end user with the information about all the problems.

When it comes to having rules in the components, you just gather all the information and then raise the error afterwards with `Throw()` instead of after every problem. You don't have to do it this way, but it's the most direct approach.

As a matter of fact, this is a very good situation for using a custom exception, so that you let the exception have a collection with one item for each broken business rule.

Tip 4: Remember Which Layer Is Responsible for Displaying Error Messages to the Users

I've seen error messages in the stored procedures being used in the consumer tier in error dialogs more than once. (This actually means that I have done it myself several times.) Under stress, this is a common mistake but—as I say in the heading—remember that it is the Consumer Helper layer's responsibility to produce user-friendly error messages for the end users. The error messages you use in the stored procedures are for programmers.

> **NOTE**
>
> In Chapter 9, I will discuss error handling and error messages in greater detail.

Evaluation of Proposal

The evaluation of my proposal is different in this chapter than in other chapters. In this chapter, I will only have one evaluation section, even though there have been several different proposals. In so doing, I will evaluate the overall philosophy of the chapter—that all rules should be evaluated where they make most sense. For information systems, that is very often in the Data tier.

Evaluation of Proposal for Where to Locate Different Business Rules

It shouldn't matter at all which type of consumer is used for determining where the business rules should be located. The Business tier and Data tier shouldn't be influenced by the Consumer tier, and, in the case of business rules, they should definitely not be influenced by it.

However, physical restrictions influence the decisions very much. Which of the servers are fast? Which of the servers must you be extremely careful with loading? Where do you have slow connections? These are the kinds of questions you must ask yourself. If you need data from the database to evaluate a rule, the chances are that this rule should live in the Data tier. In addition, of course, the Data tier can be a bad choice, such as when complex calculations and procedural algorithms are used.

Performance and scalability will often win if the business rules are located in the Data tier, but, as always, this isn't always the case. Once again, watch out for complex calculations, for example. A large percentage of all transactions may also fail because of broken business rules. It would then be a bad decision for scalability and performance to travel all the way to the Data tier to discover this if it can be determined earlier.

Using the Data tier for business rules is great for reusability because you will get more reuse layers. I also think it is very good for reliability because there is less risk that any scenarios bypass the rules. When it comes to maintainability and productivity, the Data tier is not the way to go for some rules. Depending on your background as a developer, stored procedures might be a real productivity trap if used for business rules.

Finally, when it comes to farm and cluster enabling, the Data tier is a slightly better location for business rules because it is less common that the database is scaled out. Then, there is no problem of changing a rule at several servers at exactly the same time because the rule is only located at one server. Not a huge difference, but a difference all the same.

What's Next

For several chapters now, I have been going on about my proposal for how to access the database with the help of creating an SQL script that is sent in one go. In the next chapter, I will explore this pattern in depth. I will also discuss server-side caching and how to send a lot of data in each stored procedure call.

References

1. R. Ross. *The Business Rule Book, Second Edition*. Business Rule Solutions; 1997.
2. J. Martin and J. Odell. *Object-Oriented Methods, Second Edition*. Prentice Hall; 1998.
3. T. Halpin. *Information Modeling and Relational Databases*. Morgan Kaufmann; 2001.
4. S. Sundblad and P. Sundblad. *Designing for Scalability with Microsoft Windows DNA*. Microsoft Press; 2000.

Data Access

IN THIS CHAPTER

For several chapters now, I've been discussing how important it is to prepare for debugging, to make use of a good architecture, to focus on transactions, and so on. In this chapter, we'll look at another aspect that is extremely important when you want to build scalable, reliable, and maintainable systems—data access. As Scott Guthrie, the architect of ASP.NET, says "Think hard about data access. This is really the difference between successful applications and unsuccessful applications."[1]

This chapter will focus on an unusual, but very effective, pattern for how to interact with the Data tier. I have touched on this pattern in earlier chapters, and I will also be discussing it in the context of the architecture presented in Chapter 5, "Architecture." After that, I will discuss how to send an "array of rows" to a stored procedure, as well as look at a small sampling of server-side caching. Finally, we'll discuss how to prepare your code for future schema changes.

My Proposal for a Data Access Pattern

You have several styles to choose from when you are deciding how to call the stored procedures in the Data tier from the Business tier. Before I get into my proposal, I'd like to briefly recap how the interaction between the Business tier and the Data tier is normally handled using ADO.NET's SqlCommand class.

How Stored Procedures Are Normally Called with ADO.NET

In Listing 8.1, you can see an example of code that uses ADO.NET for calling a stored procedure called a_Errand_Delete().

LISTING 8.1   Typical Code for Using ADO.NET to Call a Stored Procedure

```
Dim aConnection As New SqlClient.SqlConnection(connectionString)
Dim aCommand As New SqlClient.SqlCommand("a_Errand_Insert", aConnection)

Try
    aCommand.CommandType = CommandType.StoredProcedure

    aCommand.Parameters.Add(New SqlClient.SqlParameter("@RETURN_VALUE", _
    System.Data.SqlDbType.Int, 4, _
    System.Data.ParameterDirection.ReturnValue, False, CType(10, Byte), _
    CType(0, Byte), "", System.Data.DataRowVersion.Current, Nothing))

    aCommand.Parameters.Add(New SqlClient.SqlParameter("@id", _
    SqlDbType.UniqueIdentifier)).Value = Guid.NewGuid()
```

LISTING 8.1   Continued

```
aCommand.Parameters.Add(New SqlClient.SqlParameter("@description", _
SqlDbType.VarChar, 50)).Value = "Problem with..."

'And so on for the rest of the parameters...
aConnection.Open()
aCommand.ExecuteNonQuery()

'More about Catch blocks in the next chapter.
Finally
    Jnsk.Db.Helper.ReleaseConnection(aConnection)
End Try
```

As you see in Listing 8.1, it's relatively straightforward to make a call to a stored procedure with ADO.NET. Most developers will be accustomed to using this technique, but I'm not totally satisfied with this approach. I see a few shortcomings with the typical ADO.NET way of calling stored procedures, including the following:

- Your code will be lengthy because you are forced to write a lot of code for every parameter.

- Your code becomes tightly coupled to ADO.NET. What happens if Microsoft changes the syntax again? Many beta testers recognized this problem between beta 1 and 2 of ADO.NET. The developers who had used custom helpers were happy, but the others were not. In a way, the short history of and move from Data Access Objects (DAO) to Remote Data Objects (RDO) to Active X Data Objects (ADO) to ADO.NET also provides support for this argument.

- You can't use pure T-SQL transactions, or rather, there is no point in using pure T-SQL transactions instead of ADO.NET-controlled transactions. You could handle the previous two disadvantages with helpers, but the disadvantage of not being able to use pure T-SQL transactions directly requires a totally different approach. It might not be so bad to use ADO.NET-controlled transactions instead, but your transactions will be slightly longer.

Another typical approach developers use for accessing the database through ADO.NET is "registering" which stored procedure to use for changed rows in a DataSet, which stored procedure to use for added rows, and which stored procedure to use for deleted rows. Listing 8.2 provides a code sample in which a_Errand_Insert() is registered as the stored procedure to use for added rows to the DataSet. (In this case, the code shown is what you can autogenerate with the help of the component designer.)

LISTING 8.2   Code for Registering a Stored Procedure to Execute Once for Each Added
Row in a `DataSet`

```
Me.SqlInsertCommand1 = New System.Data.SqlClient.SqlCommand()
...


Me.SqlInsertCommand1.CommandText = "[a_Errand_Insert]"
Me.SqlInsertCommand1.CommandType = System.Data.CommandType.StoredProcedure
Me.SqlInsertCommand1.Connection = Me.SqlConnection1

Me.SqlInsertCommand1.Parameters.Add _
(New System.Data.SqlClient.SqlParameter("@RETURN_VALUE", _
System.Data.SqlDbType.Int, 4, _
System.Data.ParameterDirection.ReturnValue, False, _
CType(10, Byte), CType(0, Byte), "", _
System.Data.DataRowVersion.Current, Nothing))

Me.SqlInsertCommand1.Parameters.Add__
(New System.Data.SqlClient.SqlParameter("@id", _
System.Data.SqlDbType.UniqueIdentifier, 16))

Me.SqlInsertCommand1.Parameters.Add _
(New System.Data.SqlClient.SqlParameter("@description", _
System.Data.SqlDbType.VarChar, 50))


...
Me.SqlDataAdapter1.InsertCommand = Me.SqlInsertCommand1
```

The disadvantages mentioned with the "manual" technique (lengthy code, tight coupling to
ADO.NET, and no pure T-SQL transactions) also apply here. A further disadvantage is that
you lose some control over exactly what is going on, and you have to learn another technique
for handling problems, apart from calling the stored procedures on your own. It might not be
completely fair to make comparisons with the dreaded `UpdateBatch()` of ADO—the new
approach in ADO.NET is much better because you have some control over what methods will
be used in different cases. Still, the degree of control you have isn't always enough. The risk of
future changes by Microsoft and no direct opportunity to use pure T-SQL transactions apply
here too. Therefore, let's take a look at my new proposal, which avoids some of these problems.

My Data Access Proposal in Detail

I wrote the first version of my data access pattern in VB6 for an application in which I had a
slow connection between the Business tier and the Data tier. Since then, I've used it for applications with ordinary configurations too. (If you want to read about the VB6 version, you'll
find an article called "Round Trips Are Evil—Reduce Them!" in Pinnacle Publishing's *Visual*

Basic Developer, July 2001.[2]) Let's discuss my new version of the data access pattern, rebuilt from scratch for .NET.

The first goal of the pattern was to reduce round trips between the Business tier and the Data tier by doing more between those tiers at each round trip. Therefore, I collect all necessary information about all the stored procedure calls that will execute together, and I build an SQL script that is executed in one round trip.

The second goal was to come up with an efficient approach for how to use pure T-SQL transactions when a transaction has to span several stored procedure calls, which is, of course, a common requirement. The SQL script solution solves this too.

A bonus with the proposal is that you have a great debugging opportunity because you can intercept the SQL script, copy it, and execute it in the SQL Query Analyzer. Change the SQL script slightly until you get the expected result, and then make the necessary changes in the code so that the desired SQL script is generated.

> **NOTE**
>
> Normally, I hate scripts such as those written in VBScript for old ASP, for example, but autogenerated SQL scripts are something else!

Yet another benefit of my proposal is that you get a helper for decreasing the amount of code: Your code is decoupled from ADO.NET to better handle future changes, and your productivity is increased.

The Generated SQL Script

Before we get going on how my data access pattern proposal can be used and how it works, let's take a look at the result we hope to achieve. In Listing 8.3, you can see an example of an SQL script created with the data access pattern. In the SQL script, the public stored procedure a_Errand_Insert() is called.

> **NOTE**
>
> In the code in Listing 8.3, I decided to only show two parameters. Adding more parameters doesn't really add any value to the description. This applies to several of the code examples in this chapter.

LISTING 8.3   Script Created with the Data Access Proposal

```
DECLARE @theSource uddtSource
, @anError INT
, @anErrorMessage uddtErrorMessage
, @aReturnValue INT

SET NOCOUNT ON
SET @anError = 0
SET @anErrorMessage = ''
SET @theSource = 'SQL script used by ErrandReport'

EXEC JnskTrace_Begin @theSource

DECLARE @theTranCountAtEntry INT
SET @theTranCountAtEntry = @@TRANCOUNT
IF @theTranCountAtEntry = 0 BEGIN
  SET TRANSACTION ISOLATION LEVEL READ UNCOMMITTED
  BEGIN TRAN
END

EXEC @aReturnValue = a_Errand_Insert
@id='A9FC3FAB-B17D-464f-9DFF-2EFF99AFEF69'
, @description='Problem with...', ...

SET @anError = @@ERROR
IF @anError <> 0 BEGIN
  SET @anErrorMessage =
  '@@ERROR-problem with call to a_Errand_Insert'
  GOTO ExitHandler
END
ELSE IF @aReturnValue <> 0 BEGIN
  SET @anError = @aReturnValue
  SET @anErrorMessage =
  '@aReturnValue-problem with call to a_Errand_Insert'
  GOTO ExitHandler
END

ExitHandler:
  IF @theTranCountAtEntry = 0 AND @@TRANCOUNT > 0 BEGIN
    IF @anError = 0 BEGIN
      COMMIT TRAN
    END
    ELSE BEGIN
      ROLLBACK TRAN
```

LISTING 8.3   Continued

```
   END
END

IF @anError <> 0 BEGIN
  EXEC JnskError_Raise @theSource
  , @anError, @anErrorMessage
END

EXEC JnskTrace_End @theSource
```

Note that in reality, I wouldn't use an explicit transaction in the script shown in Listing 8.3 because only one stored procedure is called. I am only using an explicit transaction to show how it is done and how it looks in the script. If the stored procedure a_Errand_Insert() needs a transaction, it will start one on its own. The developer who writes the code that generates the SQL script shouldn't have to know about the internals of the stored procedures. This is especially important if a stored procedure is going to be changed so that a transaction is needed even though it wasn't needed before. The exception to this is when a script has to decide what Transaction Isolation Level (TIL) to use. Then, the developer must know a great deal about the internals of the stored procedures. Once again, if no explicit transaction has to be started from the script, but the stored procedure needs a transaction, the stored procedure (or rather the developer of the stored procedure) will decide what TIL to use.

> **NOTE**
>
> As you can see in Listing 8.3, there are many similarities between the generated SQL script and the standardized code structure for stored procedures that was discussed in Chapter 5. The SQL script also involves a great deal of error handling, which I will discuss in detail in Chapter 9, "Error Handling and Concurrency Control."

The SQL script shown in Listing 8.3 will then be sent to the database and executed without any extra round trips between the Business tier and the Data tier. This is what we are after. Note especially how the transaction is handled. It's exactly the same approach as the one I discussed for T-SQL transactions in stored procedures in Chapter 6, "Transactions." If there is already an active transaction when the SQL script starts to execute (for example, a COM+ transaction), I don't handle transactions in the SQL script.

External Design of My Data Access Proposal

When I refer to "external design," I mean the part of the design that the consumer of the pattern will see and interact with. To speak plainly, these are the classes and their public members.

As far as the consumer of the data access proposal knows, he or she is supposed to create a Jnsk.Db.BatchCommand instance and call AddSprocCall() one or more times. The BatchCommand will remember what calls to stored procedures should be done. Finally, the BatchCommand instance should be sent to the Acme.HelpDesk.PersistentAccess.paHelper class for executing all the stored procedure calls. You can see the class diagram for the classes that are at the center of my data access proposal in Figure 8.1.

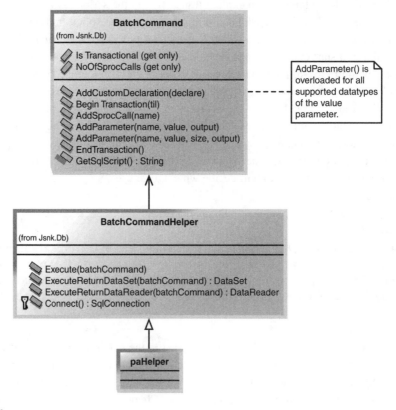

FIGURE 8.1

Class diagram for my data access proposal.

As you can see in Figure 8.1, paHelper inherits from BatchCommandHelper. The Connect() method is Protected and will often be overridden in paHelper, but the rest of the methods don't typically have to be overridden.

It's also worth mentioning that the BeginTransaction() method of BatchCommand requires the TIL. Deciding on what TIL to use can be difficult. It's seldom that SERIALIZABLE is needed, but some developers use SERIALIZABLE just in case. I prefer to use the TIL that is the lowest but still sufficient and correct for the situation.

> **NOTE**
>
> Tim Ewald's *Transactional COM+: Building Scalable Applications*[3] gives you several concrete tips on how to choose the correct TIL.

Figure 8.1 shows the static view of the design. In Figure 8.2, you can see the classes in action. I have added a few classes—ErrandReport from the Application layer and doErrand from the Domain layer—in this figure to give a complete example. I will discuss those classes in more detail later in the chapter.

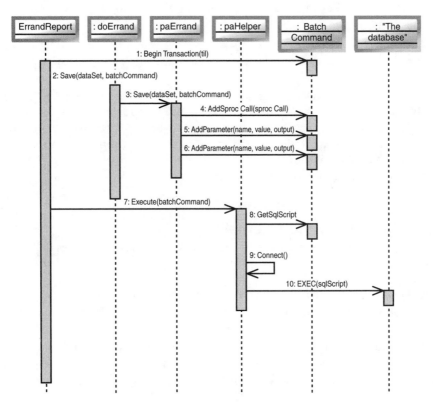

FIGURE 8.2

Interaction diagram for my data access proposal.

> **NOTE**
>
> It is commonly regarded as bad design if public methods must be called in certain sequences to give the correct result. As you notice from Figure 8.2, there is a strict sequence to follow to get the expected result. For example, you have to call `BeginTransaction()` before you call `AddSprocCall()` for the stored procedure calls that you want to have in the transaction. This is natural to most developers, so it shouldn't cause any problems. For example, a similar protocol also applies for transactions in ADO.

As you can see in Figure 8.2, the design uses an instance of `BatchCommand` as a stream, or bag, of what is to be done. The instance is sent around between the layers and finally used by the `paHelper` class in the Persistent Access layer to execute all the stored procedures in one round trip to the database. You can also see in Figure 8.2 that it is the Application layer class `ErrandReport` that decides when the transaction will start and end and that controls the complete scenario.

> **NOTE**
>
> My proposal is fairly similar to the Command Processor pattern that is discussed in Frank Buschmann, Regine Meunier, Hans Rohnert, Peter Sommerlad, and Michael Stal's *Pattern-Oriented Software Architecture: A System of Patterns*.[4] The Command Processor pattern in its turn is related to the Command pattern that is discussed in *Design Patterns: Elements of Reusable Object-Oriented Software* by Erich Gamma, Richard Helm, Ralph Johnson, and John Vlissides.[5]

Sample Code Using the External Design

Enough is enough, let's get down to business and look at some code that uses the external design.

Code that Generates an SQL Script and Sends It for Execution

First, the SQL script has to be generated. You can see how that is done in Listing 8.4, where the `BatchCommand` instance is first instantiated and a transaction is started. (Once again, an explicit transaction isn't needed in this specific example. I have used it for demonstration purposes only.) Next, the `BatchCommand` instance is sent to `doErrand` to get a stored procedure call added (`doErrand` will delegate the task to `paErrand`, but that is transparent to the code in Listing 8.4).

LISTING 8.4　ErrandReport.Report()

```
Public Sub Report(ByVal dataSet As DataSet)
    Const theSource As String = theTypeName & ".Report"

    Dim aBatchCommand As New Jnsk.Db.BatchCommand(theSource)
    Try
        aBatchCommand.BeginTransaction(IsolationLevel.ReadUncommitted)

        Acme.HelpDesk.Domain.doErrand.Save(dataSet, aBatchCommand)

        Acme.HelpDesk.PersistentAccess.paHelper.Execute(aBatchCommand)

    'Some Catch blocks...
    End Try
End Sub
```

> **NOTE**
>
> The constructor of the BatchCommand class takes fromSource as a parameter. This is used (as you can see in Listing 8.3) when building the SQL script and when adding trace calls, for example.

Finally, when the ErrandReport instance has collected all the data in the BatchCommand instance, it sends it to paHelper for execution against the database. As you see, I didn't call EndTransaction(). You don't have to do this. If you have called BeginTransaction(), the script will end the transaction anyway. The reason for having the EndTransaction() method is if you want to end the transaction before the script ends, which is highly recommended if you are going to call more stored procedures at the end of the script that don't need to be in the transaction.

Am I Promoting a Weak Protocol?

It might seem that I am promoting a weak protocol in saying that the programmer doesn't have to end the transaction explicitly because the script will end the transaction automatically. Of course, I don't want to encourage sloppy programming. The reason why you don't have to call EndTransaction() explicitly in this design is that the error-handling technique I use for SQL scripts and stored procedures requires an ExitHandler section that will handle open transactions, if appropriate. You will find more information about this in Chapter 9.

> **NOTE**
>
> If you decide to do work before and after the transaction starts in the SQL script, you get different semantics, depending on whether COM+ transactions are used or not. When COM+ transactions are used, the pre- and post-work will be done inside a transaction, which is a very important point to consider.

In Listing 8.5, you can see how the paErrand adds a call to the stored procedure a_Errand_Insert(). (We came here from doErrand.Save().) As you can see, many constants are required, not only for the names of the stored procedures, but also for the names of the parameters in the stored procedures. (The constants are called, for example, Sprocs.DataTables.errand and Sprocs.Names.a_errand_Insert.)

LISTING 8.5   paErrand.Save()

```
Public Shared Sub Save(ByVal dataSet As DataSet, _
ByRef batchCommand As Jnsk.Db.BatchCommand)
    Dim aDataRow As DataRow
    Dim aDataTable As DataTable = _
    dataSet.Tables(Sprocs.DataTables.errand).GetChanges(DataRowState.Added)

    For Each aDataRow In aDataTable.Rows
        batchCommand.AddSprocCall(Sprocs.Names.a_Errand_Insert)

        batchCommand.AddParameter(Sprocs.Parameters.id, _
        CType(aDataRow(Sprocs.Parameters.id), Guid), False)

        batchCommand.AddParameter(Sprocs.Parameters.description, _
        CType(aDataRow(Sprocs.Parameters.description), _
        String), Sprocs.ParameterSizes.description, False)

        'And so on for all parameters...
    Next
End Sub
```

> **NOTE**
>
> At first, I used a SprocCall class that was instantiated once for each call to a stored procedure and then the instances were added to the BatchCommand instance. I find the current design without the SprocCall class to be slightly more encapsulated. If a SprocCall is used internally in the BatchCommand or not, that is invisible to the consumer of the BatchCommand.

Code That Executes the SQL Script

It's now time to use the SQL script and send it to the database. There are three different methods for doing this, depending on whether there will be a resultset from the SQL script or not and how that resultset should be used. In Listing 8.6, I show you the first part of the Execute() method, which is used when no resultset is expected.

LISTING 8.6   BatchCommandHelper.Execute(): Part 1

```
Public Shared Sub Execute(ByVal batchCommand As BatchCommand)
    Dim anSqlScript As String = batchCommand.GetSqlScript()
```

As you can see in Listing 8.6, the BatchCommand instance (sent as a parameter) to the Execute() method is asked for the total SQL script with the help of the GetSqlScript() method.

This is the reason for the existence of the get only property NoOfSprocCalls. If you discover that it is more efficient to use an SqlCommand when there is only one or two stored procedure calls to make, you can check NoOfSprocCalls and determine whether you should use a future sibling of GetSqlScript() called, for example, GetSqlCommands(), that returns an array of SqlCommand objects.

> **NOTE**
>
> In a way, you can see the solution with the proposed helper as a simple optimizer. Instead of optimizing SQL statements as the optimizer in SQL Server, this optimizer can investigate all the stored procedure calls and execute them in an appropriate way. You can, of course, also extend the helper to make it configurable, so that you can provide information in a .config file.

The code in Listing 8.7 is from the BatchCommandHelper class, but the call to Connect() will actually go to the paHelper class, which overrides Connect() in BatchCommandHelper.

> **NOTE**
>
> The connection string is dealt with in a .config file and cached in the way that was discussed in Chapter 4, "Adding Debugging Support."

LISTING 8.7   BatchCommandHelper.Execute(): Part 2

```
Dim aConnection As SqlClient.SqlConnection
Try
    aConnection = Connect()
```

Finally, it's time to send the script to the database. Doing this is straightforward, as you can see in Listing 8.8.

LISTING 8.8   BatchCommandHelper.Execute(): Part 3

```
    Dim aCommand As New SqlClient.SqlCommand(anSqlScript, aConnection)
    aCommand.CommandType = CommandType.Text
    aCommand.ExecuteNonQuery()

'And some catch blocks...

Finally
    Jnsk.Db.Helper.ReleaseConnection(aConnection)
End Try
End Sub
```

Internal Design of My Data Access Proposal

I have tried to make the external design as free as possible from the implementation itself and from the fact that in the end, an SQL script will execute against the database. For example, the AddParameter() methods have a bunch of overloaded versions, one for each supported data type, even though the SQL script will, of course, be in plain text. By not exposing implementation details in the external design, you can change the implementation and use a plain ADO.NET implementation instead, for example, internally. You might wonder what you have gained by doing this. Well, you have a helper that helps you write less code, and you decouple a lot of your code from ADO.NET syntax. I definitely recommend that you use a helper to become more productive, regardless of whether you like my proposal.

As you know, I like my SQL script solution, so that is the implementation I use internally right now, but I have also prepared the design for other future implementations. I'd now like to tell you about a few of the key decisions of the internal design.

Storage

There are several possible solutions to choose from when it comes to remembering what stored procedure calls the SQL script should contain, when the transaction should be started and ended, and so on. I can use some sort of collection and when GetSqlScript() is called, the requested type of output is created. I currently only support SQL scripts as a result stream and so I store the SQL script as a `StringBuilder` that is built during the generation of the SQL script. Finally, when `GetSqlScript()` is called, the complete script is done, except for the end section that is added, and then the SQL script is returned as a `String`.

Using a `StringBuilder` in a situation like the one just discussed is fast, but not as memory saving as might first be expected. Each `AddSprocCall()` will add many bytes to the `StringBuilder`, mainly because of error handling. This applies to each stored procedure call. Meanwhile, because the storage design is totally internal to `BatchCommand`, you can easily alter the decision without affecting the `BatchCommand` consumer. Only the `BatchCommandHelper` will be affected.

> **NOTE**
>
> When `BatchCommand` supports different output methods in the future, it might be possible to add a constructor to `BatchCommand` that takes a parameter and describes what storage type to use, namely the same one that will be used when the output method is called. That could help make it easier to optimize the construction slightly.

Named Parameters

When `AddSprocCall()` is used, it will finally lead to a call for a stored procedure in the SQL script. Each call to `AddParameter()` will add a parameter to the stored procedure call. So as not to create yet another order dependency for the order in which to make the calls to `AddParameter()`, I decided to use named parameters instead. The result in the SQL script can be seen in Listing 8.9.

LISTING 8.9   Example Showing That Named Parameters Are Used for Calling Stored Procedures

```
EXEC @aReturnValue = a_Errand_Insert
@id='A9FC3FAB-B17D-464f-9DFF-2EFF99AFEF69'
, @description='Problem with...', ...
```

Another advantage of using named parameters, apart from the fact that the parameter order doesn't matter, is that you can choose to use only certain parameters. It's also a big help when you debug malfunctioning SQL scripts.

However, as usual, there are some disadvantages to using named parameters too. One disadvantage is that if the name of a parameter changes, your code breaks. In addition, it will be more tedious to write a stored procedure call. (This isn't a problem when `AddParameter()` or a similar helper is doing the job for you, of course.)

Encoding Dangerous Parameters

When you use the built-in solution in ADO.NET (and similar techniques) for adding parameters to stored procedure calls, you will automatically get help with dangerous signs, such as extra quotes in strings. When you build a solution on your own, you are not given that luxury automatically, but `AddParameter()` will take care of the problem. The encoding will be dealt with according to which `AddParameter()` method is used. For example, the `Boolean` version will translate `True` to 1 in the SQL script and `False` to 0. The `Date` version will translate dates to dates formatted in a specific way in the SQL script. All the `Decimal` versions will output dot as the decimal separator and, of course, the `String` version of `AddParameter()` will handle the quote problem.

Beware of the ISO Date Format!

When you are formatting dates to write to the SQL script, you must be careful if you want your code to be insensitive to regional date settings. My friend Tibor Karaszi (SQL Server Microsoft MVP) warns that we must watch out for the ISO format. The code shown in Listing 8.10 illustrates the danger of the ISO date format.

LISTING 8.10   The Danger Inherent in the ISO Date Format

```
SET language us_english
SELECT CAST('1998-03-25' AS datetime)
SET LANGUAGE french
SELECT CAST('1998-03-25' AS datetime)
```

Try `sp_helplanguage` and you will see that language carries the "ymd" format. In other words, Karaszi says that if you're about to use ANSI SQL date formatting, see to it that your connection has `SET DATEFORMAT ymd` set. Alternatively, you can format the date as shown in Listing 8.11.

LISTING 8.11   An Alternate Date Format

```
SET language us_english
SELECT CAST('19980325' AS datetime)
SET LANGUAGE french
SELECT CAST('19980325' AS datetime)
```

YYMMDD is "safe." It is okay to drop the separators according to ISO 8601, but not according to ANSI SQL. As Karaszi notes, this is strange because ANSI SQL is said to build on ISO 8601 regarding representation of dates and times.

Debugging

As I mentioned earlier in the chapter, the debugging experience with the data access pattern is very good. You can set a breakpoint in BatchCommandHelper.Execute(), copy the complete script, and use it in SQL Server Query Analyzer over and over again until you have found the problem.

> **NOTE**
>
> Whether the script can be executed repeatedly in SQL Server Query Analyzer with the same result depends on what the script is doing. It isn't always possible.

Note especially how @anErrorMessage is used in Listing 8.3. It holds context information so that if the SQL script has several stored procedure calls, you will see exactly which call had the problem in the error message. If the same stored procedure is called several times, the @anErrorMessage variable can also contain information about which of the calls it was.

Another benefit of the centralization of all the stored procedure calls to a helper is that you can easily add trace calls that show all the parameter values used when calling the stored procedures. The AddParameter() (or AddSprocCall()) can be changed, so it helps generate script code for tracing, as shown in Listing 8.12.

LISTING 8.12 Extract from SQL Script Where Tracing Code Has Been Added Automatically for Tracing All Parameter Values

```
SET @aTraceMessage =
'@id=A9FC3FAB-B17D-464f-9DFF-2EFF99AFEF69
, @description=Problem with..., ...'
EXEC JnskTrace_Message @theSource, @aTraceMessage

EXEC @aReturnValue = a_Errand_Insert
@id='A9FC3FAB-B17D-464f-9DFF-2EFF99AFEF69'
, @description='Problem with...', ...
```

You can call GetSqlScript() to see what the SQL script currently looks like at any time during the build process, which can also be good for debugging purposes. Just one word of caution: The GetSqlScript() method will add an end section to the SQL script, but this section will "disappear" if you continue to call AddSprocCall() (that is, GetSqlScript() adds that section).

8

DATA ACCESS

Connection Strategy

A common discussion in newsgroups is how the connection to the database in n-tier applications should be handled. Some developers have decided to go all the way with the "fast in, fast out" method in which they open a connection and close it in every method, even if they need the connection again in another method during the same scenario (by scenario, I mean a method call to the Application layer). Because of connection pooling, this works quite well, but even so, connection pooling takes resources to manipulate, and there will be a short delay when fetching a connection from the connection pool, of course.

I think the rule of thumb should be to open the connection as late as possible during a scenario and then keep that connection open throughout the complete scenario to be used by all methods. As you know by now from my data access helper, it will try to make only one call to the database during a scenario, but this rule of thumb also applies for scenarios where several calls are made to the database. However, as always, there are exceptions to the rule, so don't use it blindly. Be especially careful that you don't send a connection over a process boundary.

OUTPUT Parameters

If you want to catch the OUTPUT parameter from one stored procedure and use it in another stored procedure, you can use the AddCustomDeclaration() method of the BatchCommand to declare the variable. For the stored procedure call with the OUTPUT parameter, you use AddParameter() as usual, but the output parameter must be True, and the value parameter should be the name of the variable—for example, @id. For the stored procedure that is then to use the variable, you just use the name of the variable again as the value parameter when you call AddParameter().

> **NOTE**
>
> This part of the proposal shows internal information about the SQL script solution. If you're about to add support for GetSqlCommands(), for example, you need to take a closer look at this.

Tricky Cases of SQL

Two of the problems with using only stored procedures for interacting with the database are when you have to use an IN clause in your SELECT statement or when the user should be able to decide which column to use for the ORDER BY clause. In both cases, I still use stored procedures. I typically pack the IN clause as a VARCHAR that I send to the stored procedure. The stored procedure will then have to use dynamic SQL. One of the problems with dynamic SQL is that the user must have granted rights to use the object that is used by dynamic SQL. It's not enough to have granted rights to the stored procedure that executes the dynamic SQL. To take care of this problem as much as possible, I always use views or user-defined functions (UDFs) from the dynamic SQL and see to it that it's obvious from the name of the view or UDF that the user must have granted rights to it.

> **NOTE**
>
> When I say the user must have granted rights, the user is the one who acts as the principal for executing the COM+ application, not the end user. That is, you should use a dedicated account (that doesn't belong to an end user) for executing the COM+ application.

In the case of the ORDER BY clause, the stored procedure will take a parameter describing the ORDER BY clause that is requested. I often stay with static SQL, so I have to repeat the same SELECT statement once for each possible ORDER BY clause. When there are too many possible ORDER BY clauses for this approach, I use dynamic SQL, as I did with the IN clause.

Disadvantages with the Proposal

As usual, I will evaluate the data access proposal at the end of the chapter against the criteria we discussed in Chapter 2, "Factors to Consider in Choosing a Solution to a Problem." However, I'd like to discuss some possible disadvantages here first, because so far I have only told you how terrific the proposal is.

One likely problem is that the proposal is targeted at developers who also find T-SQL worth mastering. If you think that you are only going to be a VB programmer, the data access solution is probably hard to use and debug. In addition, the design is similar to Handles in the Win32 API. Because of this, it doesn't feel so up-to-date. Not that I think trends should govern design decisions, of course. Use whatever gets the job done well. While we are at it, it could be a bad idea to toss objects around between layers, because layers can live in different processes. On the other hand, you should have optimized for few round trips between tiers because that is the place where there will be process-to-process communication and not between layers within a tier.

In addition, the generated SQL script often becomes quite large because of the error handling, and more data will be sent to the Data tier compared to when usual ADO.NET code is used. Furthermore, the SQL script code is dynamic, so it has to be compiled each time. Also, in Visual Studio .NET, there are built-in Rapid Application Development (RAD) tools for quickly

8

DATA ACCESS

writing the code to call a stored procedure. With my data access proposal, you can't use those tools, but it's quite easy to write a few of your own tools to tackle the most time-consuming and repetitive work. An additional disadvantage with the proposal is that all parameters must be converted to text. This costs CPU cycles, of course.

Another problem is that it's hard to get results back from the SQL script, except via SELECT to a DataReader (or a DataSet).

Finally, although it's not really a problem with the proposal, as you can see from the interface of BatchCommand, I have decided not to have methods for logic other than just calling stored procedures. It would be possible to use IF clauses and such in the script too, but I chose not to do this because the helper solution would then be an SQL script–only solution.

Other Approaches to Data Access Helpers

Recently, I have learned that Microsoft has been working hard on a suite of tools called Development Accelerators for .NET. Developers will be able use this suite of tools as helpers for the efficient handling of different tasks. One of the accelerators in the suite is called the Data Access Accelerator[6] and is definitely worth a look.

As I said earlier, you can also use the built-in wizards in Visual Studio .NET and let them write a lot of the tedious code for you, but then you become much too dependent on ADO.NET, with all the drawbacks that entails. Moreover, while it may be fast to write the code, it takes time to maintain the code.

The Data Access Proposal in the Architecture

In Chapter 5, I established my favorite architecture, and in this section I'd like to put the data access proposal in the context of that architecture.

In Figure 8.2, you saw a complete call stack for a scenario in which an Application layer class (ErrandReport) controls the process of calling the stored procedure a_Errand_Insert(). As you saw, the proposal affects all three layers in the Business tier. In a way, this is not strictly layering but often some classes are "global" to several layers in layered architectures. In the data access proposal, classes in several layers are aware of and use the BatchCommand class.

Another example of a class that several layers often are aware of and use is the ADO.NET DataSet. Because I often use DataSets for carrying data, DataSets will often be sent to the consumer too.

What to Use for Carrying Data

I have just said that I often use DataSets for carrying data between layers. Before I take this idea further, I'd like to make it clear that I don't use DataSets as soon as there is data to return from a stored procedure. It depends on how far the data will be transported and whether a consistent interface to the Persistent Access layer is wanted.

In Chapter 5 (and illustrated in Figure 5.10), I explained that I like to have a consistent way of working with the classes in the Persistent Access layer. Therefore, I need a way to send and return data without having to continually change the interface. There are several alternatives to choose from, one being DataSets that comes free with ADO.NET and has several good features. One of my favorite features is that you can put several DataTables in one DataSet. (In VB6, I used several different "hack" approaches for this, the best one being to use arrays of Recordsets.) Other great features include the opportunity to create strongly typed DataSets and to have constraints in the DataSet so that some erroneous data can be caught before going into the DataSet at all. Actually, I sometimes even use a DataSet for returning one row. The DataSet is good in this situation because it has a lot of metadata, but the drawback is large overhead.

You can, of course, build a mechanism similar to DataSets yourself. One reason for doing this might be to add a shield against future Microsoft changes in DataSets. For now, I have decided to use DataSets for my transportation needs.

But what if the data won't leave the Persistent Access layer? In this situation, using DataSets is overkill. If the result is only one row, using OUTPUT parameters of the stored procedure is the most efficient approach. If there are several rows in the result, you should use a DataReader instead of a DataSet.

8

DATA ACCESS

NOTE

Be very careful when sending around DataReaders. A connection must be open to the database, and you should be sure to close connections as fast as possible for scalability reasons. That is, if one request doesn't need a connection for, say 10 seconds, if the connection is closed so it can go back to the connection pool, the connection can help to serve hundreds of other requests.

One last comment: You may wonder whether the SQL script or the stored procedure should decide whether several resultsets are to be fetched. In Chapter 5, I let the stored procedure decide, but in reality I prefer to let the SQL script do this instead, thereby creating more primitive stored procedures that can be used for other purposes. In Chapter 5, returning several resultsets was mostly used for demonstration purposes.

Saying More in Fewer Words When Calling Stored Procedures

Compared to an ordinary programming language, T-SQL and stored procedures have several problems. One of the worst problems is that arrays can't be used as parameters to stored procedures. In a way, the data access pattern that I have proposed in this chapter makes this less of a problem because when the pattern is used, the number of round trips between the Business tier and the Data tier will be reduced to a minimum. Still, in some situations, sending several rows in one stored procedure call can be very useful. Let's take a look at a few techniques you can use.

XML

SQL Server 2000 comes with some native XML support. One possible way to benefit from the built-in support for XML in SQL Server 2000 is to use stored procedures to parse XML documents. Thanks to this support, you can send several rows to insert in an XML document in a parameter to a stored procedure.

Assume you have an XML document with a couple of errands that have to be reported. The document is then sent to a stored procedure that uses `sp_xml_preparedocument()` to parse the document and to instantiate an object model. Listing 8.13 shows how this may look.

LISTING 8.13   Parsing an XML Document in T-SQL

```
EXEC sp_xml_preparedocument @aDocument OUTPUT, @xml
```

When this is done, you can use `OPENXML()` to find information in the XML document. In Listing 8.14, you can see an example in which I use an XML document as the source for an `INSERT`.

LISTING 8.14   Using an XML Document as the Source for an `INSERT`

```
INSERT INTO problemsolver (id, firstname, lastname)
SELECT * FROM OPENXML(@aDocument,
'/root/problemsolver')
WITH (id UNIQUE IDENTIFIER '@id',
firstname VARCHAR(50) '@firstname',
lastname VARCHAR(50) '@lastname')
```

Finally, it's important to remove the document, so we free resources, as shown in Listing 8.15.

LISTING 8.15   Removing the XML Document from Memory

```
EXEC sp_xml_removedocument @aDocument
```

Other Formats

Before XML was even created, I used custom formats to achieve the same effect I showed in the previous section. For example, I packed strings with order numbers separated by commas. I have also simulated an array by separating columns with tab and rows with linefeed. (This technique wasn't really useful until SQL Server 7 was released because the maximum size then for VARCHAR was changed from 255 to 8000.) At the receiver side, the structure has to be unpacked, which can easily be done with a stored procedure or a UDF. As a matter of fact, I have written an eXtended stored Procedure (XP) that takes a two-dimensional array and outputs it as a resultset that can be caught and put in a temp table for, say, further processing. However, in SQL Server 2000, a UDF is a better solution. In any case, XML is most often the preferred format to use.

Bitmaps

By sending a bitmap as a parameter, you make it possible to send several values in one parameter. In a way, it will break type safety because you can add another value without having to add another parameter. Although you can't use this technique all the time and it is somewhat awkward to use, when you need an optimization technique, it can often be very efficient.

You can also use bitmaps in your database design. Assume that problem solvers that work with the Acme HelpDesk sample application (and are also represented as rows in the database) are marked with one or more of the following descriptions:

- Smart
- Committed
- Lazy
- Fast

You can store these descriptions in the database as usual just by having a table related to a problemsolver table. You can also skip this extra table and just have an INT column in the problemsolver table. Let 1 mean Smart, 2 mean Committed, 4 mean Lazy, and so on. If you store 3 in the column, it means that the problem solver is Smart and Committed.

> **NOTE**
>
> Storing bitmaps in this way breaks the first normal form of the relational model because several values are stored in a single column and that is exactly what the first normal form forbids. Therefore, use this tip carefully.

Let's discuss this a little further. If you are about to register a new problem solver, you only have to write one row if you use a bitmap, even if the specific problem solver has three different descriptions. With the ordinary solution, you would have to write four rows, one to the problemsolver table and three to the problemsolverdescription table.

When it is time to search only for the problem solvers that are Smart and Lazy, because you want to try to stimulate them to become Smart and Committed, you can pack a bitmap like the one shown in Listing 8.16.

LISTING 8.16   Packing a Bitmap in an INT Variable with the Use of "or"

```
SET @aBitmapOfDescriptions = 1 | 4
```

You then send the bitmap to a stored procedure, and the stored procedure uses the bitmap parameter in a SELECT statement like the one shown in Listing 8.17. This time, you use "and" instead of "or."

LISTING 8.17   Unpacking a Bitmap with the Use of "and"

```
SELECT id, firstname, lastname
FROM problemsolver
WHERE @bitmapOfDescriptions & description <> 0
```

Finally, note that you don't have to stay with the data type INTEGER. You could use, for example, a BIGINT to have twice as many different values, and you can also have a large number of parameters. Another tip is to use—for example, POWER(2, 3)—for setting and getting values in the bitmap for making the code easier to read.

Data Transportation Between Stored Procedures

When one stored procedure needs to call another stored procedure, the same techniques that were just discussed can, of course, be used again, but there are also other alternatives, as we'll now see.

Temp Tables and Cursors

Perhaps the most common solution to the problem (well, the most common after not writing modular code, that is) is to create a temp table and send its name to be used with EXECUTE (string) in the called procedure, or to just let the called procedure have the name hard-coded.

Another solution is to create a cursor and, for example, return the cursor to the caller. The caller can then continue to use that cursor without knowing what the WHERE clause for the cursor was. In Listing 8.18, a cursor is created and returned to the caller.

LISTING 8.18 Creating a Cursor and Returning It to the Caller

```
CREATE PROCEDURE Sample_CursorReturn
(@cur CURSOR VARYING OUTPUT) AS
  DECLARE aCursor CURSOR LOCAL FOR
  SELECT id FROM problemsolver

  OPEN aCursor
  SET @cur = aCursor

  DEALLOCATE aCursor
```

Both temp tables and cursors create tight coupling between stored procedures, which is not a good thing. And, as you know, you should think twice (at least) before using cursors at all.

UDFs

Often, a secondary stored procedure that creates a resultset for use by a root-stored procedure can be rewritten as an Inline Table Valued Function (ITVF) or Multistatement Table Valued Function (MTVF) instead. If you rewrite this secondary stored procedure, you don't have the problem of catching the rows and putting them somewhere before using them because the UDF can be used in SELECT statements, for example, just as a table or a view.

Server-Side Caching

It doesn't matter how fast something is, not doing it at all is faster and also conserves resources. Caching is one way of achieving this ability to "do nothing." Instead of going to the database server to fetch the list of problem solvers, you can cache the list in memory in the application server, and then you don't have to do anything. The operation is much faster and you also save resources at the database server. This sounds too good to be true, right? The catch is that you will have trouble keeping the cache in sync with the original data. This is especially hard if you have scaled out the application server—that is, set up a farm of application servers each running the same application. Be careful! In an environment where you have scaled out the application server, you should probably only cache static data; otherwise, you risk the main goal of your application, namely correctness.

When you only have one application server, you can use server-side caching for semistatic data too, as long as all updates of the data are done via the application server and not directly to the data source. However, you must be very careful. I recommend that you skip caching until you really need it, and analyze the complete picture thoroughly before using caching. Going to the database each time is usually a quick-enough solution. It is also simple and has fewer risks.

> **NOTE**
>
> I created several caching solutions in the years before .NET. There are two articles you can read more about the tested methods and conclusions, namely "Server-Side Caching in COM+ and VB"[7] and "Server-Side Caching (or Buy Speed with Cache)."[8]

New Server-Side Caching Potential with .NET

With the help of .NET, two new techniques open up that are great for server-side caching, one being the use of the COM+ Component Service Object Pooling and the other being the use of ADO.NET DataSets for carrying complex structures of data, for example, in pooled objects. You can also use shared properties instead of pooled objects, but then you have only one item for which you have to write thread-safe code on your own which is always dangerous, and this also might become a bottleneck. With pooled objects, you can adjust the size of the pool to decrease contention, but then you have a new problem when the cache is to be updated, because all cached items must be updated at the same time.

> **NOTE**
>
> It's very apparent when you think about caching that there is no such a thing as a free lunch. If you save some here, you pay there. If you use object pooling and have several objects in the pool, you will also have the same data several times in memory. If it's a lot of data to cache, having several instances of it is a waste of resources.

Finally, an even better place to use caching than in the Business tier is in the Consumer tier, for example in ASP.NET or in the local executable. By using caching in this tier, you conserve resources at the application server, and operations where cached data are used will be even faster. For server-side caching, you should most probably only cache shared data, but it's all right to cache personal data if it is held at the user's workstation.

Let me state again that there can be enormous benefits to server-side caching in some situations. You actually buy speed and pay with memory. However, the risks are also enormous, so don't use caching before you have completely understood the consequences.

Dealing with Schema Changes

Yet another topic that I'd like to discuss (and hopefully provide a little inspiration along the way) is how to prepare the code for future schema changes. Sooner or later, and usually sooner, the database schema will change. Make sure that you are prepared so that you don't have to change the code at every schema change, or even worse, that your code breaks.

As always, information hiding, code generalization, and automatic testing are your friends when it comes to dealing with changes. In this section, I will discuss a couple of other techniques that you can consider.

Using User-Defined Data Types

If you use User-Defined Data Types (UDDTs) for your data types, both in the tables and in the stored procedures, it will be much easier to increase the length of a VARCHAR, for example, and have the change take effect in all the stored procedures with the minimum amount of work. However, this will not solve the whole problem. For example, it won't help you that much if you want to change from INTEGER to UNIQUE IDENTIFIER, because a lot of the code might assume INTEGER.

> **NOTE**
>
> UDDTs can't be used with the TABLE data type, which is unfortunate because the TABLE data type is crucial for UDFs.

When it comes to VB code, UDDTs are of little use. You can map them up as structures in VB too, but I haven't tried this because it doesn't feel like a straightforward proposal. In fact, as far as I know, this topic hasn't been investigated much, and no really good proposals exist.

Using Too-Large CHAR and VARCHAR Parameters

One strategy for finding bugs—because of changed database schemas, for example—is to use too-large CHAR and VARCHAR parameters for the stored procedures. If we assume that the description column is of data type VARCHAR(50), it can then be declared as VARCHAR(51) in the stored procedure. Subsequently, the first thing to do in the stored procedure would be to assert that the DATALENGTH() of the @description parameter is less than 51.

I normally use UDDTs, so to use the approach discussed here, I would have to have two UDDTs for each string data type—one that is the correct length to use for the table and one that is one sign larger to use for the parameters.

A better approach is probably to let some of the AddParameter() methods take a size parameter as well (and that is exactly what I did, as you can see in Figure 8.1). Then it's easy to check that the provided string value isn't larger than the size, and if so, raise an exception or let an assertion signal. To avoid creating a maintenance problem, you need to hold more metadata in your .NET components about the stored procedures and their parameters, which is exactly what the next section discusses.

Dragging Out Parameters from Stored Procedures and Using Them as Constants

As you saw in Listing 8.5, when AddParameter() was called, I had constants for all the parameter names in the stored procedures. The names are very important because I use named parameters. A simple approach to use for determining whether any parameter names that affect the VB code have changed is to drag out all the parameters (both names, data types, and sizes) for the public stored procedures with a utility and create one or more classes with the parameters as constants. The classes should not be written to at all by hand.

Subsequently, when you want to check that the stored procedure is as you would expect, you just rerun the utility and compare the new result of the utility with the old classes to see whether the classes are identical to the previous ones. If it isn't, you'll have to determine whether the only differences are newly added parameters with good default values. This is so that the new parameters don't have to get values when the stored procedures are called from old VB code that is unaware of the new parameters.

In Listing 8.5 earlier in this chapter, you saw that I used constants called, for example, Sprocs.Parameters.description and Sprocs.ParamterSizes.description, and that was an example of the approach discussed here.

Using Views and/or UDFs

Views and UDFs can serve very well in making many schema changes transparent to the stored procedures. Often, it feels like overkill to map every table with one or more views/UDFs, but it's well worth the effort when changes need to be made in the table structure.

Evaluation of My Proposal

It's now time to evaluate the data access proposal I presented in this chapter. I'll evaluate the proposal not only in its use of an SQL script, but also as a helper that can be expanded to use in ways other than generating SQL scripts.

The proposal focuses on reducing round trips between tiers, which is very good for flexibility when it comes to different physical restrictions and possibilities. However, be careful that you don't introduce process boundaries between the layers in the Business tier because then the architecture will not be a good one. (The architecture itself agrees with this too. Process boundaries should be between tiers, not between layers.)

Performance and scalability lies at the heart of the proposal. At the book's Web site at `www.samspublishing.com`, you can compare the throughput between ordinary ADO.NET code and my data access proposal, both for when several stored procedure calls are made in a single transaction and with only one stored procedure call and no explicit transaction.

Scalability will increase with my proposal because the transactions will be shorter, and there will be no round trips during a transaction. Shorter transactions mean shorter locks, which in turn decreases contention.

I don't see any major advantages or disadvantages with the proposal regarding reliability, reusability, testability, and interoperability, but I think the effect on debuggability is positive. I mentioned earlier in the chapter the easy way to automatically trace parameter values and to run a complete scenario by copying the script and executing it over and over again in SQL Server Query Analyzer.

Maintainability is increased thanks to the fact that the proposal is constructed as a helper routine. (This effect will be achieved by most other helpers too, of course.) The productivity is increased due to the helper, but also because debuggability is increased. I suggest you write a couple of generators that, for example, generate all the code for calling a stored procedure, to increase productivity even more.

What's Next

The next and final chapter will discuss error handling and concurrency control. It can be extremely tricky to handle errors correctly in all situations, especially in T-SQL code, and there is a lot to consider regarding .NET code too. We'll start by discussing error-handling templates for certain situations and will then look at preparing for typical errors so you don't have to find them out the hard way. Finally, we'll discuss how to deal with concurrency control in disconnected scenarios, with both optimistic and pessimistic solutions.

References

1. S. Kirk and J. Boylan. "Tech Ed 2001: .NET Application Architecture Panel Discussion," June 2001, `http://msdn.microsoft.com/library/en-us/dnbda/html/bdadotnetarch10.asp`.

2. J. Nilsson. "Round Trips Are Evil—Reduce Them!" Pinnacle Publishing's *Visual Basic Developer*, July 2001, `http://www.pinnaclepublishing.com/VB`.

8

DATA ACCESS

3. T. Ewald. *Transactional COM+: Building Scalable Applications*. Addison-Wesley; 2001.

4. F. Buschmann, R. Meunier, H. Rohnert, P. Sommerlad, and M. Stal. *Pattern-Oriented Software Architecture: A System of Patterns*. Wiley; 1996.

5. E. Gamma, R. Helm, R. Johnson, and J.Vlissides. *Design Patterns: Elements of Reusable Object-Oriented Software*. Addison-Wesley; 1995.

6. Development Accelerators for .NET. No public Web address yet.

7. J. Nilsson. "Server-Side Caching in COM+ and VB."
   `http://www.vb2themax.com/HtmlDoc.asp?Table=Articles&ID=360`.

8. J. Nilsson. "Server-Side Caching or Buy Speed with Cache." `http://www.vbxml.com/conference/wrox/2000_vegas/text/jimmy_cache.pdf`.

Error Handling and Concurrency Control

I once heard a developer say, "I don't judge the coolness of an application from its feature list, but from how gracefully it handles exceptions." Even if you're not striving to write the "coolest" application ever, it's extremely important to prepare up-front for strategies relating to error handling. How many times have you worked on projects and told yourself that error-handling code can always be added later? Even if this has only happened to you once, you know that adding error-handling code to your application as an afterthought is very difficult, error-prone, time consuming, and almost never a good idea.

As you know, for an application to be considered robust and reliable, it's extremely important that it catches errors and deals with them effectively. This is easily said, but is often not done sufficiently in real-world applications. I'll start this chapter with an in-depth discussion of how to handle errors, both in stored procedures and in .NET components. After that, I will discuss a couple of typical errors that your application will most likely come across. I will describe these errors and propose efficient approaches for handling them. The chapter ends with a lengthy discussion on several different approaches for concurrency control of data that has been disconnected from the database. I'm obviously not going to attempt to say all there is to say about concurrency control here, but I will look at the main approaches.

My Proposal for How to Handle Errors

In Chapter 4, "Adding Debugging Support," we discussed how to log errors to provide valuable debugging information so that a problem could be understood and tracked down. For this error-logging function to work, you must consider several points in both the stored procedures and in the .NET components. For a start, errors must be caught. Therefore, let's start this chapter by taking a close look at how error handling can be implemented efficiently in stored procedures. In this discussion, you'll see the obvious differences between the T-SQL and Visual Basic .NET languages when it comes to error handling.

Handling Errors in Stored Procedures

There are four different types of cases that you have to think about when you are handling errors in stored procedures. These are:

- EXEC of stored procedure
- INSERT/UPDATE/DELETE
- SELECT
- Violation of business rule

In this chapter, I will include template code that you can use for handling errors in stored procedures in each case but, as usual, the appropriateness of the template code depends on your particular situation. Don't use it without proper consideration. However, before we investigate the four different cases for error handling in stored procedures, let's look at the general approach that I use for error handling in stored procedures.

The General Approach for Error Handling in Stored Procedures

In Chapter 5, "Architecture," I shared with you the typical code structure that I use for stored procedures. In this section, I'd like to discuss some details of the code structure that concern error handling. Listing 9.1 describes a few variables needed for the error handling to work. I have talked about those variables in earlier chapters, but I think a brief recap is in order.

First, I have a variable, @theSource, for storing the name of the current stored procedure. Then there are two variables for storing information about the error, @anError and @anErrorMessage. @anError is used for storing the error code, while @anErrorMessage is used for saving context information about the problem so that you can determine where in the stored procedure the error occurred, because the same error can occur in several places.

@theTranCountAtEntry is used for storing the number of active transactions when the stored procedure is entered, while @aReturnValue is used for capturing the return value from an EXEC call to a secondary stored procedure. (Quite often, @aRowCount is also used. It is used for tracking how many rows were affected by a SELECT, INSERT, UPDATE, or DELETE statement.)

LISTING 9.1 Error-Handling Related Variables

```
DECLARE @theSource uddtSource
, @anError INT
, @anErrorMessage uddtErrorMessage
, @theTranCountAtEntry INT
, @aReturnValue INT
```

9

As you have seen in several chapters of this book, I use an ExitHandler at the end of all my stored procedures. After each "dangerous" statement, I check to see whether there was an error. If there was, @anError will get the error code and then GOTO the ExitHandler, as shown in Listing 9.2 and later in Listing 9.3.

LISTING 9.2   The `ExitHandler` of a Stored Procedure: Part 1

```
ExitHandler:
  IF @theTranCountAtEntry = 0 AND @@TRANCOUNT > 0 BEGIN
    IF @anError = 0 BEGIN
      COMMIT TRAN
    END
    ELSE BEGIN
      ROLLBACK TRAN
    END
  END
```

Let's look at the first part of the `ExitHandler`. As you'll see, I start by investigating whether the stored procedure will end a transaction. I use the `@theTranCountAtEntry` variable to determine whether there was an active transaction when the stored procedure started. If there wasn't, this stored procedure is responsible for the transaction itself and will end it if it is still active. We know whether the transaction is active through `@@TRANCOUNT`.

> **NOTE**
>
> The transaction might be inactive if it was explicitly ended earlier in the stored procedure to make the transaction as short as possible. Even if the transaction was explicitly ended earlier in the stored procedure, we will still have the end transaction section in the `ExitHandler`. This is because we might encounter an error before the explicit transaction ending has been reached, and SQL Server will ensure that it is harmful to leave the stored procedure if `@@TRANCOUNT` has a different value than when the stored procedure was entered.

Assume when the stored procedure concludes that the transaction has to be ended. Then `@anError` is investigated, so a decision can be made regarding whether `COMMIT TRAN` or `ROLLBACK TRAN` should be used.

In the second part of the `ExitHandler`, shown in Listing 9.3, there will be a call to the stored procedure `JnskError_Raise()` if there is an error. I will discuss the implementation and reason for `JnskError_Raise()` later in this chapter, but for now you need to know that its main task is to perform a `RAISERROR()` so that the information on the error can be caught by the .NET component and used for logging. Finally, the `ExitHandler` is ended with a trace call and the `@anError` is returned to the caller.

LISTING 9.3   The ExitHandler of a Stored Procedure: Part 2

```
IF @anError <> 0 BEGIN
  EXEC JnskError_Raise @theSource
  , @anError, @anErrorMessage
END

EXEC JnskTrace_End @theSource

RETURN @anError
```

Reasons for Using Both RETURN() and RAISERROR()

You might think that I'm using both a safety net and a wire because I use both RAISERROR() and RETURN() of the error code when an error is encountered. I used to think so too, but this is still the best solution I'm aware of. First of all, the caller must be aware of an error so that it can take the correct action. For example, the caller probably shouldn't make another stored procedure call after an error, but should just go to the ExitHandler instead and end the stored procedure. Second, I want to have as much contextual information as possible for the logging solution.

Using RETURN() for communicating the result of a stored procedure is considered a de facto standard among T-SQL programmers. The RETURN() value can also be used from the .NET component, which would then know what went wrong, although the information will often be vague. For example, the following questions can't be answered:

- Where in the call stack of the stored procedures did the error occur?
- Which errors did the involved stored procedures raise from the error and "up"? (that is, the error stack)
- Where in the stored procedure did the error occur?

This last question is an interesting one if the same error could occur in several places in one stored procedure, which is a common situation.

The other approach is to use RAISERROR() instead of RETURN(). This solves the problems concerning lack of context information. However, RAISERROR() introduces new problems in the context of stored procedures. There are two ways to use RAISERROR(). You can either use RAISERROR() with custom error codes (which means 50000 or higher, and the code must have been added in the sysmessages table), or you can use RAISERROR() with a string.

9

ERROR HANDLING
AND CONCUR-
RENCY CONTROL

For example, assume that you catch the @@ERROR for a duplicate key (the duplicate key error code is 2627) and want to tell the calling stored procedure about the error. The problems you will encounter are

- You can't raise that error to the caller because RAISERROR() may not use error codes of less than 50000.
- If you put the error 2627 together with a description of where the problem is in a string and use that string with RAISERROR(), the caller stored procedure can't get to the string. Typically, the caller won't catch an error at all, but you can at least have that effect by using WITH SETERROR with RAISERROR() to give @@ERROR a value.

I could create new error codes by just adding 50000 to each one of those that already exists in sysmessages. I could then catch reserved errors, raise them again by taking their old value and adding 50000, and then use WITH SETERROR. (In this case I would also have to add my custom error codes to sysmessages.) The advantage would be that I never have to check the return value of a stored procedure but only @@ERROR, but I find this technique to be clumsy and a bit of a hack. Thus, my conclusion remains to use both RETURN() and RAISERROR() and let them solve different problems, so to speak. This solution works very well, although I do have to check for both return values and @@ERROR after a stored procedure call.

Another reason for using RETURN() to communicate problems back to the components is that when SQL Server raises an error (such as 2627 because of duplicate keys, for example), it will be visible to the components as an exception, even if the stored procedure is prepared for the problem and handles it gracefully. In this case, the RETURN() will send 0 and the component knows that the exception can be skipped.

> **NOTE**
>
> You can decrease the number of situations in which SQL Server raises errors that the component shouldn't see by taking proactive actions. Before you do an INSERT that you know might give a duplicate key error, you can check the situation with a SELECT first.

Let's now take a look at the four different types of cases that you have to think about when you are handling errors in stored procedures. I'll start with the first type of case—error handling after EXEC of a stored procedure.

Error Handling After EXEC of a Stored Procedure

The built-in error handling in T-SQL is, to put it nicely, outdated. With it, you have to check @@ERROR after each statement to see whether it is different from 0. If it is, a problem has occurred. This feature makes the T-SQL code cluttered and unnecessarily long, but you don't have a choice—you *must* check for errors. In addition, @@ERROR will be set to 0 after each successfully executed statement. This means that you can't check @@ERROR and then use the value afterward. After you check the value, it is set to 0.

In Listing 9.4, you can see how my typical code looks after a stored procedure call. The called stored procedure's return value is caught in @aReturnValue for later use. Then @@ERROR is stored in a local variable called @anError. If the @anError or @aReturnValue is different from 0, there was a problem of some kind. If @anError was equal to zero, @aReturnValue must have been different from zero, and @anError gets that value. Finally, GOTO is used to jump to the ExitHandler.

LISTING 9.4   Error Handling After a Stored Procedure Call

```
EXEC @aReturnValue = Errand_Insert
@id, @description, ...

SET @anError = @@ERROR
IF @anError <> 0 OR @aReturnValue <> 0 BEGIN
  SET @anErrorMessage = 'Insert problem...'
  IF @anError = 0 BEGIN
    SET @anError = @aReturnValue
  END
  GOTO ExitHandler
END
```

It's obvious that I'm paranoid because I check for @@ERROR after a stored procedure call. You should almost never find that @@ERROR is different from 0 after a stored procedure call. However, you might find this to be the case if the called stored procedure doesn't exist, although this should never happen in an operational system, of course. In any case, it's better safe than sorry, and the effect of checking for @@ERROR after a stored procedure call can be dramatic. For example, assume that you have two stored procedures that must be called in the same transaction and, for some reason, somebody by mistake has changed the name of one of the two stored procedures without changing all the calls. If only @aReturnValue is used for checking for success, the transaction will probably COMMIT, even though one of the stored procedures wasn't found.

Error Handling After INSERT/UPDATE/DELETE Statements

The error handling will be similar in the case of INSERT, UPDATE, and DELETE statements, but it is slightly different from stored procedure calls. For INSERT, UPDATE, and DELETE, you don't have a return value to check; instead, @@ROWCOUNT tells you how many rows were affected. Listing 9.5 shows an example of the error handling used after INSERT, UPDATE, and DELETE

9

ERROR HANDLING
AND CONCUR-
RENCY CONTROL

statements. As you can see, I need to catch both @@ERROR and @@ROWCOUNT in one statement, so I use SELECT instead of SET. If I don't do it like this, but first catch the @@ERROR value instead, for example, @@ROWCOUNT will be lost when I try to grab it.

LISTING 9.5   Error Handling After INSERT, UPDATE, and DELETE Statements

```
INSERT INTO errand
(id, description, ...)
VALUES
(@id, @description, ...)

SELECT @anError = @@ERROR, @aRowCount = @@ROWCOUNT
IF @anError <> 0 OR @aRowCount = 0 BEGIN
  SET @anErrorMessage = 'Problem with insert...'
  IF @anError = 0 BEGIN
    SET @anError = 80001   --Unexpected error.
  END
  GOTO ExitHandler
END
```

In the error handling for a stored procedure call, I typically want to keep the error code I find. In the case of error handling for INSERTs, UPDATEs, and DELETEs, I keep the error code as it is because @@ERROR was different than 0. If the error is because @@ROWCOUNT is 0, I have to decide what error code to set on my own. A common reason for why @@ROWCOUNT equals 0 after UPDATE and DELETE is that there was a concurrency conflict, which I will discuss later in this chapter.

> **NOTE**
>
> You can, of course, redefine an error on its way up the call stack so that the Business tier doesn't have to be aware of so many possible errors. Still, I have the same problem between the Consumer tier and the Business tier, and that is where I focus my efforts at handling the problem.

How to Choose Custom Error Codes

As you know by now, you are free to choose error codes from 50000 and greater. Below 50000 is reserved for SQL Server's own use. If you want, you can save error codes in the sysmessages table and then use RAISERROR() with the code to get the text from sysmessages. I actually prefer to use a table of my own with my own error messages, because I prefer to use a custom string to RAISERROR() instead of an error code. The custom string is formatted as XML to make it easy for the logging solution to find all the information it needs for every error.

Error Handling After a SELECT Statement

Getting a catchable @@ERROR presents only hypothetical risks after SELECT statements. Most errors, such as incorrect column names, will abort the batch so you can't deal with the @@ERROR. In any case, there are some instances when you can find a value in @@ERROR different from 0, so I use error handling for it all the time. Listing 9.6 shows an example of error handling after a SELECT statement.

LISTING 9.6 Error Handling After a SELECT Statement

```
SELECT e.id, e.description
FROM errand e
WHERE e.id = @id

SET @anError = @@ERROR
IF @anError <> 0 BEGIN
  SET @anErrorMessage = 'Problem with select...'
  GOTO ExitHandler
END
```

NOTE

Examples of @@ERROR problems you can catch after a SELECT statement are:

- Arithmetic overflow as when you CAST a value to a too-small data type.
- Division by zero.
- Timeout when a lock couldn't be granted, after LOCK_TIMEOUT has been SET to a value different than 0.

Although it's not common, it is also sometimes an error for SELECT if @@ROWCOUNT is 0 (that is, it might be an error if the SELECT doesn't find any rows). In these cases, you can easily switch to the construction used for INSERT, UPDATE, and DELETE instead.

Error Handling After Violation of a Business Rule

Finally, the fourth typical situation for error handling is one in which you find that there is a problem, for example, because the values of some of the parameters aren't as expected. In other words, a business rule has been broken. In Listing 9.7, you can see example code for such a situation and how the error is handled. As you can see, the handling of this situation is straightforward.

LISTING 9.7   Example Code for When a Business Rule Has Been Broken

```
IF @payment < @theExpectedPayment BEGIN
  SET @anError = 81001   --For example...
  SET @anErrorMessage =
  'The provided payment is too low.'
  GOTO ExitHandler
END
```

> **NOTE**
>
> Note that in Listing 9.7, it would be valuable to add the real values of the two variables to the @anErrorMessage string as well. Providing information like this is invaluable for quickly detecting what the problem is. The runtime cost is most often negligible, at least when it is not the normal situation, but only an abnormal exception.

An Additional Stored Procedure: `JnskError_Raise()`

As you saw in Listing 9.3, the `ExitHandler` centralizes the raising of errors through a stored procedure called `JnskError_Raise()`. I'd like to discuss the implementation of this stored procedure before we look at exception handling in .NET components.

Listing 9.8 shows the first part of the implementation of `JnskError_Raise()`. As you can see, two parameters seem a bit obscure at first—`@specificErrorMessage` and `@severityLevel`. `@specificErrorMessage` is typically the `@anErrorMessage` from the caller-stored procedure that gets its value as close to when the problem has been found as possible. (You have already seen examples of this in Listings 9.4, 9.5, 9.6, and 9.7.)

LISTING 9.8   The Implementation of `JnskError_Raise()`: Part 1

```
CREATE PROCEDURE JnskError_Raise (@source uddtSource
, @error INT, @specificErrorMessage uddtErrorMessage
, @severityLevel INT = 11)
AS

  DECLARE @aBuffer VARCHAR(255)
  , @aStandardErrorMessage uddtErrorMessage
```

LISTING 9.8   Continued

```
SET NOCOUNT ON
SET @aBuffer = ''

IF @error >= 50000 BEGIN
  SELECT @aBuffer = j.description
  FROM jnskerror_message j
  WHERE j.id = @error
END
```

As you see in Listing 9.8, the `@severityLevel` gets the default value 11, as was the case in Listing 9.3. There was no explicit value provided for this parameter (which is most often the case), so the default value will be used.

Then, two local variables are declared. In `@aBuffer`, the complete string will be constructed to be used by `RAISERROR()` later. `@aStandardErrorMessage` is the opposite of the `@specificErrorMessage` parameter. In `@aStandardErrorMessage`, I will store a string that I might find from my custom table of error messages. Assume that error 80001 is labelled as an "Unexpected error." It doesn't have to be SET each and every time it is used; indeed, the only thing that should be SET when the problem occurs is context-specific information.

Next, I make a few initializations before I read from my custom error message table to see if there is standardized text to be added to the error message.

> **NOTE**
>
> As I have mentioned already, I could have used the sysmessages table instead of my custom-built one, but I like to add information to the table, such as probable reasons, for the operation staff to use. This way, the documentation will also be a part of the system and you can, of course, output the "reason" column in the error log too. You can also give this kind of information for the reserved error codes smaller than 50000 in the custom table. That is not possible with the sysmessages table. If so, you have to change the implementation of JnskError_Raise() slightly so that it doesn't check whether the value is 50000 or greater for the error before reading from the custom error message table.

In the second part of the implementation of `JnskError_Raise()`, as you can see in Listing 9.9, I format an XML string with information about the problem. This XML string will subsequently be used as the string to `RAISERROR()` and also for the trace call, signalling an error.

LISTING 9.9   The Implementation of JnskError_Raise(): Part 2

```
SET @aBuffer = '<errorMessage error="'
+ CAST(@error AS VARCHAR(10)) + '"'
+ ' description="'
+ @specificErrorMessage + '|'
+ @aBuffer + '"'
+ ' source="' + @source + '">'

RAISERROR (@aBuffer, @severityLevel, 1)

EXEC JnskTrace_Error @source, @aBuffer
```

Listing 9.10 shows an example of the content of @aBuffer from Listing 9.9.

LISTING 9.10   Example of the Content of @aBuffer

```
<errormessage error="80001"
description="Problem with insert...|Unexpected error." source="Errand_Insert">
```

Note that one problem with centralizing the error raising in T-SQL, as I do with JnskError_Raise(), is that you will get incorrect source information when you execute the stored procedure from SQL Server Query Analyzer, as you can see in Listing 9.11. Instead of the faulty stored procedure, JnskError_Raise() will be mentioned as the problematic stored procedure and the line number where RAISERROR() was called. However, I don't consider this a big problem, especially because the description string will contain the real source.

LISTING 9.11   Example of Output in SQL Server Query Analyzer (Shown with Line Feeds)

```
Server: Msg 50000, Level 11, State 1, Procedure JnskError_Raise, Line 40

<errorMessage error="80001"
description="Programming error. Incorrect parameter!|Unexpected error"
source="a_Errand_FetchList">
```

> **NOTE**
>
> Whether it's a good idea to send the complete @aBuffer to JnskTrace_Error() is open to discussion, because @source will be provided twice, so to speak—both as a parameter on its own and also as part of the @aBuffer. This is a minor problem, but one that is perhaps worth looking at.

Note that when there is a value in @@ERROR different from 0, SQL Server will make a RAISERROR() call for you, and that will, of course, not be formatted like the one in Listing 9.10. The .NET code that examines the error stack and writes to the error log is prepared and will reformat that RAISERROR() message accordingly. This leads us nicely into exception handling in .NET, our next subject of discussion.

Handling Exceptions in .NET Components

Error handling in T-SQL is hopeless, even worse than it was in VB6. Thankfully, the exception handling in .NET is state of the art. Certainly, I think exception handling in .NET also has its caveats. As you know, I always take pride in trying to find issues with everything, but exception handling in .NET is wonderful to work with.

Most books about .NET programming include a chapter on how exception handling works and is programmed in .NET. I'm not going to discuss all the details in this section; instead, I will focus on the strategies particular to the server-side layers and apply the technique to the architecture and other previous discussions you've read about in this book. Note that I use the words "exception handling" instead of "error handling" in this section. When it comes to VB6 and T-SQL, the most common term to use is "error handling," but in .NET, it's mostly referred to as "exception handling."

> **NOTE**
>
> As I said, there is a wealth of information about exception handling available to you. If you want to learn more about handling exceptions, see Daniel Appleman's *Moving to VB.NET: Strategies, Concepts, and Code*[1] and Keith Franklin's *VB.NET for Developers*.[2] You should also read Eric Gunnerson's articles, "Writing Exceptional Code"[3] and "The Well-Tempered Exception."[4] Finally, a very good white paper is Kenny Jones and Edward Jezierski's "Exception Management in .NET."[5]

I'd like to start this section by recapping how I think Try, Catch, and Finally should be used.

Recap of the Basic Structure of Try, Catch, and Finally

Although we discussed the basic structure of Try, Catch, and Finally in Chapter 5, let's recap the basic ideas. Assume that you are going to use a resource—say an instance of a class called doErrand and a method called Escalate()—to check whether an errand is old enough and important enough to escalate to the next level of problem solvers. In this case, the instantiation of the object is usually done before the first Try clause. If the instantiation fails, the previous method in the call stack will handle the exception. This is similar to when Using() is used in C#. (Instantiations seldom fail, but if you find this is a problem, you can always add an outer Try block to the structure I'm proposing here.) When the resource is used, it will be protected by a Try block. Finally, a Finally block will call IDisposable's Dispose().

This is more or less what we discussed in Chapter 5. But what should be done between Try and Finally if there is an exception? This section discusses this scenario further.

Seven Different Approaches for Handling an Exception

There are actually more than seven approaches for how to handle an exception, because there are more combinations than those I'm about to explain. I have chosen to discuss only seven cases because, by doing so, I touch on all the basic "ingredients." Before we get to the examples, let's take a look at the different elements of exception handling and the combinations that are possible:

- *Catch*—Will the exception be caught or not?
- *Compensate*—Will there be code compensating or acting because of the exception?
- *Throw*—How should the exception be raised back to the calling method? There are several mechanisms for throwing an exception. First, you can use Throw just to rethrow the exception, Throw e to throw a new exception of the same type that was caught, and Throw New to throw a new exception of another type. (I will discuss the differences later in this section.)
- *Inner*—Will the caught exception be wrapped as an inner exception and sent with the Throw so that the receiver can see both the exception and the previous exception?

You can see that there are 15 combinations of these elements in Table 9.1. To give an example of how to read the table, let's take a look at the third example in the table. There, the exception will be caught, but no compensating action will be used. The exception will be raised to the caller by using Throw, but without wrapping the original exception as an inner exception to the Throw statement.

TABLE 9.1   Combinations of Exception Handling Elements and Their Validity

Combination	Catch	Compensate	Throw	Inner
1	No	-	-	-
2	Yes	No	No	-
3	Yes	No	Throw	No
4	Yes	No	Throw	Yes
5	Yes	No	Throw e	No
6	Yes	No	Throw e	Yes

TABLE 9.1 Continued

Combination	Catch	Compensate	Throw	Inner
7	Yes	No	Throw New	No
8	Yes	No	Throw New	Yes
9	Yes	Yes	No	-
10	Yes	Yes	Throw	No
11	Yes	Yes	Throw	Yes
12	Yes	Yes	Throw e	No
13	Yes	Yes	Throw e	Yes
14	Yes	Yes	Throw New	No
15	Yes	Yes	Throw New	Yes

Let's now look at the seven most typical approaches for how to handle an exception.

Don't `Catch`

If you don't have a `Catch` block, you won't `Catch` the exception, and it will bubble up the call stack. In VB6, this approach was uncommon because of the necessity of always explicitly cleaning up all method-instantiated resources in the method. Therefore, errors had to be caught locally to allow the method to do the cleanup before reraising the error. This is not a problem in .NET because you have the `Finally` clause, so the cleanup is decoupled from the catching of exceptions.

> **NOTE**
>
> This is not to say that explicit cleanup isn't important in .NET. I'm sure you remember the discussion about `IDisposable` from Chapter 5. When you instantiate resources that implement `IDisposable` at the method level, they should always be disposed of in a `Finally` block.

If you're not going to do anything special with a problem locally, there is really no point in catching the exception at all. Of course, sooner or later you will have to `Catch` the exception, but this doesn't necessarily mean it has to be at the lowest level.

This solution—not using `Catch` at all—is the easy one. Let's now turn our attention to techniques to use when exceptions are caught.

Catch and Eat

It's very simple just to `Catch` an exception and then not do anything about it. It's doable, but it's just as dangerous, as it is for other platforms. If you treat very specific exceptions this way, of course it won't be a problem, but if you have a last resort `Catch` that eats every problem, there is potentially a high risk of future bugs occurring.

Catch and Compensate

Sometimes you find that you can `Catch` an exception, investigate it, and then use some compensating code that deals with the exception as a whole so you don't have to raise a new exception to the caller. A typical example would be a retry mechanism.

Catch and Throw

When you use `Catch` and `Throw`, you are more or less saying that you had to `Catch` the exception because you had to use some compensating code, but then you don't want to deal with the real exception. Rather, you want the caller to take care of that so you just rethrow the exception. You will later see that this might be a common approach for transactional serviced components when `AutoComplete` isn't used.

Catch and Throw e

Catching an exception—for example, `As Exception`—and then using that variable to `Throw` is often a bad habit to get into. It means that you treat all exceptions as one and then you give that information to the caller. If you use an inner exception, it is possible for the caller to find the previous exception, but this is not the way the caller wants to find out what the problem was. The caller will have to use much too much code in this situation.

> **NOTE**
>
> I have decided to use e for exceptions, even though it is also the common variable name for events. It should be obvious from the context with which we are dealing.

Catch and Throw New

With `Catch` and `Throw New`, the exception is caught, but when it's time to raise an exception, a new exception is created and thrown. This solution is typical at "borders," such as in the classes in the Application layer, so that the consumer will only see nice, neat exceptions. Only show the consumer exceptions that you have documented as coming from you and exceptions that reveal as little as possible about your inner workings. For example, if you let the consumer receive a serviced component-related exception, you have revealed information to the consumer that he or she shouldn't know.

Catch and Throw (in Any Way) with Inner Exception

As long as Throw is used without an inner exception, the receiver of the exception won't know that there were previous exceptions or what those exceptions were. This is, of course, unfortunate in some situations. (One example is regarding the error-logging solution proposed in Chapter 4. Therefore, in most situations when you use Throw after Catch, you should also wrap the caught exception as an inner exception.

To simplify adjusting to the error-logging protocol, I propose that a helper be used for raising exceptions. I call the helper method Jnsk.Instrumentation.Err.Raise(), discussed in the next section.

My Centralized Method for Raising Exceptions

Without further ado, Listing 9.12 shows the Raise() method of the Jnsk.Instrumentation.Err helper class.

LISTING 9.12   Implementation of Jnsk.Instrumentation.Err.Raise()

```
Public Shared Function Raise(ByVal exceptionToThrow As Exception, _
ByVal caughtException As Exception, _
ByVal log As Boolean, _
ByVal exeOrDllName As String, _
ByVal source As String, _
ByVal userId As String) As Exception

    If log Then
        Jnsk.Instrumentation.Err.Log(exeOrDllName, _
        source, caughtException, userId)
    End If

    Jnsk.Instrumentation.TraceError(exeOrDllName, source, _
    caughtException, userId)
    Return exceptionToThrow
End Function
```

9

ERROR HANDLING
AND CONCUR-
RENCY CONTROL

> **NOTE**
>
> The code in Listing 9.12 looks a bit unintuitive. Be patient; it will be explained in just a few paragraphs.

It is worth mentioning that if the log parameter is True, no inner exception will be used when throwing the exception. The reason is that your consumers will probably receive the exception, and you don't want them to get all the information about previous exceptions.

I initially planned to let the helper do the `Throw` too, but the main drawback with having a helper for raising exceptions is that the exception stack is affected with more calls than are conceptually involved. The `Throw` will happen in the wrong method, so to speak. This wouldn't be a problem for my error-logging solution, because I could filter out calls to my `Raise()` method. However, it can be a problem for other consumers who want to browse the exception stack. Apart from this, I find there are mainly advantages to this solution. For example, logging an exception doesn't need another method call, a certain exception-handling protocol is forced (positively) on the components, and if you want to change exception-handling behavior, you have only one place to go. To eliminate the last drawback (the exception stack being affected), I use a little less intuitive call to the `Raise()` method. In Listing 9.13, you can see when `Raise()` is being called from a `Catch` block.

LISTING 9.13   `Raise()` Called from a `Catch` Block

```
Catch e As Exception
    Dim aNewException As New Exception(Exceptions.UnexpectedException)
    Throw Raise(aNewException, e, _
    True, AssemblyGlobal.exeOrDllName, theSource, "")
```

The code in Listing 9.13 also helps explain the implementation of the `Raise()` method shown in Listing 9.12. As you can see, the `Throw` is actually taken care of by the `Catch` block itself, not by the `Raise()` method. Because of this, the exception stack isn't affected, but the error logging and tracing is still centralized to the `Raise()` method.

In the code in Listing 9.13, the `log` parameter is `True`, and `aNewException` doesn't get an inner exception. This code is extracted from an entry method in the Application layer.

Also worth mentioning about Listing 9.13 is that `Exceptions.UnexpectedException` is a constant, containing the value `"Unexpected Exception"`.

NOTE

Even though I didn't show it here, there is also a `ServicedErr` class that uses the `ServicedTrace` class for tracing. I discussed this in Chapter 4.

Different Strategies for Different Layers

It's been a while since I presented my architecture proposal in Chapter 5, "Architecture." You'll recall that the Business tier has three layers—the Application layer, the Domain layer, and the Persistent Access layer. Figure 9.1 presents the architecture for your review.

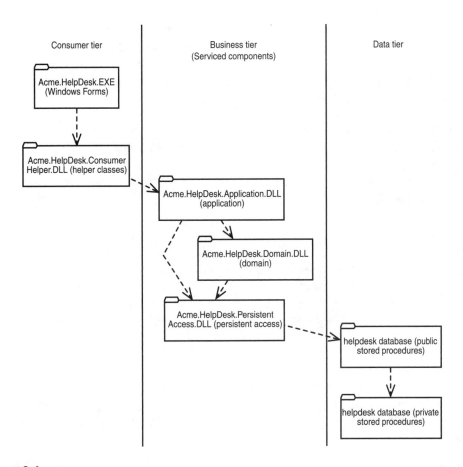

FIGURE 9.1

Tiers and layers in the architecture.

When we consider exception handling in terms of my architectural proposal, we must look at whether all layers must catch exceptions or not. I noted earlier that if you aren't going to do anything with an exception, don't catch it. On the other hand, sooner or later you reach the entry point, which is the Application layer. You then have to decide what the exception will look like for the consumer.

> **NOTE**
>
> It's probably also the case that only the Application layer will log problems. You decide this by giving True to the log parameter of the Raise() method previously discussed.

9

ERROR HANDLING AND CONCURRENCY CONTROL

As I said in Chapter 5, the Consumer Helper layer will translate exception information from programming information to user-friendly information. When I said that, I was thinking about what text to expose. The programmer of the consumer wants to see descriptive information from the Application layer, but on no account should you expose sensitive information. You need to strike a delicate balance.

Code with Manual Voting

In Chapter 5, I recommended you use AutoComplete() for the methods of your transactional classes. However, sometimes you need to manually vote for the outcome of automatic transactions. Of course, this is easy to do, but it also forces you to Catch exceptions, even when you have preferred to leave that to the caller instead.

> **NOTE**
>
> If you follow the architecture that I proposed in Chapter 5, the need for negative voting, which forces a Catch, won't be a problem, even if you can't use AutoComplete(). This is because you will normally only have one method to do the voting, and it will be located in the Application layer, which will need to Catch the exception anyway.

There are two common styles to choose from when using manual voting. For simplicity's sake, I'm assuming you use SetComplete()/SetAbort() for the voting. In the first case, you start the Try block by using SetAbort() and then the last statement of the Try block is SetComplete(). This means that if you reach the last statement of the Try block, the method votes yes; otherwise, the vote is no.

The second approach is to move SetAbort() to each of the Catch blocks. This usually requires a little more work, and there is the risk that you might forget to add SetAbort() to one Catch block. On the other hand, there is also a better chance to control the voting, because you might not want to vote no in the case of certain exceptions.

Writing Your Own Exception Classes

When you want to raise exceptions that aren't already found in the .NET Framework, you should gather those exceptions as subclasses to a custom exception class that inherits from ApplicationException. If we assume your superclass is called AcmeException, the consumer can easily group its Catch blocks to see whether the exception is coming from your application, at least if the exception is an uncommon one.

Should you want to give the user information about, say, several broken business rules in one single exception, this might be a good situation for adding custom behavior to your exception so that you can add all the problem information. This way, the consumer can find information about each problem in one exception.

> **NOTE**
>
> VB6 lacked a good method to catch unhandled errors high up in the call stack. We can now do this thanks to the `UnhandledException`·event in .NET. It might be useful as a last resort, but right now I don't really see the need for it, because I let my Application layer classes catch all exceptions and throw appropriate exceptions to the consumer.

Exceptions to Be Prepared For

In some of my sample code, in articles and course material, I force a division by zero on purpose to show what happens when an exception occurs. In reality, division by zero isn't one of the most significant problems you'll face, because most developers know how to prevent it. In this section, I'll discuss three different exceptions that you can't prevent completely, as well as the related problems for which you should be prepared to deal. Because I'm discussing them here, there is no excuse for waiting until you actually have the problems in your application to add exception handling to deal with them. In addition, you'll see that the Consumer Helper we discussed in Chapter 5 is our ally when it comes to helping us with all three exception situations.

Deadlock (1205)

Even though you may have used all the tips I gave you in Chapter 6, "Transactions," to lessen the risk of deadlocks, you will sometimes experience them anyway. Sooner or later, you will get error code 1205 from SQL Server, letting you know that you have been selected as a deadlock victim. Unfortunately, the error handling in your stored procedures is of no help whatsoever, and the stored procedure in which the deadlock occurred will be interrupted and so will the calling batch. Therefore, you're right back in the Persistent Access layer again.

> **NOTE**
>
> You will get a `System.Data.SqlClient.SqlException` and to find 1205, you have to investigate the `sqlErrors` in the `sqlErrorCollection` for the `SqlException`.

If you do use COM+ transactions, the transaction is doomed, and you have to leave the transaction stream. You do this by going all the way back to the Consumer Helper.

The Consumer Helper layer class can then restart the scenario and call the Application layer class again, and a new COM+ transaction will be started (if the Application layer is transactional). The Consumer Helper will often repeat this behavior a couple of times after a random-length pause before it gives up and tells the user that there is probably something very wrong because the transaction has been interrupted over and over again.

What Is Deadlock?

A simple way to describe a deadlock is that two transactions are both requesting resources exclusively held by the other transaction. Neither transaction will release any resource until it has grabbed the second resource, but this won't happen; thus, deadlock occurs.

Timeout

A similar situation to deadlock that is found in a Resource Manager (RM) is when the COM+ transaction times out. The exception will show up as System.Data.SqlClient.SqlException: "Timeout expired" in your .NET component. This may be because there is a distributed deadlock or because you have set the timeout to a value too short for the current load.

NOTE

The default value for transaction timeout of 60 seconds is not appropriate for operational applications, but only for debugging. You should probably decrease it to, say, 3 or 5 seconds instead. The shorter the better, until timeouts only occur because the given timeout attribute is too low.

Whatever the reason, there is nothing you can do about the problem in the current COM+ transaction. Instead, you have to trust the Consumer Helper layer class to take care of the problem again, by retrying the call to the Application layer class a couple of times before giving up.

NOTE

Unfortunately, you won't get the exception until the CommandTimeout of the SqlCommand object has been reached, and the exception is also the same as when the CommandTimeout has been reached because of another reason than that the COM+ transaction timeout has occurred.

Shutdown

Sometimes, the COM+ application terminates and you get
"System.Runtime.InteropServices.COMException: The RPC server is unavailable.
(0x800706BA)" when you try to use the Application layer instance from the Consumer Helper
layer. The reason for this problem could be that there is a serious problem and COM+ has
decided to terminate the COM+ application and restart it, or else an administrator has decided
to shut down the application.

<table>
<tr><td>NOTE</td><td></td></tr>
</table>

> It doesn't matter if you use Just-In-Time (JIT) activation or not, because this problem
> can show up in both situations. Of course, the risk of this exception occurring is
> greater if you keep a reference during a period of time and don't tear down the ref-
> erence between requests, but it doesn't matter. You should prepare for the exception
> anyway.

In any case, the Application layer instance will be lost for the Consumer Helper layer class.
Once again, the Consumer Helper layer class will help you out here, and the solution is simple—the Consumer Helper layer class just creates a new instance. Exactly as in the case with
the deadlock situations, the Consumer Helper layer class will retry a couple of times before
giving up.

Approaches to Concurrency Control for Disconnected Scenarios

The term "concurrency control" is a broad one. In the next couple of pages, I will discuss it in
very specific, but still common, scenarios—optimistic and pessimistic concurrency control.

In the first scenario, called optimistic concurrency control, you read data from the database
(let's call this time A), but disconnect the data so all locks are released. Then, when the user
has made some changes to the data and it is ready to be written back to the database (at time
B), you want to be sure not to save changes that overwrite changes made by someone else to
the very same rows (between time A and B). This process is called *optimistic concurrency control* because it is most likely possible to save changes because nobody else has made interfering changes to the same data.

> **NOTE**
>
> Never hold locks in the database while waiting for user interactions. Keeping lock periods as short as possible is perhaps the singlemost important tip for achieving high scalability.

In pessimistic concurrency control, you want to be sure that you will be able to change what you have read from the database without there being a risk that someone else has made changes that make it impossible for you to update. I will discuss pessimistic concurrency control later in this chapter, but for now, let's look at optimistic concurrency control.

> **NOTE**
>
> If you want to read up on concurrency in general for database applications, a good source would be a general textbook on databases. For example, C. J. Date's *An Introduction to Database Systems*[6] or Thomas Connolly and Carolyn Begg's *Database Systems: A Practical Approach to Design, Implementation, and Management.*[7]

Optimistic Concurrency Control

You may be wondering why we have to think about optimistic concurrency control at all. Well, sometimes it might be acceptable to not care, but usually there is a real need for a concurrency control mechanism. Let's investigate one of the problems associated with optimistic concurrency control, called the Lost Update problem, but this time in a situation in which you are disconnecting from the database between read and write.

In Table 9.2, you can see that I have two transactions working with the same data (called x in the example). Transaction A is reading the value x at time t1; Transaction B reads the same value at t2 and saves a change to the value at t4. When Transaction A is going to save its change to the same value at t6, the value in the database isn't the same value as it was when Transaction A read the value at t1.

TABLE 9.2   Example of the Lost Update Problem

Transaction A	Time	Transaction B
SELECT @x = e.x FROM errand e WHERE e.id = 1	t1	
Disconnect from database. Locks are released, no matter what was the Transaction Isolation Level (TIL).		
		BEGIN TRAN
	t2	SELECT @x = e.x FROM errand e WHERE e.id = 1
	t3	"Change" @x
	t4	UPDATE errand SET x = @x WHERE id = 1
		COMMIT TRAN
"Change" @x	t5	
Connect to the database.		
UPDATE errand SET x = @x WHERE id = 1	t6	

> **NOTE**
>
> In a way, calling it Transaction A is a misnomer because it is actually two transactions. First the one that reads the value and then, after reconnect, there is a second transaction when the value is written.

Note that Transaction B might look naïve to you because the same task could be done with code, such as that shown in Listing 9.14. That said, I decided to use the same approach as for Transaction A for reasons of clarity. It might also be the case that Transaction B makes a similar disconnect as Transaction A, but after time t2. Anyway, the main problem would be the same, no matter which approach Transaction B uses.

LISTING 9.14   A Better Approach for Transaction B

```
UPDATE errand
SET x = x + @something
WHERE id = 1
```

Was the Lost Update problem presented in Table 9.2 a serious one or not? It might depend on what x is. Assume x is some kind of description. All that happens is that Transaction A changes the description so that as far as Transaction A knows, the description value Transaction B gave at t4 has never existed. Perhaps Transaction A (or rather the user requesting the transaction) wouldn't have wanted to make the change if it had known about the value at t5.

On the other hand, if x is a numeric value that is accumulated over time, the Lost Update problem is always a nasty one. Assume that x is 100 at t1. Transaction B adds 20 to the value at t3. x is then 120 at t4. Transaction A adds 50 to the value at t5, but Transaction A makes the addition to 100 so x is written as 150 at t6. It should, of course, be 170 instead, after both Transaction A and B have executed.

> **NOTE**
>
> In Table 9.2, I'm not using stored procedures, but this is only to provide as concise an example as possible. Nothing in the example is really affected by not using stored procedures. I have also used an INTEGER for the ID column in the example, even though you know that I used UNIQUEIDENTIFIER before. I have used an INT here because UNIQUEIDENTIFIER occupies several rows without really adding any valuable information to the table.

So, what is the typical solution to the Lost Update problem? The most typical solution is to let the database take care of the problem by using locks. If we forget about the fact that Transaction A disconnects from the database for a moment, it could make BEGIN TRAN at time t0 and COMMIT TRAN after time t6. If it uses Transaction Isolation Level (TIL) REPEATABLE READ or SERIALIZABLE, the shared lock will be taken at time t1. That makes it impossible for Transaction B to get the exclusive lock that it is asking for at time t4. Transaction B is thus in a wait state. Unfortunately, Transaction A won't get an exclusive lock either at time t6 (at least not if Transaction B uses a suitable TIL) because Transaction B has a shared lock from t2, so Transaction A also stops in a wait state. This is a deadlock, and hopefully SQL Server will decide on a victim so that this transaction can be aborted and the other transaction can be fulfilled. The aborted transaction can then be restarted and there is no lost update.

This was quite a drastic solution to the problem. In Chapter 6, I said that it's better to take an exclusive lock directly if you know that you are going to escalate a shared lock to an exclusive lock later. If that methodology is applied to Table 9.2, it would mean that optimizer hint (UPDLOCK) would be used at time t1 and time t2 so that the SELECT statement would appear as it does in Listing 9.15.

LISTING 9.15   SELECT Statement That Asks for an Exclusive Lock

```
SELECT @x = e.x
FROM errand e (UPDLOCK)
WHERE e.id = 1
```

The result of this would be that Transaction A is granted an exclusive lock at time t1. Transaction B won't be granted an exclusive lock at t2, but stops in a wait state. Transaction A can continue all the way to after time t6 (where COMMIT TRAN is executed); the lock is then released and Transaction B's wait state is over. Transaction B gets an exclusive lock and can move on.

So far so good, but there's just one problem. Before these explanations, I said that we should forget that Transaction A is disconnecting from the database. Assume we can't forget it. Assume that Transaction A needs user interaction inside the transaction so it knows how to change x in time t5. Having that user interaction would be a minor disaster for throughput if the exclusive lock were kept. Imagine that you are Transaction B. If you're lucky, you would have to wait for seconds, and if you're less lucky, minutes. Meanwhile, the connection used by Transaction A is occupied during the user interaction, so that resource can't be used by another user. This methodology would greatly harm scalability.

Do we have a problem that's impossible to solve here? Of course not, but it requires an approach that is a little different than what most classic database textbooks discuss. I'd like to discuss three different approaches to the problem and, while doing so, come up with a proposal for the recommendation I find to be the best.

Problem Solution 1: ROWVERSION Column

Probably the most typical solution to the optimistic concurrency problem is to use a ROWVERSION column on the table. The ROWVERSION value is read in the SELECT (time t1 in the example in Table 9.2) and remembered until it's time to save the changes. The UPDATE statement in a stored procedure might then look as is shown in Listing 9.16.

> **NOTE**
>
> In the code in Listing 9.16 and most often after that, I have just added comments as placeholders for the regular declarations, initializations, error handling, and ExitHandler.

LISTING 9.16   ROWVERSION Version of Concurrency Control

```
CREATE PROCEDURE Errand_Update (@id UNIQUEIDENTIFIER
, @x uddtX, @rowVersionOld ROWVERSION AS)

  --The usual declarations and initializations.
  UPDATE errand
  SET x = @x
  WHERE id = @id
  AND rv = @rowVersionOld
  --The usual error handler and ExitHandler.
```

In Listing 9.16, you can see that the old ROWVERSION value (found at time t1) is compared to the current ROWVERSION value at time t6. (The ROWVERSION column is called rv in the example.) If they are different, @@ROWCOUNT will get the value of 0. As you probably remember from the INSERT/UPDATE/DELETE example of error handling earlier in this chapter, the error-handling code considers @@ROWCOUNT = 0 an error, so the user can be notified. The user can then reread the row and make the same changes again, if he or she still thinks the changes should be made. Of course, you can also implement so that the user can compare earlier values and current values to his or her own changes so that the user can decide what values should be used of those three possible versions.

NOTE

ROWVERSION was called TIMESTAMP in versions before SQL Server 2000. I believe ROWVERSION is a better name, because there is no time in the value, it's just an ordinal.

Problem Solution 1: Pros and Cons

The pros of the ROWVERSION solution are as follows:

- It is commonly used and well known.
- It is in a sense automatic and not much extra code is needed.
- It will also work when changes are done to the data from other code or by hand, without the other code having to know about the protocol.

And the cons of this solution are as follows:

- Sometimes it is too coarse granular. Assume you want to change the column called `description` and another user has changed the column called `responsible`. Should that really stop your UPDATE? Probably not, but that is exactly what might happen when ROWVERSION is used for concurrency control, because there can only be one ROWVERSION on a table. This is particularly a problem for wide tables, or rather tables that are used for several different purposes.

- You can't use Distributed Partitioned Views (DPVs) for tables with a ROWVERSION column. This is because the ROWVERSION series is local to each machine. With DPV, the table will be partitioned over several machines.

- You can't use merge replication for tables with ROWVERSION columns. Well, you can if you say that those columns shouldn't be replicated, but then your mechanism for concurrency control doesn't really work. On the other hand, concurrency control in replication scenarios is a completely different story and not within the scope of this book.

Problem Solution 2: Before and After Values

In the second problem solution, we use the values from the SELECT at time t1 and check that the values are still the same at time t6 before you make the update. A typical solution to an UPDATE stored procedure would be to use code shown in Listing 9.17.

LISTING 9.17   Before and After Values Version of Concurrency Control: Example 1

```
CREATE PROCEDURE Errand_Update (@id UNIQUEIDENTIFIER
, @xNew uddtX, @xOld uddtX) AS
  --The usual declarations and initializations.
  DECLARE @theCurrentX uddtX

  SELECT @theCurrentX = e.x
  FROM errand e (UPDLOCK)
  WHERE e.id = @id
  --The usual error handler.

  IF @theCurrentX = @xOld BEGIN
    UPDATE errand
    SET x = @xNew
    WHERE id = @id
    --The usual error handler.
  END
  ELSE BEGIN
    SET @anError = 80004
```

LISTING 9.17   Continued

```
    SET @anErrorMessage = 'Conflict in update.'
    GOTO ExitHandler
END
--The usual ExitHandler.
```

> **NOTE**
>
> It's important to understand that the code in Listing 9.17 must execute in an active transaction to work correctly.

The implementation shown in Listing 9.17 is a bit clumsy, especially if you imagine that you have 50 before and after values with which to work. I earlier complained about the implementation of UpdateBatch() in ADO, but through it I learned another way of doing this, which I think is a much better solution. In Listing 9.18, you can see that I use the old columns in the WHERE clause instead. If @@ROWCOUNT = 0, I know that some of the values have changed.

LISTING 9.18   Before and After Values Version of Concurrency Control: Example 2

```
CREATE PROCEDURE Errand_Update (@id UNIQUEIDENTIFIER
, @xNew uddtX, @xOld uddtX) AS
    --The usual declarations and initializations.
    UPDATE errand
    SET x = @xNew
    WHERE id = @id
    AND x = @xOld
    --The usual error handler and ExitHandler.
```

Problem Solution 2: Pros and Cons

The pros of the before and after values solution are as follows:

- It is as granular as you want. You can have column-level concurrency control instead of row-level concurrency control, although I don't recommend this. (Row-level concurrency control is what you always get when ROWVERSION is used.)

- Assuming you want to audit changes by writing before and after values to an audit table in your stored procedure, you don't have to read from the table to collect the before values, because they are provided as parameters to the stored procedure.

- It is not imperative that the consumer reread the row before updating it directly again. This depends on whether the stored procedure that handles the update changes any of the columns. If it doesn't, the consumer has all the required information. He or she can simply move the newly saved values to the variables holding the old values.

- The solution will work when changes are made to the data from other code or by hand, without the other code needing to know about the protocol.

> **NOTE**
>
> In addition, the disadvantage of handling the business rule to check that a status change is valid disappears. Business rules are discussed in Chapter 7, "Business Rules."

The cons of this solution are as follows:

- There is more data to keep track of, more data to keep at the consumer, more parameters to set before calling the stored procedure, more data to send to the stored procedure at the time of UPDATE, and more data to use in the WHERE clause. This may not seem to be a big problem at first, but when you have 50 columns to update in one stored procedure, you will have 100+ columns in the parameter list to the stored procedure. Furthermore, even if you have only updated one column of these 50, you still have to compare 50 different columns in the WHERE clause.

- There might be problems with precision when you toss float numbers over to .NET components and back to the stored procedure to be used in the WHERE clause.

Problem Solution 3: Custom Columns

The third solution to the concurrency problem is completely manual. It's best illustrated by an example, which can be seen in Listing 9.19. Here you can see that I keep a SMALLINT column called rv (just as with the ROWVERSION column in the first solution) in the table. When the row was read from the database at time t1, the rv was fetched too. When it's time to UPDATE the row at time t6 (as is shown in Listing 9.19), the code checks that the rv value is the same as it was when it was read. If it is, the rv value will also be increased.

LISTING 9.19 Custom Value Version of Concurrency Control

```
CREATE PROCEDURE Errand_Update (@id UNIQUEIDENTIFIER
, @x uddtX, @rvOld SMALLINT) AS
  --The usual declarations and initializations.
  UPDATE errand
  SET x = @x
```

LISTING 9.19   Continued

```
, rv = CASE WHEN rv < 32767 THEN rv + 1 ELSE 1 END
WHERE id = @id
AND rv = @rvOld
--The usual error handler and ExitHandler.
```

Note that the rv column in Listing 9.19 is a good example of a column that should use a user-defined data type. On the other hand, you will have to change the border value in the code (see 32767 in Listing 9.19) if you change the datatype for the user-defined datatype. I miss global constants in T-SQL very much. Or even better, I wish we had available a possibility similar to the one in .NET as is shown in Listing 9.20.

Also worth mentioning is that I could use negative values too, an often-forgotten technique in situations like this. That doubles the size of the span for the interval of values.

LISTING 9.20   How to Ask for the Max Size of a Variable in Visual Basic .NET

```
Dim anInteger As Integer
Console.WriteLine(anInteger.MaxValue.ToString())
```

It's no secret that T-SQL isn't at all as powerful as the .NET languages, but it still frustrates me.

Problem Solution 3: Pros and Cons

The pros of the custom columns solution are as follows:

- It has full flexibility. Because you program this solution on your own, you have a certain amount of freedom.

- You can "partition" the row in as many concurrency control pieces you want by using several rv columns.

- You can actually see how many times a row has been changed, which might be useful in some situations. (If so, you should perhaps use INT instead of SMALLINT as I did in Listing 9.19.)

- You are not obliged to reread the row before updating it directly again. This depends on whether the stored procedure handling the UPDATE changes any of the columns. If it does not, the consumer has all the necessary information. The consumer can just move the newly saved values to the variables holding the old values, and the current rv is the old rv + 1.

The cons of this solution are as follows:

- It's completely manual, so you have to program this solution completely on your own. (As you saw in the previous "pros" section, I listed this as an advantage also. Whether it's an advantage or disadvantage depends on the situation.)

- You must watch out for borders. No matter what data type you use for the rv column, there is a value border to watch out for.

- The protocol doesn't work if other UPDATE requests don't follow the protocol. However, if all UPDATEs are done through a stored procedure, this is not a problem.

What If I Don't Like Stored Procedures?

As you know by now, I'm very fond of stored procedures, and I did the checking in a stored procedure for all three solutions. However, each solution can, of course, be used from the .NET components and with dynamic SQL instead. However, I find this task is very close to the database. Also, watch out for overhead if you use several round trips with the third solution because the throughput will be damaged.

Problem Solution 4: Taking Care of the Concurrency Control in a .NET Component

All three solutions discussed so far have been located in stored procedures. Each of the mechanisms of those solutions can be used for solving the concurrency control problem in .NET components instead of as in stored procedures. I don't think this is a good idea though, because you will get longer transactions and longer locks. In the evaluation later in this chapter, this approach will be discussed some more.

My Proposal for Approaching Optimistic Concurrency Control of Disconnected Data

As always, coming up with a recommendation is very difficult, because it depends so much on the situation at hand. In the case of the different techniques for optimistic concurrency control of disconnected data, this is certainly the case. All three solutions work just fine, and work best in different situations. As usual, the best approach is to use the best solution for the situation.

If you find that my recommendation in the previous paragraph was kind of a nonrecommendation, I can say that if I had to choose only one solution to use all the time, I prefer solution 3, the custom columns solution, because it is the most flexible. Just one word of caution though—as you know, flexibility often means more work.

Pessimistic Concurrency Control

We have now discussed several solutions for how to get optimistic concurrency control when the data has been disconnected from the database. In certain situations, you need pessimistic concurrency control instead. Assume that you are thinking of buying two flight tickets to Sweden for you and your loved one. (What's that? You'd rather go to France? Trust me, you should visit Sweden....) So, you ask the airline if any tickets are left and they tell you that you are in luck, they have just two. The sales clerk asks you if you want them; you think for 10 seconds and say you do. Right at that moment, you think those tickets are yours. However, if the sales clerk had been using an application that used optimistic concurrency control, anyone could have bought the tickets while you were making up your mind.

A similar example can be taken from our sample application Acme HelpDesk. When a problem solver inspects a reported errand, he expects that nobody else will take on the responsibility of solving that errand until he has decided if he is a suitable problem solver himself. Although it involves more work, it is possible to implement pessimistic concurrency control for disconnected scenarios. Let's take a look at my recommended solution for adding pessimistic concurrency control for disconnected scenarios to your applications.

NOTE

· Once again, remember that I want the data to be disconnected from the database and the connection to be released during the time the user is thinking. Otherwise, an easy solution would be to not disconnect from the database and keep an exclusive lock on the rows in the database for those tickets or the errand. As a matter of fact, this isn't a good solution anyway, because you don't want a user to decide the length in time for the locks. This can't be said often enough. Keep in mind too that when the Consumer tier is a classic Web application, it's also a problem keeping a connection open over several requests.

Problem Solution: My Proposal for Approaching Pessimistic Concurrency Control of Disconnected Data: Custom Lock Table

Let's continue with the errand sample where I show a solution proposal to the problem. An easy solution for achieving pessimistic concurrency control is to add a lock table, such as the one shown in Figure 9.2. If the id of the lock table is of data type UNIQUEIDENTIFIER, the same table can be used, even if several tables (all must have UNIQUEIDENTIFIERs, of course) need to use this custom solution for pessimistic concurrency control. If you don't use UNIQUEIDENTIFIERs in your tables but perhaps use INT for your primary keys, you must have one lock table per table that can be handled the way I'm about to show. Of course, you could also have a composite primary key of id and table name in the lock table and then you only need one lock table. In any case, this is a situation when UNIQUEIDENTIFIER is very good.

FIGURE 9.2

Lock *table for custom locks.*

If all your reading of errands goes through a stored procedure (which I recommend anyway), you can use code like that shown in Listing 9.21.

LISTING 9.21 Use of Lock_GrantRead()

```
EXEC @aReturnValue = Lock_GrantRead@id
, @userId

SELECT @anError = @@ERROR
IF @anError <> 0 OR @aReturnValue <> 0 BEGIN
  SET @anErrorMessage = 'Problem when granting read.'
  IF @anError = 0 BEGIN
    SET @anError = @aReturnValue
  END
  GOTO ExitHandler
END

SELECT e.id, e.description ,...
FROM errand e
WHERE e.id = @id
--The usual error handler.
```

If the user tries to read an errand from the database that isn't locked, he or she will receive 0 as the return value from the Lock_GrantRead() stored procedure. The Lock_GrantRead() stored procedure will also INSERT a row to the lock table with the @id, the @userId, and the time for when the lock was acquired. Because 0 was returned, the user will get the information back about the errand.

On the other hand, if the errand was already to be found in the lock table, and the lock still is valid and owned by somebody else, Lock_GrantRead() will return the error code associated with the problem that a custom lock can't be granted, and the SELECT will not take place. If there is already a row in the lock table for the id but the lock is more than 10 minutes old (if that is the validity time for this example), the user will be granted the lock and 0 will be returned.

I think it's important to set a time when the lock is no longer valid; otherwise sooner, rather than later, you will get into the situation where an administrator has to change a lock manually.

The inner workings of the `Lock_GrantRead()` stored procedure looks as shown in Listing 9.22.

LISTING 9.22   Implementation of `Lock_GrantRead()`

```
CREATE PROCEDURE Lock_GrantRead (@id UNIQUEIDENTIFIER
, @userId uddtUserId) AS

  --The usual declarations and initializations.

  DECLARE @aCurrentUserId uddtUserId
  , @aLockedDatetime DATETIME

  SET @theTranCountAtEntry = @@TRANCOUNT
  SET TRANSACTION ISOLATION LEVEL SERIALIZABLE
  IF @theTrancountAtEntry = 0 BEGIN
    BEGIN TRAN
  END

  SELECT @aCurrentUserId = userid
  , @aLockedDatetime = lockeddatetime
  FROM lock (UPDLOCK)
  WHERE id = @id

  SET @anError = @@ERROR
  IF @anError <> 0 BEGIN
    SET @anErrorMessage = 'Problem with SELECT from lock table.'
    GOTO ExitHandler
  END

  IF @aCurrentUserId IS NULL
  OR @aCurrentUserId = @userId
  OR DATEADD(n, dbo.LockValidNMinutes(), @aLockedDatetime)
  < GETDATE() BEGIN
    DELETE FROM lock
    WHERE id = @id

    SET @anError = @@ERROR
    IF @anError <> 0 BEGIN
      SET @anErrorMessage = 'Problem with DELETE from lock table.'
      GOTO ExitHandler
    END

    INSERT INTO lock
    (id, userid, lockeddatetime)
```

LISTING 9.22   Continued

```
VALUES
(@id, @userId, GETDATE())

SELECT @anError = @@ERROR, @aRowcount = @@ROWCOUNT
IF @anError <> 0 OR @aRowcount = 0 BEGIN
  SET @anErrorMessage = 'Problem with INSERT to lock table.'
  IF @anError = 0 BEGIN
    SET @anError = 80001
  END
  GOTO ExitHandler
END

END
ELSE BEGIN
  SET @anError = 80004
  SET @anErrorMessage = 'Read lock can not be granted.'
END

--The usual ExitHandler.
```

As you can see, the lock is granted in one of the following circumstances:

- When there is no lock for the row
- When I have the current lock for the row
- When there is a lock for the row, but it is too old

It is also worth mentioning that in the implementation of Lock_GrantRead(), I use a scalar UDF called LockValidNMinutes() for providing the constant of how many minutes the lock is valid.

In Listing 9.22, the stored procedure for granting a read (and taking a lock) was shown, but you also need a similar stored procedure to be used before you update the row. The same rules apply as in Listing 9.22, but the row will be unlocked instead of locked. My implementation of that stored procedure is called Lock_GrantUpdate() and can be downloaded from the book's Web site at www.samspublishing.com.

You also need an a_Lock_Release() procedure. As you saw, I prefix a_Lock_Release() with a_ and that usually means that this stored procedure can be called from the Persistent Access layer. That is exactly the reason this time too. Locks will be released with the help of Lock_GrantUpdate() that is called by the UPDATE stored procedure. But what if the user that is granted the lock decides not to UPDATE the errand? Then the lock is left in the database until its validity time is at an end.

What if the user doesn't click the Close button of the form but just terminates the application? This is a particular problem with Web applications because you have very little control of how the user uses the application. There will always be situations when a lock isn't released, but that is exactly the problem that the time validity will solve gracefully.

Weak Spots in the Proposed Solution

Although later in this chapter we will evaluate this proposal against the criteria we established in Chapter 2, "Factors to Consider in Choosing a Solution to a Problem," let's look at a few of the specific weak spots with having a custom `lock` table. The first, and probably the most important one, is that it consumes a lot of resources, so don't overuse this solution. You might find yourself using the solution for each and every table. If so, this is a sign of a possible design error or an incorrect perception of customer requirements. Is it really important to only let one user at a time update the information about a specific customer, for example? Why can't it be treated with optimistic concurrency control of disconnected data instead? The moral of the story is to push optimistic concurrency of disconnected data and only use pessimistic concurrency control of disconnected data when it's absolutely necessary. Think about pessimistic concurrency control of disconnected data as reserving something. You don't use the reservation mechanism all the time. You would also think that it's all right to first take a look at the item and then explicitly reserve it. What I mean is, let the user show his or her intent to update and at that point grab a lock.

Even if you have a correct implementation of the proposed solution for pessimistic concurrency control of disconnected data, it doesn't have exactly the same semantics as the pessimistic locking handled natively by the database. The reason is that the lock will only be valid for *n* minutes. If you think for too long, the lock is gone when you think that you still have it. You could implement a mechanism in the consumer, giving a warning to the user when the lock will soon become invalid. In addition, after you have updated the row, you have to read the row again if you want to keep the lock. This is not a huge problem, but it adds to the overhead.

It's not always enough only to have locking for a `userId`. If so, the user might kick up two different browsers and take a look at the same errand in both of them. This is perfectly valid, because both browsers are used by the same `userId`. Unfortunately, when he or she clicks the Close button in one of the browsers, the lock is released for both browsers, without them knowing. You can add `sessionId` as another piece of information for the lock, and then each browser will be treated as two different requesters. If one browser has a lock, the other one won't be granted that lock, even if the `userId` is the same. A slightly improved protocol would be to only let the `sessionId` that holds the lock release it and use the lock for updating. Still, the same `userId` is always granted rights to read the row.

> **NOTE**
>
> There are several ways to create a `sessionId`, but a common one is to generate a GUID and store it as a cookie for Web applications, for example. A GUID works perfectly well in the case of Windows Forms consumers too.

Some users aren't authorized to change a specific errand, in which case there is no point in letting them grab a lock either. The same goes for calls to `a_Lock_Release()`. It's no use calling that stored procedure if the user looks at an errand that he or she isn't allowed to update. If you build logic like this in your application, you will decrease the overhead of the solution. Finally, another way to decrease the overhead is to take care of the pessimistic locking at a coarse granular level. Don't use the custom locking on separate actions, but only on the complete errand.

Evaluation of Proposals

It's now time to evaluate the proposals I presented in this chapter against the criteria we established in Chapter 2. We'll first evaluate the complete proposal for how to catch errors in both stored procedures and .NET components, and then we'll look at the optimistic concurrency control proposal. Finally, we'll look at the pessimistic concurrency control proposal I just presented.

Evaluation of Proposal for Handling Errors

The proposal for how to deal with errors is actually quite a large one. First, a complete protocol must be fulfilled in the stored procedures and then, in the .NET components, a centralized method will be used for "raising" exceptions. The type of consumer factor is only of interest in the case of .NET exceptions, because the only consumer to the stored procedures should be the Persistent Access layer. Even so, the type of consumer shouldn't affect the .NET exceptions at all. The Application layer will raise an exception and, if the consumer wants to see exceptions another way, the Consumer Helper layer will take care of that.

As you may guess, performance and scalability will be affected when error handling is used, but then, do we really have a choice? We need to handle errors and the cost isn't all that great. We can use different strategies, but there isn't usually much overhead with the solution I use. In the case of abnormal situations, there is a lot of overhead, but exceptions should happen so rarely that this is not really a problem.

As you might guess, I find the solution both maintainable and reliable. It's maintainable because it's a distinct model for how to treat error handling. Consistent code means maintainable code. One example of how reliability is increased is the paranoid error handling used in the stored procedures. As I mentioned in the chapter, I even handle errors due to missing stored procedures.

I discussed the error-logging solution in detail in Chapter 4. Thanks to this error logging, debuggability is greatly increased. I think the reuse situation is good for both the stored procedures and the .NET components. Because the stored procedures use both RETURN() and RAISERROR(), it will be possible for them to be reused by most other stored procedures, and vice versa. The main problem as I see it with reusing stored procedures and components from other sources is that I expect XML-formatted error descriptions from RAISERROR() for the error logging solution to work just as expected. I also want raised exceptions that are lower than the entry point to use inner exceptions so as not to lose the error stack. Writing a custom exception schema for the .NET components could mean that exactly the same schema could be used for COM components, so they could both be better integrated instead of relying on interop. Still, in this case, I definitely prefer to play with the cards we have. Finally, as I said earlier, consistent code means maintainable code, and thanks to this, productivity gains too.

Evaluation of Proposal for Approaching Optimistic Concurrency Control of Disconnected Data

In this chapter, I actually listed two different proposals for approaching optimistic concurrency control of disconnected data. One was to use the best technique for the situation at hand, and the other was to use the custom column approach because it has less constraints. In this evaluation, I will look at the conceptual proposal for dealing with optimistic concurrency control in stored procedures in general, and also the custom approach I recommend. In this evaluation, you will find that there will be quite a few factors that aren't affected at all. Let's start with performance and scalability.

Performance and scalability fare very well thanks to the use of stored procedures for the solution, even though yet another column has to be changed at every UPDATE. However, this doesn't affect the performance and scalability much because the row has to be read and locked anyway. At the book's Web site at www.samspublishing.com, you can see a diagram comparing the differences in throughput between the three proposals, and also the fourth solution for taking care of the control in a .NET component. (Please remember that the results will be affected by several factors and are only correct in the actual situation used for the test.)

Maintainability is better than using before-after values, because the control solution isn't affected at all when an additional column is added. There are also fewer parameters to send to stored procedures. Reliability is just fine, but a problem occurs when the tables are written to by sources that don't follow the protocol. It is exactly the same for reusability, of course. Productivity is fine too, especially compared to when before-after values are used.

Evaluation of Proposal for Approaching Pessimistic Concurrency Control of Disconnected Data: Custom Lock Table

Even here, in the case of concurrency control, I decided to handle it in my stored procedures. When I come to the factor of farm-/cluster-enabling, you will see that this has advantages, but let's start from the beginning.

Performance and scalability will definitely be negatively affected when you use the proposed solution. Don't overuse it—I repeat, don't overuse it! To give you a picture of the overhead, I have compared the recommended solution for pessimistic concurrency control of disconnected data with the recommended solution of its optimistic sibling. You can see the result at the book's Web site at www.samspublishing.com.

Because all the locking work is done in stored procedures, it is relatively encapsulated and therefore maintainable. Reliability may be a problem, because if not all requesting parties follow the protocol, it fails. It is also the case that after n minutes, your lock is gone, and it may not be possible to save the changes you make.

Reusability is positively affected this time, but in a different way than usual. The structure and solution can be reused for all the different tables and resources for which you want to use pessimistic concurrency control.

Another solution to the problem is to let COM+ handle the locks, for example, with the help of the Shared Properties Managers (SPM). A big advantage with my recommended approach is that you don't get farm/cluster problems. On the other hand, you can first use a SPM-based solution and, when you need to support farms/clusters, you change the solution to use my recommended solution instead. I don't recommend this approach, because I think it will be a pretty large change when the time comes, and my approach is also more reliable—for example, if the COM+ application terminates without the user noticing it at all.

9

ERROR HANDLING AND CONCUR-RENCY CONTROL

What's Next

Because this is the last chapter in the book, what's next is what the future has to bring. The new platform of .NET is the most promising and powerful platform so far, no question about that. Still, there are a lot of new problems and design decisions waiting around the corner. I hope this book has inspired you with ideas of how to deal with some of the problems you will face and has helped you prepare for what must be done early on when building enterprise applications. Good luck!

References

1. D. Appleman. *Moving to VB.NET: Strategies, Concepts, and Code*. Apress; 2001.

2. K. Franklin. *VB.NET for Developers*. Sams; 2001.

3. E. Gunnerson. "Writing Exceptional Code," `http://msdn.microsoft.com/library/en-us/dncscol/html/csharp07192001.asp`.

4. E. Gunnerson. "The Well-Tempered Exception," `http://msdn.microsoft.com/library/en-us/dncscol/html/csharp/08162001.asp`.

5. K. Jones and E. Jezierski. "Exception Management in .NET," `http://msdn.microsoft.com/library/en-us/dnbda/html/exceptdotnet.asp`.

6. C. J. Date. *An Introduction to Database Systems*, *Seventh Edition*. Addison Wesley; 2000.

7. T. Connolly and C. Begg. *Database Systems: A Practical Approach to Design, Implementation, and Management*. Addison-Wesley; 1998.

Suggestions for Further Reading

The following is a list of books you may find helpful as you learn about .NET and SQL Server 2000 and for developing your professional skills in general. You'll notice that, while I haven't mentioned books that focus on COM, I've included several COM+ books. This is because most of the information in these COM+ books is still valid because the programming model for writing serviced components in .NET is very similar to writing COM+ components, say, in VB6. The number of .NET books is on the thin side because I wrote this book early on in the days of .NET. Good .NET books will certainly enter the market in the coming months; therefore, you can find an up-to-date reference list at this book's Web site at `www.samspublishing.com`.

Appleman, D. *Moving to VB.NET: Strategies, Concepts and Code*. Apress; 2001. ISBN 1-893115-97-6

Beck, K. *Extreme Programming Explained: Embrace Change*. Addison-Wesley; 1999. ISBN 0-201-61641-6

Ben-Gan, I. and T. Moreau. *Advanced Transact-SQL for SQL Server 2000*. Apress; 2000. ISBN 1-893115-82-8

Bernstein, P.A. and E. Newcomer. *Principles of Transaction Processing*. Morgan Kaufmann; 1996. ISBN 1558604154

Booch, G., Rumbaugh, J., and I. Jacobson. *The Unified Modeling Language User Guide*. Addison-Wesley; 1998. ISBN 0-201-57168-4

Brill, G. *Applying COM+*. New Riders; 2001. ISBN 0-7357-0978-5

Brown, R., Baron W., and W. D. Chadwick III. *Designing Solutions with COM+ Technologies*. Microsoft Press; 2001. ISBN 0-73561127-0

Buschmann, F., Meunier, R., Rohnert, H., Sommerlad, P., and M. Stal. *Pattern-Oriented Software Architecture: A System of Patterns*. Wiley; 1996. ISBN 0-471-95869-7

Celko, J. *SQL for Smarties, Second Edition*. Morgan Kaufmann; 1999. ISBN 1-55860-576-2

Connolly, T. and C. Begg. *Database Systems: A Practical Approach to Design, Implementation and Management, Second Edition*. Addison-Wesley; 1998. ISBN 0-201-34287-1

Date, C. J. *An Introduction to Database Systems, Seventh Edition*. Addison-Wesley; 2000. ISBN 0-201-38590-2

Delaney, K. *Inside SQL Server 2000*. Microsoft Press; 2000. ISBN 0-7356-0998-5

Ewald, T. *Transactional COM+: Building Scalable Applications*. Addison-Wesley; 2001. ISBN 0-201-61594-0

Fleming, C. C. and B. von Halle. *Handbook of Relational Database Design*. Addison-Wesley; 1989. ISBN 0-201-11434-8

Fowler, M. *Analysis Patterns*. Addison-Wesley; 1997. ISBN 0-201-89542-0

Franklin, K. *VB.NET for Developers*. Sams Publishing; 2001. ISBN 0-672-32089-4

Gamma, E., Helm, R., Johnson, R., and J. Vlissides. *Design Patterns*. Addison-Wesley; 1994. ISBN 0-201-63361-2

Gunnerson, E. *A Programmer's Introduction to C#, Second Edition*. Apress; 2001. ISBN 1-893115-62-3

Gray, J. and A. Reuter. *Transaction Processing: Concepts and Techniques*. Morgan Kaufmann; 1993. ISBN 1-55860-190-2

Heinckiens, P. M. *Building Scalable Database Applications*. Addison-Wesley; 1997. ISBN 0-201-31013-9

Henderson, K. *The Guru's Guide to Transact-SQL*. Addison-Wesley; 2000. ISBN 0-201-61576-2

Hunt, A. and D. Thomas. *The Pragmatic Programmer*. Addison-Wesley; 1999. ISBN 0-201-61622-X

Kernighan, B. W. and R. Pike. *The Practice of Programming*. Addison-Wesley; 1999. ISBN 0-201-61586-X

Kline, K., Gould, L., and A. Zanevsky. *Transact-SQL Programming*. O'Reilly; 1999. ISBN 1-56592-401-0

Lowy, Juval. *COM and .NET Component Services*. O'Reilly; 2001. ISBN 0596001037

Meyer, B. *Object-Oriented Software Construction, Second Edition*. Prentice Hall; 1997. ISBN 0-13-629155-4

Pattison, T. *Programming Distributed Applications with COM+ and Visual Basic 6.0, Second Edition*. Microsoft Press; 2000. ISBN 0-7356-1010-X

Platt, D. S. *Introducing Microsoft .NET*. Microsoft Press; 2001. ISBN 073561377X

Pfister, G. F. *In Search of Clusters, Second Edition*. Prentice Hall; 1998. ISBN 0-13-899709-8

Robbins, J. *Debugging Applications*. Microsoft Press; 2000. ISBN 0-7356-0886-5

Schmidt, D., Stal, M., Rohnert, H. and F. Buschmann. *Pattern-Oriented Software Architecture: Volume 2: Patterns for Concurrent and Networked Objects*. Wiley; 2000. ISBN 0-471-60695-2

A

SUGGESTIONS FOR
FURTHER READING

Schulmeyer, G. G. and J. I. McManus. *Handbook of Software Quality Assurance, Third Edition*. Prentice Hall; 1998. ISBN 0-13-010470-1

Sommerville, I. *Software Engineering, Sixth Edition*. Addison-Wesley; 2001. ISBN 0-201-39815-X

Stonebraker, M. and P. Brown. *Object-Relational DBMSs: Tracking the Next Great Wave, Second Edition*. Morgan Kaufmann; 1999. ISBN 1-55860-452-9

Sundblad, S. and P. Sundblad. *Designing for Scalability with Windows DNA*. Microsoft Press; 2000. ISBN 0-7356-0968-3

Sunderic, D. and T. Woodhead. *SQL Server 2000 Stored Procedure Programming*. Osborne; 2000. ISBN 0-07-212566-7

Szyperski, C. *Component Software: Beyond Object-Oriented Programming*. Addison-Wesley; 1997. ISBN 0-201-17888-5

INDEX

SYMBOLS

A